PROVINCIAL
PEWTERERS

PROVINCIAL PEWTERERS

A Study of the craft in the West Midlands and Wales

R. F. Homer
& D. W. Hall

Phillimore

1985

Published by
PHILLIMORE & CO. LTD.
London and Chichester

Head Office: Shopwyke Hall
Chichester, Sussex

Ronald F. Homer and David W. Hall

ISBN 0 85033 572 8

Typeset in the United Kingdom by:
Fidelity Processes - Selsey - Sussex

Printed and bound in Great Britain by
REDWOOD BURN LTD.,
Trowbridge, Wiltshire

CONTENTS

LIST OF PLATES

(between pages 18 and 19)

LIST OF ILLUSTRATIONS

LIST OF FAMILY TREES

PREFACE

For almost a hundred years old pewterware has been collected, studied and described and several thousand makers were recorded by H. H. Cotterell in *Old Pewter its Makers and Marks* in 1929. Despite this, and later cataloguing of names and marks, virtually nothing has been known of the personal lives of the pewterers themselves, or, outside of London, of the social history and practical operation of the craft which supplied essential household utensils to rich and poor alike for over four centuries. In the provinces, where we now know that far more pewterers plied their trade than worked in the capital, limited investigations have been carried out in the past on a few major towns and cities, but published information usually comprises little more than a list of names culled from registers of freemen or fortuitously discovered in old documents.

The first extensive, though necessarily superficial survey of the provincial scene, was published in 1974 in Hatcher and Barker's *History of British Pewter* which revealed the scope which existed for further study. In this book we have concentrated our attention on Birmingham and its neighbours as the focal point of the West Midland metalworking industries; on the towns bordering the River Severn, for centuries a major trade artery; and on the Welsh border and Wales itself, the last a country previously erroneously believed to be devoid of pewterers. Our studies have revealed many hundreds of craftsmen who worked in pewter in the cities and towns of the area, and scarcely a market town has been examined which did not support at least one pewterer, and frequently several, at any given time in the 17th century; the heyday of the pewter trade.

We have sought to describe the growth and decline of the craft, the history of some of the families who dominated it and the economic circumstances which influenced and surrounded it. Above all, we have tried to bring to life what might otherwise be yet another catalogue of names which revealed nothing of the background to a once essential and ubiquitous traditional craft which had its origins in medieval times and which died only within living memory.

To pewter collectors we hope to bring a new perspective against which they can enjoy their treasures and to the social and economic historian a perhaps uniquely detailed overall study of a once vital industry.

RONALD F. HOMER
DAVID W. HALL

ACKNOWLEDGEMENTS

Many organisations and individuals have contributed information and help and in particular we wish to thank the Leverhulme Trust for a Research Grant, The Worshipful Company of Pewterers for permission to quote extensively from its archives and for certain financial guarantees, and the University of Reading for the use of its library. The staff of the following Record Offices: Clwyd, Dyfed, Glamorgan, Hereford and Worcester, Lancashire, Lichfield, Shropshire, Surrey and Worcester Guildhall; and of the libraries at Aberystwyth (National Library of Wales), Birmingham, Cardiff, Guildhall (London), Hereford, Newtown, Oswestry, Shrewsbury, University College of North Wales (Bangor), Walsall and Worcester have been unstinting in their help. Other organisations who have provided assistance include: Brecknock Borough Council, the Ludlow Historical Research Group, Monmouth Museum, the Powysland Club, Tenby Museum, the University of Birmingham Faculty of Commerce and Social Studies, The National Trust (who kindly provided access to the pewter at *The Fleece Inn*, Bretforton) and The Pewter Society. Among individuals we are much indebted to Dr. A. S. Law who placed at our disposal the fruits of his detailed research on Birmingham pewterers. Others who have provided valuable information include Douglas J. Elliott, Gertrude V. Freeman, Paul H. Gibbons and John H. Harvey.

Our thanks are due also to all those secretaries and typists who have struggled over the years with our manuscripts and to our wives and families who have tolerated and supported our efforts. Finally, 'if any be overlooked or forgot', we tender our apologies.

Many of the marks in the Appendix are reproduced from *Old Pewter its Makers and Marks* (Batsford, 1929) and others have been specially drawn by Arthur Muir. For the text illustrations we are indebted to Worcester City Council, The Hereford and Worcester Record Office, the Lichfield Joint Record Office, Messrs. Hemingway, Bewdley, Bewdley Museum, and the Worshipful Company of Pewterers. To those who have supplied photographs and generously agreed to their publication we are most grateful: plates 3-5 at the *Fleece Inn*, Bretforton; plate 12, Sotheby's; plates 22, 27 and 29, Peter R. Hooper; plate 35, Brecknock Museum and plate 38, Englefields, London.

ABBREVIATIONS

Used in the Tables

app	apprenticed	g.son of	grandson of
b	born	f. of	father of
B	made a burgess	m	mentioned
b. of	brother of	MPM	*More Pewter Marks*
br	brazier	n. of	nephew of
Cott.	*Old Pewter its Makers and Marks*	p	pewterer
d	died	s. of	son of
d. of	daughter of	w. of	wife (widow) of
f	free		

REFERENCES

In the Text

Cotterell or Cott., Cotterell, H. H., *Old Pewter its Makers and Marks* (1929, reprinted 1963)

MPM., Peal, C. A., *More Pewter Marks* (1976)

INTRODUCTION

UNTIL QUITE RECENTLY collectors and students of old pewter have only been superficially aware of the importance and extent of pewtering outside London during the 16th to 18th centuries. It is true that Bristol and the West Country, York, Wigan and later Birmingham were recognised as important centres many years ago, and instances of pewterers in other towns were recorded in isolation by local historians and by the early collectors. Nevertheless no overall view of pewtering country-wide became available until the publication in 1974 of Hatcher and Barker's *History of British Pewter* to commemorate the 500th anniversary of the grant of the first charter to The Worshipful Company of Pewterers of London. Their book contains extracts from the Country Search Books of the London Company for 1640, and an analysis of the market distribution of pewterware made in a number of provincial towns at this time indicates a well-organised production and distribution chain even at so early a date.

The archives of the Company, extant from 1451, were studied and selected extracts were published by Welch in 1902.[1] However, Welch was concerned with writing a history of the Company and he largely ignored the Search Books and such other accounts of provincial activity as are contained in these records. As early as 1474–5, immediately following the grant of their charter which gave them the right of search and seizure of sub-standard pewter throughout England and Wales, the Company organised search parties who rode on horseback to many English towns on the Company's behalf. Records of these searches reveal the names of pewterers working in the East Midlands, the West Country, the South of England and East Anglia in the 1470s. Twenty-three towns were visited, but the nearest these early searches came to the area covered by this book were Coventry, where Robert Burnett and John Yalle were fined in 1474–5 for producing sub-standard ware, and Bristol where four pewterers were named, William White, John Caulse, Alson Caylye and John Avys. Although it is now clear that pewtering was being carried on in West Midlands and Welsh Border towns at this time, either they were not searched, or the records have perished. Not until the mid-17th century do the surviving records of searches cover these areas. Invaluable though these London records are, the bulk of the information now published here for the first time derives from local records, guild books, burgess lists, parish registers, wills and inventories and the incomparable contemporary business documents of the Bewdley pewterers of the 18th century preserved, by a lucky accident, in the Hereford and Worcester Record Office. From these sources we are now in the position of knowing far more about the individuals, their businesses and their customers in Birmingham and the West Midlands and in Wales, than we do of all but a handful of pewterers who plied their craft in London. The rise and fall of family concerns, the close-knit world of those who practised the craft, who inter-married, witnessed each other's wills and inventories, and borrowed each other's expensive moulds, and the eventual emergence of modern mass production and business methods are clearly apparent.

The area covered by this study is a rough triangle with its apex at Birmingham and fanning out to embrace much of Worcestershire, Herefordshire and Shropshire, with a little of South Staffordshire and Warwickshire, and extending into the hitherto unexplored area of pewtering, Wales. In the Principality, already by the late 17th century a growing iron-producing area, there were pewterers active in the main towns at this time. Much of the area covered in this book was served by the River Severn as its main trade artery and, from the 1760s, by the growing network of canals serving the industrial midlands and other centres of population.

The Severn was a free and navigable river for some hundred and fifty miles and was then one of the busiest in Europe. The main port for the midlands, before the building of the canals, was Wribbenhall lying on the opposite bank of the river to Bewdley to which it was joined by a bridge in the 15th century. The watermen of the town plied their trade up and down the river as early as the 14th century and Leland wrote in 1539 'To this bridge resort many flat long vessels to carry up and down all manner of merchandise to Bewdley and above Bewdley'. In the 17th century carriage was by sailing trows of forty to eighty tons burthen and by barges of about twenty tons. In 1758 there were 47 scheduled trows from Bewdley and 75 from Bridgnorth, itself a not insignificant pewtering town. Further downstream the ancient city of Worcester supported many pewterers and was also an important centre for the river trade.[2] Carriage down-river, with the current was 10s. 0d. a ton from Bewdley to Bristol and 15s. 0d. a ton in the reverse direction.

The border towns, such as Shrewsbury and Oswestry supplied much of the Welsh market, and shipments by river and sea from other towns and cities on the Severn and its tributaries enabled a significant part of England and Wales to be supplied from these midland pewtering towns. By the end of the 18th century, with improved communications, this scattered industry had been eclipsed by the dominance of Birmingham which absorbed pewter manufacture into its already divers metal trades and became the main supplier of pewter measures and drinking pots to the public house market during the 19th century.

An Act of Parliament of 1503 reinforced the London Company's right of search and included a right of search for sub-standard brassware as well as pewter. The extent to which, at least during the 17th and 18th centuries, the trades of pewterer and brazier were combined is one of the interesting features which is only now being recognised and which makes more understandable this hitherto rather curious dual provision of the 1503 Act. One man may describe himself indifferently as either pewterer or brazier, and frequently as both, and inventories show that many craftsmen had stock-in-trade and tools relevant to both occupations. The point is well illustrated by the advertisement placed in the *Ludlow Post-Man* on 20 November 1719 by Randolph Phillips of Hereford, self-styled brazier, who proclaimed that he took in old pewter and cast it into spoons. Indeed from the latter part of the 18th century distinctions become even more blurred and many self-styled ironmongers were also engaged in pewtering and braziery. Trades directories as a source of information for this later period must therefore be used with a certain discretion.

The ramifications of some family pewtering concerns extended over very long periods and sometimes operated from several towns, either at the same time or as the family moved from place to place. Robert Banks, whose ancestors were pewterers in

Wigan from the early 1500s, appears in the late 17th century in Bewdley to found a dynasty of Banks's who were originally pewterers and later brassfounders there until the late 1800s. The Ledesham or Ledsham family who made pewter in Chester in 1530-50 are almost certainly the same family as the Lettsomes or Ledsams of Worcester who made pewter there from before 1600 to the 1720s, and who also practised the craft in Bewdley in the late 16th century. John Rosengrove of Shrewsbury must surely be related to Seth Rosengreve of Chester who flourished about 1540. Members of the Cumberlidge family appear in Walsall, Wolverhampton and Warwick in the 17th century, and Worcester was the home of the extensive Greenbank family of braziers, plumbers and pewterers from the late 16th century to well after 1700. The metal trades of pewtering, brazing and ironmongery in Walsall were pervaded by many members of the Nicholls family and later the Seneys for over a century and a half. Interesting also is the frequency with which widows took over their late husbands' businesses, sometimes to hold in trust until children came of age, but sometimes to run in their own right.

The distribution of pewterware from a single provincial maker can be discovered in many cases from the London Pewterers' Company's searches. Other valuable sources are the trade debtors listed in the inventory of Sampson Bourne of Worcester (d. 1689), the surviving daybook of John Duncumb of Birmingham and Bewdley for 1718-24 and the ledgers of Ingram and Hunt, also of Bewdley, from 1769 to the early 1800s. John Duncumb whose annual turnover in the 1720s was about £2,000, supplied 124 customers over the five years covered by the surviving records, which includes the period of his move from Birmingham in 1720, most of them within a 40-mile radius and many of them now known also to have been fellow pewterers. Others were the wholesale ironmongers established by ironmasters such as Sampson Lloyd of Birmingham and the Molineux family of Wolverhampton.

As well as organised river transport there were frequent wagon and pack-horse services. Before 1700 there were regular wagon services linking the towns of Walsall, Birmingham, Wolverhampton, Bridgnorth and Dudley to Shrewsbury and to London. In 1745 a Wolverhampton wagoner had services to Liverpool, Kendall, Whitehaven, Newcastle-upon-Tyne and Glasgow and collected from Birmingham, Bewdley, Worcester and Kidderminster. In addition many husbandmen and farmers used their horses as pack animals during the slack season. Much finished pewter is recorded as being dispatched in pack-cloth bundles or in barrels and sent by pack-horse or wagon to the customer, or for the customer's collection from a convenient market town.

Ingram and Hunt's much more extensive business, turning over some £6,000 per annum in 1805, supplied over seven hundred customers throughout England and Wales, again some identifiable as pewterers, but most of them at that time wholesalers who are to be found in other contemporary records as ironmongers or merchants. Trade between pewterers and the loaning of moulds enabled them to hold comprehensive stocks of various types of ware even though, as evidenced by inventories, they may have themselves owned moulds for only a limited range of flatware or hollowware. Some ware was supplied 'rough', that is as-cast, for finishing by the purchaser who presumably added his own touchmark.

As to the techniques of fabricating pewter there are very few early accounts. The oldest surviving description of the casting and working of pewter is the one written in the 12th century by Theophilus Presbyter, a German monk.[3] He describes the casting of a cruet in a clay mould by the lost-wax process, a one-off method which is not relevant to the later English techniques with which we are concerned. However, having poured the metal into the mould his account continues 'when the mould is entirely cold, break the clay off the outside and . . . then mount the work on the lathe and turn it evenly all over. Finally polish it with shave-grass'. The finishing process of turning and polishing is one which is in essence that still used even today in the making of pewter by traditional methods.

Four hundred years later Biruguccio, in his *Pirotechnia* of 1540, describes the methods then in use in northern Italy. 'The [pewter] vessels, as perhaps you have seen, are cast one by one in moulds made of white tuff. Several pieces fastened together are then put on the axle of a wheel turned by hand and they are turned with a slightly bent tool which has a cutting edge. In this way they are made thin and of good shape. They are then polished with a piece of linen cloth and a little powdered tripoli, and thus they are finished. Other vessels as well as round ones are made of pewter, such as flasks, containers for preserves, and salt cellars. They are cast in halves in moulds made of white tuff, and then fitted together and soldered. With rasps and scrapers and other cutting tools they are smoothed and polished, and made beautiful'. Save for the replacement of his moulds of tuff — a soft volcanic stone — by ones of bronze the methods Biruguccio recounts would equally aptly describe those used in England during the 15th to 19th centuries.

A uniquely early inventory of the contents of a London pewterer's workshop, which appears to have been overlooked by earlier writers,[4] records the working tools of Thomas Filkes, pewterer, who died in 1426 or 1427, and was prepared to enable provision to be made for his son, William, through the sale of the 'instruments used in his Mistery'. These included:

> a small charger mould of brass; a middle platter mould of brass; a small platter mould of brass; a great dish mould; a counterfeit dish mould; a middle dish mould; a great saucer mould; a hollow plate mould; a new charger mould; 14 'prynts', [presumably dies or stamps of some kind]; 7 pairs of clamps; a wheel, an arbour and a 'tower', i.e., a lathe and fittings; a pair of clipping shears; a burnisher; 8 turning hooks, i.e., lathe tools; 4 anvils; 2 swages; 7 'clene' hammers; 2 scoring 'flotes'; 2 chisels; 1 pair of lifting tongs; 2 bellows; 2 casting pans; a stirring staff; soldering irons; 3 casting stocks; 4 'strake stones'

This clearly indicates the casting, turning and hammering processes which were used in the production of English pewter as early as the first decades of the 15th century, and is as relevant to the provincial scene as it is to London. Much of the terminology is found still in inventories three centuries later in date.

Biruguccio's mention of the turning of several pieces fastened together may refer to the ingenious method used for finishing plates. Here the first plate is fixed to the face-plate of the lathe and the outer face turned. A second plate is then fixed to the first by means of three blobs of solder at the edge, and the second plate turned on its exposed face. The process is repeated until a stack of plates is formed in the lathe. These are then reversed on the face-plate, the newly exposed face of the outer one is turned, and the solder then cut away to remove it. This is repeated until the stack has been dealt with.

A brief but succinct comment in the *Universal Director* of 1763 describes the London pewterers of that time as 'Mechanic Artists whose ingenuity and industry are of public utility, as they furnish us with a variety of necessary and convenient kitchen furniture; which they likewise finish in such a neat and masterly manner, that they have a great demand for exportation. The making of Pewter, which is a metal composed of Tin and Lead, forms one part of their art; the casting of it in moulds a second; the turning it, a third; and the hammering it, a fourth and last'.

This sketchy background can be filled out in some detail from probate inventories. Such inventories were in theory obligatory for every executor or administration but the number which survive is comparatively small and tracing them can be both difficult and time consuming. Until 1857 probate proceedings were handled by a variety of ecclesiastical courts and even some civil courts. The ecclesiastical courts concerned were those of the archdeacon, the bishop and the archbishop. Although many of these are accessible through the County· Record Offices, the Public Record Office and the National Library of Wales, finding the papers relating to one particular individual may present considerable difficulty.

Obviously with such a variety of jurisdictions and the haphazard nature of some clerical work at the time, the surviving inventories are very different in character and contents. Some are detailed lists recording every item of stock held and every tool, all personal property, furniture, bed-clothes and linen, domestic and farm animals, leases and debts. Others vaguely record and value goods and property under a few broad headings. The accuracy of the detailed inventories is often vouched for by the practice of including one or more professional colleagues of the deceased among the appraisers selected to prepare the inventory. Such pewterers and braziers would obviously have as good an idea as any contemporary of the price of pewter items and the value of the tools and materials.

In addition to the use of inventories as a source of details of specific interest to the student of particular subjects, they have been much used in recent decades by historians as a source of general information about economic and social life. During this study 56 pewterers' inventories have been located and although this is not a large enough number to produce statistically significant results, it is possible to compare them with the other more general studies made of contemporary inventories. In this way an insight into the general prosperity of provincial pewterers can be obtained to supplement and reinforce the picture presented by other sources. However inadequate this may be, the following table represents the only extensive list of pewterers' inventories so far published.

Name	Place of Residence	Date of Death	Inventory Total £	s.	d.
Richard PARKER	Walsall	1534	24	7	4
Nicholas GREEN	Worcester	1541	155	0	0
Elizabeth PARKER	Walsall	1541	18	2	1
Henry JERMAN	Worcester	1558	2	18	10
Henry GREEN	Worcester	1569	112	1	0
Widow GREEN	Worcester	1570	37	9	8
William NICHOLLS	Walsall	1578	108	18	0
John BAYSIE	Worcester	1585	41	10	5
Gilbert CLARE	Worcester	1589	10	17	0

Name	Place of Residence	Date of Death	Inventory Total		
			£	s.	d.
Henry LEDSHAM	Worcester	1593	47	9	4
William HOPKINS	Worcester	1602	18	16	5
John ROSENGROVE	Shrewsbury	1601	13	2	4
James GREENBANK	Worcester	1603	71	11	8
Margaret GREENBANK	Worcester	1604	89	18	0
Richard COLLINS	Shrewsbury	1611	69	15	2
William HANSON	Walsall	1614	83	16	3
Thomas JENNINGS	Walsall	1616	195	8	6
Richard NICHOLLS	Walsall	1628	8	10	6
John NICHOLLS	Walsall	1629	61	11	2
Joseph SENY	Walsall	1630	5	14	4
Francis TRAPP	Worcester	1633	388	0	6
Robert EBB	Walsall	1637	91	17	8
Robert WOOD	Birmingham	1637	136	1	0
Thomas LETSOME	Worcester	1643	4	6	6
William WOODWARD	Worcester	1644	2	18	4
Elizabeth TOM(P)KINS	Leominster	1644	90	3	0
Christopher NICHOLS	Walsall	1655	33	18	8
William WOOD	Birmingham	1665	219	13	0
Thomas TOM(P)KINS	Leominster	1667	265	11	7
William SENEY	Walsall	1673	8	16	6
Thomas FELTON	Oswestry	1675	300	12	8
John TRAPP	Worcester	1675	255	11	3
Ann TRAPP	Worcester	1677	201	12	10
John TOM(P)KINS	Leominster	1677	150	16	4
Gwen FELTON	Oswestry	1678	343	10	8
Thomas GORTON	Birmingham	1683	184	15	6
Joseph BRADNOCK	Birmingham	1684	264	11	7½
Francis TRAPP	Hereford	1689	108	18	6
Francis GREENBANK	Worcester	1689	176	14	8
Sampson BOURNE	Worcester	1689	3,275	15	7¼
Richard PLUMMER	Ludlow	1692	417	13	8
Abraham DEAKIN	Walsall	1679	130	10	10
Francis TRAPP	Hereford	1699	32	12	6
John TRAPP	Worcester	1713	270	2	1½
Nathaniel GREEN	Lichfield	1715	63	12	3½
Thomas FOSTER	Shrewsbury	1718	258	14	11
Thomas SMITH	Bewdley	1719	313	18	5
William HALL	Birmingham	1723	37	19	4
Henry GOODE	Bewdley	1726	19	10	6
Samuel BROWN	Shrewsbury	1727	4	3	9
Francis KING	Worcester	1730	63	12	1
Hopwood HARPER	Worcester	1733	308	4	0
Sampson LETSOME	Worcester	1737	592	16	3
Edmund LEETH	Worcester	1746–7	56	10	10

WALES

John BERROW	Brecon	1706	56	10	0

Average values (without Wales)

	£	s.	d.
up to 1619 (17 inventories)	64	15	5
1620–1659 (10 inventories)	82	6	2
1660–1710 (13 inventories)	339	11	1¾
1711– (9 inventories)	178	19	9

Dyer, in his study of Worcester in the 16th century,[5] undertook a detailed analysis of 817 probate inventories extant for the City for the period 1529–1619. The list on the previous pages of pewterers' and braziers' inventories includes 17 individuals from this period, several of whom are from Worcester itself. The average value for Dyer's 817 inventories is £45.8 while the average for the 17 pewterers listed is £64.76. This would suggest that pewterers were more prosperous than most of the city residents who had sufficient property or movable wealth to justify their executors or heirs obtaining Letters of Administration and probate. In this period it is to be noted that two of the £100+ figures are for pewterers who were also bellfounders. Without this dual occupation it seems doubtful that they would have achieved what was, for the period, such considerable wealth.

The evidence which exists suggests that pewterers in the 16th century were reasonably prosperous, at least in comparison with other shopkeeper–artisans, but the trade did not in itself afford the opportunities for the ambitious to achieve that transition into status and land-owning which some other trades and occupations could offer. Between 1620 and 1660 the evidence is rather unclear. One or two pewterers were clearly prosperous — one exceptionally so. Some of the other inventories present in contrast a picture of real poverty, in particular two from the Civil War which seem to imply that at least Worcester may have suffered some economic dislocation. The average value of the 10 inventories dating from this period is £82. After 1660 the picture is a far more consistent one and indicates reasonable overall prosperity. This apparent increase in wealth is confirmed from other sources such as wills and municipal records. The average value[6] for 1660–1710 is £399, five times that of the period from 1520–1619 and four times that of the period 1620–60. Obviously price rises will have influenced these figures as inflation is nothing new, but the trends appear valid.

Hatcher and Barker[7] have published an index of the retail prices of new pewterware covering the period 1411–1700. This index shows that new pewter rose in price between 1521 and 1620 by 130 per cent., that by 1661–70 it was up by a further 55 per cent. but by 1690 it had dropped below the 1620 level. Typically pewterware cost 3d. to 4d. per pound in the 15th century, 8d. by 1550, one shilling by 1620 and 14d. by 1670. Thereafter there was a fall to 10d. in 1700.

M. B. Rowlands[8] gives the following table covering probate inventories of 484 metalworkers dating from between 1660 and 1710:

Trade	No. of cases	£	s.	d.
Nailers	298	38	12	5
Locksmiths	42	46	19	1
Lorimers	20	28	17	3
Bucklemakers	10	25	19	1
Blacksmiths	20	80	10	0
Scythesmiths	26	212	4	3
Scythegrinders	17	49	6	1
In comparison				
Pewterers and braziers	16	339	11	1¾

Traditionally this period has always been seen as the high period of pewter production, marked by the quality of the metal used, the excellence of design and innovation in styles. It seems also to have been a period when provincial pewterers were prospering. In this context it is perhaps desirable to keep two facts in mind, the retail price of pewter had risen, as far as the surviving evidence shows, faster than that of many other products, and our investigation has shown that in the West Midlands pewterers were broadening the range of their wares to include more items of brass and copper.

Twelve inventories have been found for the period after 1710, a small number from which to generalise. However the inventories show a widely scattered range of values. Five of them are for small sums and another, that of Hopwood Harper, is abnormal. His inventory seems superficially similar to those of the late 17th century but in fact it includes a substantial legacy and an annuity. Without these items Hopwood Harper's inventory would look very similar to those of Francis King, William Hall and Henry Goode if not quite so desperate as that of Samuel Brown. On the other hand those of Thomas Foster of Shrewsbury, Thomas Smith of Bewdley and Sampson Letsome of Worcester reflect considerable prosperity. We can perhaps speculate that these individuals had managed to adjust to, and benefit from, the new environment of the 18th century, whereas their poorer colleagues had not.

TABLE I

Town	Before 1500	1500–1600	1600–1700	1700–1800
Shrewsbury	4	12	27 (28)	15 (46)
Oswestry	—	1	4 (8)	5 (6)
Ludlow	—	9	11	9 (12)
Worcester	—	13	36 (37)	25 (42)
Hereford	—	2	4 (5)	2 (26)
Birmingham	—	—	14	20 (33)
Bewdley	—	15*	12 (14)	13
Walsall	2 (4)	13 (15)	44 (49)	1 (6)
Bridgnorth	—	—	7 (8)	4 (12)
Lichfield	—	—	10 (11)	5 (15)
Leominster	—	—	6 (7)	—
Tewkesbury	—	—	5	—
Wales				
Haverfordwest	—	4	3 (5)	—
Carmarthen	—	2	1	1 (3)
Conway	—	1	—	—
Denbigh	—	—	2 (3)	1
Swansea	—	—	2 (3)	2
Brecon	—	—	1	2 (6)
Wrexham	—	—	1	3 (4)
Monmouth	—	1	—	(3)
Cardiff	—	—	1	—

Approximate total numbers of pewterers and braziers working in the principal West Midland pewtering towns and in Wales. The higher figure in parentheses includes individuals who were, or who may have been, braziers only.

* Not possible to differentiate between pewterers and braziers.

From the inventories listed it is possible to form a reasonable picture of the equipment and tools which furnished the workshop of a master pewterer of the period. Fundamental of course was a means of melting the metal. A number of inventories refer to a furnace, mention perhaps depending on whether it was portable or not, to coals, bellows and to melting pots, presumably of clay or iron. Ladles for handling the the molten metal are also mentioned, sometimes they were used for melting small amounts of metal and then were styled melting ladles.

The most valuable asset of a pewterer was his stock of moulds and the quantity of these belonging to a reasonably prosperous craftsman could be considerable. Richard Plummer of Ludlow had 11 hundredweight (1,232 pounds) of moulds at his death in 1692, Thomas Gorton of Birmingham had 1,200 pounds weight in 1693 and Francis Trapp of Worcester 745 pounds in 1633. Numbers of moulds are seldom mentioned, but there is reference to seven hollow-ware moulds in the possession of Gilbert Clare of Worcester in 1589 and to 'twelve brasen moulds for pewter platters, saucers and dishes' owned by John Rosengrave of Shrewsbury in 1601. The types of mould are rather infrequently given but the exceptionally detailed will of Rowland Collins of Shrewsbury (made in 1654) lists 'fflagon moulds, cann moulds, candlestick moulds, saltsellar moulds, porringer moulds, quart moulds, chamber pott moulds, saucer moulds all of every sort both great and small, three spoon moulds and a trencher plate mould'. Sometimes found are the expressions box moulds (perhaps to hold casting sand for casting brass), moulding troughs (perhaps for casting ingots), and casting forms for clamping together and holding vertical the halves of plate and dish moulds of bronze.

Of finishing tools the wheel or hand-driven lathe is the most important: Thomas Gorton had three and Francis Trapp four. With the wheels, which were frequently fitted with mandrels and 'towers' (an expression of uncertain meaning) went the turning and finishing tools usually referred to as hooks and burnishers of which Francis Trapp had 69 together with a number of rasps and files. For hammering, anvils and bickorns (*beackorn*, an anvil with two pointed ends) are found, together with swages and a variety of hammers for particular jobs. These include stamp hammers, spoon hammers, tower and wheel hammers, bright hammers, rough hammers, and rapping hammers. Miscellaneous tools include vices, steadies, shears, soldering irons and grindstones. Lastly, and most important, nearly every inventory includes the scales and weights needed both for weighing out the ingredients for the metal alloy and also for pricing the finished ware, the commoner items of which were normally sold by weight.

Something needs to be said about the stocks of metal, often partly in the form of scrap, which a typical pewterer might hold. Francis Trapp of Worcester at his death in 1633 had 465 pounds of new lay, 371 pounds of plate metal, 190 pounds of old fine and 75 pounds of old lay, together with 40 pounds of old spoons. In copper and brass he had 150 pounds of shruff (scrap); in old iron 100 pounds; and 824 pounds of lead, valued all together at about £50. Richard Plummer of Ludlow had 1 cwt. of cast pewter, 3 cwt. of old pewter, 1 cwt. of yellow brass, 40 pounds of lay, 28 pounds of fine shavings and 40 pounds of trifles shavings in his shop at the time of his death, worth together almost £21. The inventory of John Trapp of Worcester, died 1713, mentions 20 pounds of tin-glass (bismuth) along with 1½ cwt. of plate metal, 2½ cwt. of trifle metal, 30 pounds of old lay, 1 cwt. of platter metal, 76 pounds of new lay and

1 cwt. of old pewter. Exceptionally, Sampson Bourne of Worcester had seven tons of old and new metal in 1689. The substantial quantities of old metal indicates the extent to which old ware was traded in and recycled — one of the reasons for the rarity of old pewter. Typically old pewter would fetch 10d. per pound when the price of new ware was 13d. to 14d.

At the beginning of the period covered by the surviving records pewtering was a skilled craft and the production units were small. A master and a journeyman or two, together with a few apprentices formed a sizeable business supplying local customers. The prosperous master pewterers owned goods and chattels valued on their deaths at £100 or more, the poorer craftsmen were worth only a few tens of pounds. The general background level of pewtering in the area in the 17th century is well illustrated by the search of the Pewterers' Company[9] when they visited a number of towns in 1636–40 and in 1673–7. In 1640, for example, Michael Nicken's shop in Lichfield yielded, 'lay by George Geson of Walsall, porringers by Thomas Cheshere of Walsall, spoons and saucers by Cheshere, and flagons by Geson and by Christopher Nichols [Walsall or Worcester] and bottles by Robert Seneres [Walsall]'. Obviously the intrusions of the searchers was resented and on 27 July 1640, there was a fracas with William Lee of Hereford where 'ware of divers sorts by William Nichols of Walsall' was assayed and found wanting, and, as the searcher wrote, 'I would have sayed [assayed] more but could not be reason that William Lee took away our say [assay] and was very troublesome both in speech and action'. Premises belonging to Thomas Arundel of Ross-on-Wye were visited the same day, and three days previously in Worcester various wares were seized at four pewterers' shops belonging to Sampson Bourne, Mr. Ten, Mr. Nichols and Mr. Greenbank. Fuller records exist for 1673 and 1677 and the variety of wares offered for sale and the purchases made by one pewterer from another are well illustrated by the following entries for William Mountford of Kidderminster and Elizabeth Arndale of Ross-on-Wye, both for 1677.

William Mountford: Candlesticks; Flagons; Tankards; Bottles by Nichols of Worcester; Candlesticks by Nichols of Worcester; Salts by Gorton of Birmingham; Candlesticks made by ditto; Saucers made by ditto; Porringers made by ditto; 2-eared taster by Banks of Wigan; Spoons by Biggs of Bromsgrove; Stool pans by James of Bristol; Chamber pots round brims; Chamber pots ordinary middle; Rough quarterns.

Elizabeth Arndale: Salts made by Plummer — Ludlow; Saucers made by him; Flagons without touches — Worcester; Chapnitt without touch; Salts made by Prire — Gloucester; Salts of another sort by him; Saucers by him; Porringers by him; Planished tankards by him; Flagons (Lyon).

The accounts for the 1677 search survive. It occupied 24 days in July and cost the party of six London pewterers £77 6s. 1½d., including £18 for the hire of six horses for 24 days, an average of £1 a night accommodation, and £4 for wear and tear to their apparel! The fines levied from the makers of substandard wares totalled £95 13s. 10d. showing a net profit of £18 7s. 8½d. on the search.

While we have comprehensive lists of the ware made by a number of the 17th and early 18th century pewterers who worked in the West Midlands it is much more difficult to identify surviving examples of their work. A number of so far unattributed touch marks can now be allocated to these makers, and some firm and some possible identifications will be found in the section on *Marks* at the end of this work. Styles of ware can also be perceived in some cases and tentative judgments of provenance can be made. The quantity and diversity of ware made in Birmingham and the West Midlands from the 17th century onwards indicates that much of it must survive and further research should allow at least some of it to be identified in the future. Indeed a considerable number of flagons and tankards of the late 17th century by William Wood of Birmingham can now be identified as a result of the discovery of his touch mark.

By the middle years of the 18th century most of these local pewterers had disappeared in the face of competition from cheap pottery, tinplate and brass, and pewter production became concentrated in a much smaller number of 'manufactures' supplying the trade markets of the tavern and public house, the naval and military establishments, hospitals and workhouses, and increasing overseas colonial markets such as North America. The emphasis of the local craftsman's business changed to a more general involvement with non-ferrous metals and they became braziers, plumbers and tinsmiths. A transition aided by the enormously increased availability of brass after the mid-18th century.

By the 1770s Birch and Villers of Birmingham were advertising in *Aris' Birmingham Gazette* to employ both braziers and pewterers in their manufactory there and industrial production had arrived. In the earlier decades of the 18th century the first move in this direction probably involved the use at least in part of out-workers on a cottage industry basis and the prolific output of the Duncumbs was perhaps achieved in this way. It is interesting that they appear to have made very largely flatware, a standard, simple product not requiring the skills of an apprenticed man to make the finish. A parallel can perhaps be drawn with the business of William Seney, brazier, ironmonger and pewterer of Walsall (successor to four generations of pewterers and braziers) who in 1716 employed 55 men, some on a casual basis only whereby they collected supplies from his warehouse and returned finished goods. This was of course the way in which the nail trade had been organised for many years in the midland's iron towns. Surviving traditional pewter manufacturers, such as Engelfields of London and (until 1983) James Smellie of Birmingham (who inherited the early Bewdley business) use methods and machinery little different from that employed two hundred years ago and their workshops — safety precautions apart — probably differ little from those of that period. Indeed many of their massive bronze moulds are of 18th century date and still in frequent use.

The towns which are studied in detail in subsequent chapters are necessarily only a selection, chosen for their importance and the ease of access or abundance of their records, but there is no reason to suppose that they are not representative of the majority of comparable towns in England. We know from the incomplete information in the Search Books of the London Company that in the 1670s over 130 towns in England had one or more pewterers practising their craft and the field for further study is thus enormous.

NOTES AND REFERENCES

Introduction

1. Welch, C., *History of the Worshipful Company of Pewterers of London* (1902).
2. Davies, S. W., *The Economic History of Bewdley to 1700* (London Ph.D. thesis, 1981) quantified the river trade for various towns.
3. Hawthorne, J. C., and Smith, C. S. (eds.), *On Divers Arts* (New York, 1963).
4. Sharpe, R. R. (ed.), *Calendar of Letter Books preserved among the Archives of the City of London*. Book K, p. 65.
5. Dyer, Alan, *The City of Worcester in the Sixteenth Century* (1973).
6. In calculating the 1660–1710 average a net value of £2,370 15s. 7¼d. has been used for Sampson Bourne rather than the gross given in the table. Using median values rather than averages, which discounts the distortion produced by Sampson Bourne's very high figure, does not affect the general trend.
7. Hatcher, J., and Barker, T. C., *A History of British Pewter* (1974), pp. 275–6.
8. Rowlands, M. B., *Masters and Men in the West Midland Metalworking Trades before the Industrial Revolution* (1975), p. 48.
9. *The Pewterers' Company Search Books* for the period 1639–89 are deposited at Guildhall Library, London (Guildhall MSS. 7105–6). The recently discovered later books are, at the time of writing, at Pewterers' Hall. Some scattered information on searches prior to 1639 is contained in the *Audit Books* (Guildhall MSS. 7086/1–10) and the *Court Books* (Guildhall MS. 7090).

SHREWSBURY

THERE ARE THREE or four towns or cities in the West Midlands where one might commence a study of pewter manufacture in individual communities. Shrewsbury has been chosen because of the abundance of material available for the study of the history of the town and, perhaps almost as important, its accessibility. Before looking at the scope and nature of the sources available some brief comment on the development of the town is perhaps desirable. Shrewsbury today is a medium-sized country town in the shadow of the conurbation of the West Midlands. Founded in the Dark Ages on a site with a strong defensive potential, it replaced the Roman city of Wroxeter a few miles to the south. It is sited on a hill within a great loop of the River Severn and this defensive position was further strengthened by the provision of town walls and the construction of a castle on the one side not protected by the river. Such defences were essential, since until the 15th century the town was a bastion against Welsh attacks and a base for offensive operations in the Principality.

With the pacification of Wales and the Marches Shrewsbury was able to exploit its natural commercial advantages. These included good communications by the River Severn to the south and Bristol, to the east along Watling Street and into mid-Wales via various valleys. Shrewsbury became the main urban centre for mid-Wales and in time secured control through its Drapers' Company of the growing Welsh woollen industry. The control of this industry, which lasted for some two hundred years, brought considerable prosperity, physical evidence of which survives in the many fine 16th, 17th and 18th century homes.

Eventually the economic changes brought about by the industrial revolution caused fundamental shifts in the patterns of industrial activity and society and with these shifts the possibility of the further growth of Shrewsbury became limited. With this kind of history, it is not surprising that municipal government was established in the town at an early date and that considerable municipal pride was evinced. Excellent records were maintained and have survived, in many cases to be published. These include the burgess rolls dating from the 13th century, guild records and parish registers. The exceptional quantity of this material has made it possible to prepare a detailed history of the craft of pewtering and the production of pewter in the town. These municipal records have produced the earliest known references (with the exception of a conjectural Walsall pewterer of c. 1399) to pewtering in the West Midlands and Wales. In 1414 William Spragge, son of Thomas Spragge of Shrewsbury, was apprenticed for eight years to John Hyndlee of Northampton, brazier, to learn first the craft of brazier and afterwards to be taught the pewterers' craft.[1]

From 1414 until 1629 the names of 20 master pewterers and four apprentices have been recovered from the municipal records.[2] Most were members of the Shrewsbury Company of Mercers, Ironmongers and Goldsmiths, which was one of the most prestigious in the borough. Of the 20 mentioned above, 16 are listed in the Mercers'

Company's books and papers, including one woman, Katherine Wylmot (*c*. 1470–90), who was the wife and later the widow of a William Wylmot who was also a pewterer.

It is not known when the Mercer's Guild was formed since its first Rules or Composition do not survive. The oldest surviving book of the Mercers' Company starts in 1424–25 and a very voluminous set of Rules exists which were granted by Edward, Prince of Wales, son of Edward IV, in the year 1480–81. This document does not indicate that pewterers were to be included in the collective membership of the fraternity, but it does mention William Wylmot by name. A certificate of examination of these rules dated 1515 lists pewterers among those in membership as well as mercers, ironmongers, goldsmiths, founders, candlemakers and copperers. A surviving list of goods belonging to the Company dated from the second year of the reign of Richard III (1484–5) does, however, show that it then owned a considerable quantity of pewter.[3]

> Goods belonging to the Company 2 Rich. 3. Rede money iij^l Itm 1 confur w^t evydens Itm vj sponys selvyr Itm j pece of selvyr Itm j Chalis w^t the paten selvyr and in parte ov' gylde content . . . m^d that hyt ys halowyd. Itm a Bras potte of Robert Ivory whiche lythe for Rent in pledge Itm a nue Baner and an olde Itm iiiji Banerrs for the Mynstrellys werying Itm xliij waxe dysshis of pewter Itm xliiij pencellys ther to Itm ij potell pottys pewtyr Itm ij pewt^r Basens and ij Ewyrs Itm ij pewtry chargerrs Itm j dos' platerrs Itm iiij dos' disshis Itm ij dos' vawcerrys Itm iiij dos' Trenchours Itm j Tabull clothe Itm ij Towell Irysshe clothe Itm iij staynyd cloeths Itm xij Stompys of Torches ii^{lb} of mayde Waxe.

It would appear that the craft was not self-sustaining in the period of domination by the Mercers, as several of the pewterers were immigrants coming from other towns in the region (as were most of the apprentices recorded). These included William Greenbank, who came from Worcester where the Greenbanks were established pewterers and braziers, Thomas Frere from Wigan, then the most important centre in the north-west for pewter production, Thomas Jenins, son of Thomas, a Wednesbury pewterer, John Rosengrove from Chester, and the Collins family together with John Worthynton from Walsall, an important early centre for pewtering. The surviving evidence is not sufficient to clarify whether many others listed were natives of the town. There are, moreover, chronological gaps in the list which make it likely that it is not comprehensive. Additional information has survived for two of those who have been identified, John Rosongrove or Rosengrove, who was made free of the Mercers' Company in 1586, and Richard Collins who was made free in 1599 and was admitted as a burgess in 1608.

John Rosongrove died in 1601–2 and was buried at St Julian's Church. In accordance with the procedures of the time, an inventory of his movable property was submitted to the Lichfield Diocesan Authorities for probate purposes. This is a detailed document which permits a real insight into his business and personal prosperity. The inventory was taken on 2 March 1601–2 by Thomas Jervis, Minister of St Julian's Church, Richard Fearnes and Roger Brown. They also witnessed the accompanying will. The following items listed seem to have formed John Rosongrove's stock-in-trade:

Five dozen and two pewter platters	40s	
Seven pewter dishes	6s	8d
Twelve pewter keevers*	4s	
Five banquetting dishes		20d
Eighteen saucers	3s	

Three pewter pottell potts	4s	
Three quart potts	3s	
One pewter chamber pott		6d
Ten pewter candlesticks	5s	
Fifteen pewter salts	5s	
Eight small brass potts	23s	
One kettell	30s	4d
One dozen spoons and half pint bottell		9d

*Keevers — either a variant of 'covers', or a type of dish.

In addition, he owned brazen moulds for plates, saucers and dishes, a lathe for finishing hollow-ware and a similar one for sadware, a quantity of brass and pewter metal, as well as various tools. The absence of moulds for hollow-ware but the presence of a hollow-ware lathe, indicates that he must have been buying-in probably unfinished items from another maker and then carrying out the final stages of manufacture himself. The total value of the goods listed, including household items, was about £12.

Richard Collins was a more prosperous and a more substantial master craftsman. At the time of his death in December 1611, the total value of his stock in trade, tools and equipment, and domestic goods was £69 15s. 2d. The items of trade stock listed include:

Thirty-eight brass kettles (great and small)	£8	17s	
Eight small brass pannes	£4		
Three brass potes		30s	
Fifteen large pewter plates		30s	
Forty small keevers		30s	
Ninety-seven fruit dishes and trencher platers		48s	6d
Three basons, a collander and a small bowl		8s	
Twenty-four platers		36s	
Two warming pans and a pair of snuffs		8s	
Four flagon potes		16s	
Seven pottle potts		14s	
Twelve three pint potes		18s	
Seventeen quart potes		2s	
Twenty-three chamber potes		24s	
Twenty candlesticks		17s	
Three brasson candlesticks		8s	
Three eleven (?)		5s	
Two . . . (illegible)		3s	
Fifteen double salts		15s	
Forty-four small salts		7s	2d
Eleven cups and two . . . potes		6s	6d
Eleven bottles		3s	
Three dozen and eight saucers		8s	
Five dozen and seven porringer dishes		22s	
Eleven dozen and half and five spoons		8s	

As for tools and related items, the inventory mentions various ladles and skimmers, seven brasson moulds, a lathe, anvils, hammers, etc., and a quantity of old brass, pewter and lead. In addition to the contrast between John Rosongrove's stock of about one hundred and fifty pieces and Richard Collins' five hundred and fifty, their life styles were markedly different. Rosengrove's domestic goods seem only to have consisted of a bed and coverings, a table and cupboard plus odds and ends. Collins lived in a well-furnished home which is described as consisting of, in addition to the shop, the hall, the great chamber over the shop, the little chamber over the shop, the cockloft and the backside. His possessions include a horse, described as being 'fleabitten grey' in colour, and £10 7s. in money. This inventory was taken by Roger Hancks, baker, Edward Buckdall, chandler, David Cadd, Edward Baker (pewterer?) and William Barnes.

In the middle of the 17th century a change of some significance took place in the organisation of the pewter craft in Shrewsbury. Those engaged in the trade ceased to be in membership of the Mercers' Company, and are to be found instead among the ranks of the more plebian 'Fraternity of Smiths, Cutlers and Braziers, etc.', which embraced most of the metal working trades.[4] This guild is not so much noted for the part it played in municipal history, as for the part it played in the Shrewsbury Show, which at the time was a municipal parade followed by feasting outside the town. The Smiths were always led by a man wearing a suit of armour which, it is recorded, weighed 44 pounds.[5] Unfortunately the records of the town do not explain why this change of Company was made. The surviving apprentice book of the Smiths, which covers a large part of the 17th and 18th centuries, is, by comparison with the books of the Mercers, a rough and ready record, kept on an apparently casual basis. This change in company is associated with a change in the term used to describe those making pewter. For some decades they are described indifferently as either pewterers or braziers, with no great significance being attached to the use of either term. This can make the definite identification of working pewterers difficult.

Between 1646 and the mid-18th century, approximately thirty pewterers have been traced, as well as a number of persons described as braziers who may have also been working pewterers. In 1677 the London Company Searchers visited Shrewsbury, as far as it is known for the first time. They listed four pewterers in their record of the search, an indication of the increasing importance of pewter manufacture in Shrewsbury which is confirmed by the fact that we find a pewterer, John Felton, reaching the top of the urban hierarchy as mayor of the town.

John was probably born in Shrewsbury in 1645,[6] although subsequently his parents moved to Oswestry where they and others of the family established themselves as prosperous braziers and pewterers.[7] In 1671, John was admitted as a burgess of Shrewsbury and in 1687 he was elected Warden of the Smiths' Company. In 1690 he was admitted as a burgess of the Montgomeryshire Borough of Welshpool, the other side of Offa's Dyke, and in 1704 was appointed High Sheriff of that Welsh county. Both he and his brother James owned land in Montgomeryshire and his daughter married into the local Welsh gentry.[8]

The records of the Smiths' Company show that during most of his active working life John had an average of three apprentices. A total of 15 of his indentures are listed in the Company Apprentice Book. Contemporary London Company regulations limited pewterers to three apprentices at any one time as being the maximum number who could be satisfactorily taught by one master. At the time of his death in 1707–8, John Felton was mayor of Shrewsbury and was the only Shrewsbury pewterer or brazier known to have been elected to this office.

Information about the nature of the pewter items produced by John Felton and his contemporaries can be gleaned from the London Pewterers' Company Search Books.

The information from this source is subject, however, to two limitations. It can be safely presumed that the visit of the searchers was unwelcome and that little co-operation would have been offered and that efforts may have been made to hide part of the stock held. Secondly, the Search Books often only contain information regarding pieces which did not pass the assay, which was a test of the alloy used. Despite these two drawbacks, the London Company records do help to show what the makers of the town were producing.

The 1677 Search Book gives the following details for Shrewsbury pewterers:

Mr. Felton:	Candlesticks rough square; Porringers; Flat Candlesticks; Flagons; Rough Salts; Spoons; Other Spoons; Small Salts made by Williams [Shrewsbury]; Chapnitt Salts made at Wigan; Bottles made by Nichols; Large porringers made by Prire [Gloucester]; Cupps made by Williams [Shrewsbury]; Chamber potts.
Mr. Williams:	Turn Spoons; Saucers; Porringers; Spoons; Blood dishes; Cans; Candlesticks; Candlesticks made by Banks [Wigan]; Bottles made by Baker of Worcester; Chappnetts made by Felton; Chamber potts; Wine quarts; Wine pints made by Banks; Chamber potts by Felton.
Mr. Sherwin:	Flagons; Stool pans; Porringers; Saucers; Salts; Blood porringers; Dishes made by Ford of Wigan; Chamber potts.
Howell Brown:	Dishes rough; Dishes made by James of Bristol; Dish made by Ford of Wigan; Porringers made by Bradshaw of Wellington; Blood porringers made by Bradshaw of Wellington; Spoons made at Wigan; Other spoons Wigan — touch ye crown; Flagons made by Sherwin [Shrewsbury]; Square Salts made by James of Bristol.

Mr. Williams was Edward Williams and Mr. Sherwin was Humphrey Sherwin who was Warden of the Smiths' Company in 1684. Once again there is clear evidence of trade between pewterers, and this time the available information highlights its considerable geographical extent. Goods were coming up river from as far away as Bristol, and from Wigan in the north.

Howell Brown, son of John Brown of Little Ness, Shropshire, was apprenticed in 1650 to the London pewterer John Bateman and would have been free of the London Company in 1657, assuming a normal seven-year apprenticeship. His whereabouts for the next 15 years are unknown and he may perhaps have worked for a while as a journeyman in London. Be that as it may, he had returned to Shrewsbury by 1672 when he is recorded as having four hearths in Stone Ward and he was admitted a burgess in 1676. It is curious that Howell Brown should have been sent to London to serve his apprenticeship when there were numerous pewterers in nearby Shrewsbury from whom he could have learned the craft. However he is only one of several provincial pewterers who have been identified as having served under a London master before returning to their own locality to practise their skills. A few years later, in 1666, the Shrewsbury pewterer Michael Betton was to send his son Robert to London to be apprenticed to Charles Tough. There does not appear to be any reference to Robert's subsequent career in either Shrewsbury or London.

The appearance in Shrewsbury of Michael Betton, son of an Aberdeen mercer, seems to have been the result of the Civil War. When he is first mentioned in the mid-1640s he is described as a cannoneer and we may safely assume that he was one of the ubiquitous Scottish professional soldiers who came to the town with the parliamentary army. In 1647 he was admitted as a burgess and in 1654 he contracted a second marriage with Elizabeth Wilkes, a pewterer in her own right and the widow of Thomas Wilkes whose business she inherited. Thus the former cannoneer became a pewterer and took over his wife's business.

Sherwin and Brown are among a number of surnames which appear in the period between 1660 and 1730. Others are Davies, with Edward, James, Thomas and a second James; Churchyard, Richard and Thomas; and finally of course Felton. Rather more information is available about some of these families than is available for the earlier pewterers. Many of them appear frequently in the parish registers, particularly those of St Chad's Church, and it is common in the registers of this particular church for occupations to be noted at least until the end of the Stuart period. Some of them appear in the business records of John Duncumb, the prolific maker of pewter who settled in Bewdley in 1720. Some also have been traced in the probate proceedings of the diocese of Lichfield including Humphrey Sherwin who died in 1686, Thomas Foster who died in 1718 and Samuel Brown, the nephew and successor of Howell Brown, who died in 1726-7. Thomas Foster's goods were appraised for his probate inventory on 10 October 1718 by Andrew Thomas and George Sherwin who was also a pewterer.

This inventory reads as follows:

	£	s.	d.
In the best chamber: joinery ware and upholstered ware	8	4	0
Silverplate and brass and iron belonging to ye Chimney in the same room	2	12	0
In the middle room joinery and upholstery were valued	2	0	6
Linen and napery ware in the same room . . .	9	0	0
In two other small rooms joinery ware and upholstery valued	4	0	6
In the little room below ye stairs joinery ware with some books	2	0	0
In the Kitchen: joinery ware and a fowling peice and all sorts of ironware and earthenware in the kitchen valued at	3	0	3
And all sorts of pewter and brass waring in the kitchen	8	4	6
In the Brewhouse and cellar: Vessels and cowpery ware and a load (illegible)	3	0	0
Goods in the shop all sorts of new and old pewter to ye value of	85	0	8
And all sorts of new and old brass and copper valued at	61	5	0
Corn and hay in the barns and stables and a horse valued at	35	0	0
Money at decease and debts owing and a Chattell lease value	35	0	0
Lumber and other fittings not mentioned		6	0
Total	£258	14	11

As well as holding a stock of brass and pewter which would appear from the monetary sum recorded to have amounted to over a ton, Thomas Foster lived a life of some comfort. He owned a horse, a sporting gun, books and, according to his will, a silver tankard and some silver spoons. This is in stark contrast with the picture given of the poverty of Samuel Brown in his probate inventory taken on 26 January 1726-7. All his movable property amounted, at least as far as the two appraisers Henry Baker and Thomas Churchyard (another pewterer) could ascertain, to two old bedsteads, a table, an old chair and form and book debts of £3 9s. 3d. The total value of these meagre domestic possessions and debts due was only £4 3s. 9d.

Only a few years before, Samuel Brown had been trading on some scale. For example, in August 1721, he ordered goods from John Duncumb of Bewdley

1. A mid-18th century dome-lid tankard with a distinctive handle shape. The hall-marks on the drum are those now attributed to Samuel Harrop of Shrewsbury; the first bears three leopards' heads resembling those on the town's arms.

2. A 20-inch charger with multiple reeding to the rim, *c.* 1690. It bears the touch and hall-marks attributed to John Felton I, Shrewsbury. *See* No. 22 in the *Marks* section.

3. A 16⅝-inch diameter charger by Sampson Bourne II of Worcester with a broad rim bearing incised reeding, *c.* 1670.

4. A 20¼-inch charger with incised reeded rim bearing the hall-marks attributed to Edward Bowen, Worcester, *c.* 1690.

5. A 22-inch diameter charger by John Trapp II of Worcester with cast multiple reeding to the rim, *c.* 1690.

6. *(above)* A 9½-inch single reeded plate by Richard Green of Worcester, *c.* 1720.

7. *(above right)* A 9-inch narrow rim plate of a type traditionally attributed to the west country but with the hallmarks of William Greenbank of Worcester on the face and the touch of his father, John Greenbank on the back, *c.* 1690.

8. *(right)* A puritan spoon, with detail of the touch, excavated in Broadway, Worcestershire, with the touch 'IT' in the bowl. Perhaps by John Trapp I, *c.* 1660-70.

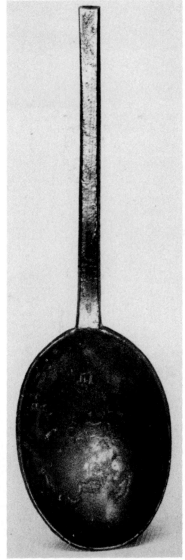

9. Two examples of work by William Wood II of Birmingham. On the left a flat-lid tankard, and, on the right a flagon, both *c.* 1680-90. Note the distinctive thumbpiece and handle terminal on the former and the equally distinctive twin-lobed handle terminal on the latter.

10. Detail of the thumbpiece of the tankard in plate 9.

11. *(left)* An early dome-lid tankard by William Wood II with ram's horn thumbpiece and denticulations at the edge of the lid, *c.* 1700. These exist in pint and quart sizes.

12. *(below)* A two-handled cup of *c.* 1680 of unusual bucket shape with twin loop handles, 6 inch overall, also by William Wood II.

13. Two Birmingham bellied measures; *left*, a quart by McKenzie and *right*, a pint by Morgan and Gaskell, both mid- to late 19th century; *below*, details of the typical later 19th century incuse maker's marks.

14. A 10-inch gadrooned-edge plate by William Tutin, Birmingham, *c.* 1790.

15. Three 19th-century Birmingham tavern pots by *(left to right)* Yates, Birch and Spooner; Villers and Wilkes, and Yates and Birch.

16. A pint dome-lid tankard by Yates, Birch and Spooner, Birmingham, with an unusual 'scallop shell' thumbpiece, *c.* 1830.

17. A pint two-handled cup by Abel Grove, Birmingham, *c.* 1830.

18. The Wribbenhall waterfront *c.* 1920. 'Wribbenhall House' is the white building in the centre background partly obscured by a tree. Pewterers' Alley lies to the left of and behind the row of buildings on the left.

19. *(above)* The old Bewdley (Wribbenhall) pewterers' guild-hall as it now stands re-erected in Ombersley.

20. *(left)* 'River House', Bewdley (with the balcony), for long the home of the Ingram family and dating from 1675.

21. A group of unusual rope-edged dishes by John Duncumb 13½-16½ inch diameter. The edging is cast separately and soldered onto otherwise normal dishes. Perhaps before 1720 and hence made in Birmingham.

22. A wavy-edged plate 10-inch diameter with cast decoration at the rim by Stynt Duncumb, c. 1760.

23. A magnificent 24-inch diameter charger by Stynt Duncumb, Wribbenhall, c. 1750.

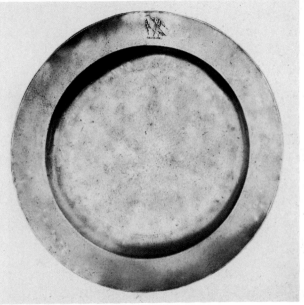

24. *(left)* An unusual small flagon 8½-inch high described as bearing the marks of 'Samuel' Duncumb but perhaps by Ingram and Hunt. (A 40-year old photograph of a piece in the Shelley collection, present whereabouts unknown.)

25. *(right)* A spire flagon by Christopher Banks II of Bewdley inscribed 'C. BANCKS, C. WARDEN 1780'.

26. *(left)* Detail of the inscription on the flagon in plate 2[5]

27. An unusually slender flagon of the late 18th-century with the hall-marks of Ingram and Hunt at the rim.

28. A hot water dish 20-inches over the handles with the hall-marks of John Ingram, Wribbenhall, and a touch of the Duncumb crest, *c.* 1780.

29. Three late 18th-century dome-lidded tankards by Ingram and Hunt. Note the characteristic handle shape and the 'plume' thumbpiece.

30. A quart (Old English Wine Standard) tavern pot by Ingram and Hunt, c. 1780. Note the distinctive twin-cusped handle terminal.

31. A quart (Old English Wine Standard) tavern pot by William Banks of Bewdley, c. 1780.

32. *(above)* A pint (Old English Wine Standard) tavern pot by Crane and Stinton with their touch in the base but with the hall-marks of Ingram and Hunt, *c.* 1810-20.

33. *(above right)* A pint tavern pot by John Carruthers Crane, Bewdley, *c.* 1825, with his touch in the base but bearing still the hall-marks of Ingram and Hunt.

34. *(right)* A Charles I bun-lidded flagon with an unusual 'button' on the lid. A touch of 'CN' in a circle, under the base, is perhaps that of Christopher Nichols of Walsall.

35. A 16th-century porringer with (originally) two fleur-de-lis handles, said to have been excavated at Strata Florida abbey, perhaps Welsh.

36. Part of a banner of the Ludlow Guild of Hammermen showing the arms of the London Pewterers' Company, *c.* 1730. From Cotterell's original photograph.

37. A group of bronze plate moulds, some of 18th-century Bewdley origin, in use by James Smellie of Birmingham until a few years ago.

38. *(above)* A typical multi-part bronze mould for casting the upper half of a bellied measure.

39. *(right)* A range of mainly cast iron moulds in the possession of A & E Williams, Birmingham, and in current use by them.

40. *(overleaf top)* Bewdley and Birmingham hall-marks, *left to right*, John Ingram, Bewdley; Ingram and Hunt, Bewdley; Yates, Birch and Spooner, Birmingham; Abel Grove, Birmingham. Note the use of the Ingram arms by Ingram and Hunt and Yates, Birch and Spooner. The Ingram and Hunt hall-marks were also used by Crane and Stinton and by John Carruthers Crane.

41. *(overleaf bottom)* Three provincial marks with pretended London provenance. *Top*, the 'horse's jamb' crest used as a touch mark by John and Stynt Duncumb and by John Ingram. It is also found on pieces by Ingram and Hunt and was used until recently on reproduction pewter made by their successors; *bottom left*, the touch mark of Birch and Villers, Birmingham, 1772-86. Note the use of a 'LONDON' label in both. *Bottom right*, the touch marks and label of Richard Green, Worcester, incorporating the arms of the London Pewterers' Company.

LONDON

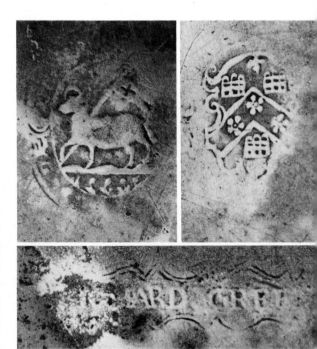

consisting of three hundredweight, three quarters, and six pounds of sadware, and one quarter and five pounds of ordinary plates. The cost of this order, including carriage, etc., was £16 12s. 10½d., four times the above inventory figure. To discover what lies behind this apparent change in fortune at this distance of time is impossible, although the likelihood of bankruptcy or commercial failures is high since by the late 1720s a change in the nature of the trade is apparent. We are moving from the pewterer and brazier to the brazier who sold some pewter which may have been bought in from one of a number of larger producers who are best described as manufacturers. The completion of this change from individual craftsmen to commercial concerns will however take nearly another hundred years. There is some evidence to suggest that in the 1720s the manufacture of pewter in Shrewsbury suffered a check and most of the families which had dominated the pewter business in the previous decades disappear.

These developments are difficult to quantify and evaluate because of changes in the character and scope of the documents and records available. The guilds and fraternities were of course in decline, a process which would accelerate as the pace of industrial change became faster. The Apprentice Book of the Smiths' Company peters out around 1760 and there is no other source from which details of apprentices can be found. For a large part of the 18th century the Shrewsbury parish registers cease to give trade or occupation as a means of identification although odd entries are found. Finally, the burgess roll, earlier a most reliable source of basic details, is distorted by considerations of national politics. Admission as a burgess carried with it the right to a vote in parliamentary elections. During the 18th and early 19th centuries when there was a contested election, it was immediately preceded by an influx on the burgess roll, while at other times there were few admissions. The rolls become as a result a less reliable guide to the economic and social history of the town.

Caution should also be used when drawing conclusions from the later Smiths' Company records, as for example in the case of Thomas Burgess. He is first mentioned in the Smiths' Company Book in 1731 but appears in the parish register of St Chad's Church as early as 1714 as a brazier and in 1719 as a pewterer. Of all those listed in that book during the 18th century as braziers and pewterers, Thomas Burgess is the person most often described as a pewterer. An intriguing question is posed by Thomas and another Shrewsbury pewterer. On 28 January 1701-2, a Thomas Burgess was given leave to strike his touch by the London Company (London Touch Plate 595), having been admitted to the Yeomanry of that Company the previous April. Pieces bearing this touch survive and have been recorded. Although it is tempting to assume that this is the same individual, this cannot be confirmed, as the London Thomas Burgess is described in his apprenticeship record as the son of Jonathan Burgess of Thame in Oxfordshire. There is nothing to connect him with Shrewsbury. The other individual about whom a similar question can be asked is Josiah Clarke, who is mentioned in the parish registers of St Chads between 1701 and 1710 as a pewterer and brazier, and was a witness to the will of John Felton. The London Company records show that a Josiah Clarke was permitted to strike his touch on 6 January 1694, but again the records of the London Company show that he was the son of a John Clarke of Congrave, Nottinghamshire, and the link cannot be confirmed.

Any list of pewterers, even Howard Cotterell's *Old Pewter: its Makers and Marks*, can appear rather formless and disjointed. In practice the world of pewter manufacture was small and closely knit through three types of links; by apprenticeship, by marriage and by descent. From the records as they exist, and some other sources it is possible to see and trace some of these links. For example in 1707–8 Samuel Brown, who has already been discussed, took as an apprentice Michael Reynolds, who became a burgess in 1734. Likewise in 1727 Michael Reynolds took as an apprentice Samuel Harrop, who was admitted himself as a burgess in 1750 and died in 1779. Samuel was a nonconformist, and in due time his daughter Elizabeth married another member of the same nonconformist chapel, who was also a pewterer and brazier, White Cooke.[9] Cooke died in 1785 aged 57 and *Minshill's Directory* of 1786 lists Mrs. Cooke as a brazier whose place of business was in Pride Hill.

This survey of the manufacture of pewter in Shrewsbury has now reached its final phase. By the end of the 18th century it is quite clear that pewterers have been replaced by braziers who sold pewter but made little of what they sold. As far at least as pewter was concerned the braziers were retailers buying their wares from specialist manufacturers. There had always been trade between different pewterers but by 1800 (as the chapter on Bewdley will show) this had become sophisticated and the methods of business in use appear to our eyes surprisingly modern. The 18th century has always been viewed as a period in which the making and use of pewter was in decline. Whatever the effect this decline may have had on the London pewterers, in the provinces the result of the decline was not to destroy the industry so much as to change its character. Whereas in 1700 any town of size would have had one or more active pewterers, by 1800 there would have been several braziers who also dealt in pewter. The decline in pewter may have been exaggerated in the past because most scholars and collectors have looked at the number of makers who were marking pieces with a touch rather than the quantity of pewter being made. By 1800 there were several shops in Shrewsbury at which a wide variety of pewter items could have been bought, but they would have been made by a far smaller number of pewterers.

There remains as far as Shrewsbury is concerned one problem. In 1796 there was a contested parliamentary election in the town, and as a result a large number of burgesses were admitted. The burgess roll surprisingly lists five men whose occupations are given as pewterers, Joseph Bevan, James Crump, Thomas Farmer, Thomas Jones and Thomas Purslow. None of these is, however, mentioned in any contemporary trade directories. It is conceivable that they were all brought in from outside in an attempt by one party or another to pack the poll. Alternatively they may be the workers or employees of a master who was engaged in the manufacture of pewter but who described himself — as did most of his contemporaries — as a brazier. Whichever is the case no evidence has been found to solve the problem except for an entry in Cotterell regarding Thomas Barrow. Cotterell notes that the *Salopian Journal* included an entry on 9 December 1795, which described him as a pewterer of Pride Hill, Shrewsbury.

Among those mentioned in 1796 is Thomas Purslow, whose son Thomas was admitted a burgess at the same time as his father, but who was not sworn because of his age. This was a common practice as it protected a male child's right to burgess status. When Thomas was sworn in 1848 he was listed as a pewterer. He was presumably the one remaining pewterer who was recorded in the 1841 Census as being a resident of the town. With him ended the manufacture of pewter in Shrewsbury which began 400 years previously.

In one way however this is not quite the end of the story. Until a few years ago there was a small shop in Grope Lane, Shrewsbury, where repairs were undertaken to items made of brass, copper and pewter, and where items in the same metals, mostly second-hand, could be purchased. This is perhaps the final, if tenuous, link in an historic chain which began with William Spragge.

Shrewsbury Pewterers and Braziers

Note: f = free of the Mercers' Company

Spragge, William	app 1414, p (app in Northampton)
Lynge, Richard	f 1462-3, p
Wylmot, William	f 1475-6, p
Wylmot, Katherine	m 1473-90, p, w. of William
Kensall, Christopher	m 1506, p
Keneston, Thomas	f 1524-5, p
Derby, Philip	f 1524-5, p (of Worcester)
Jenins, William	f 1548-9, p
Worthynton, John	f 1550, p (from Walsall)
Mooles, Thomas	B 1551, p
Nicholls(on), Thomas	f 1550, p
Watson, Thomas	m 1568, d 1597, p
Pellyter, John	m 1579-1600, p
Frier (Frere), Thomas	f 1580, p
Rosongrave, John	f 1586, d 1601, p
Blower, Richard	f 1605
Collins, Richard	f 1599, B 1608, d 1611, p (from Walsall)
Collins, Rowland I	f 1613, B 1624, d 1655, p
Davies, Timothie	m 1625, br
Collins, John	f 1626, d 1650, p, b. of Richard
Savage, Robert	d 1648, br
Greenbank, William	f 1629, B 1632, d 1649, p (from Worcester)
Wilkes, Thomas	B 1646, p
Greenbank, Cecily	m 1649, p, w. of William
Wilkes, John	app 1646, d 1663, p, s. of Thomas
Wilkes, Elizabeth	m 1649, d 1679, p, w. of Thomas
Collins, Rowland II	b 1634, f 1654, d 1699, p, s. of Rowland I
Browne, Howell	app 1650, B 1676, m 1691, p (app in London)
Betton, Michael	m 1654, d 1671, p
Davies, Edward	m 1660s, p
Sherwin, Humphrey	B 1670, d 1686, p (Warden, Smiths' Company in 1684)
Hill, John	m 1656-77, p
Felton, John I	b 1645, B 1671, d 1708, p and br (Warden, Smiths' Company in 1687, mayor in 1707-8)
Williams, Edward	b 1656(?), B 1672, d 1692, p
Churchyard, Richard	m 1682, p
Griffiths, Richard	app 1672, m 1703, br
Foster, Thomas I	B 1687, d 1718, p
Davies, James I	app 1683, d 1699, p and br·
Sherwin, George	app 1677, m 1718, p, s. of Humphrey
Felton, James I	b 1654, app 1670, B 1702, d 1717, p and br, b. of John (of Oswestry, q.v.)
Collins, Rowland III	b 1667, p, s. of Rowland II

Brown(e), Samuel	b 1670, app 1686, B 1721, p, n. of Howell
Churchyard, Thomas	app 1692, B 1721, p and br (Warden, Smiths' Company in 1713)
Clarke, Josiah	m 1700, d 1710, p
Felton, James II	app 1699, d 1710, p and br (*see also* Oswestry)
Clemson, William	app 1706, B 1721, p and br
Davies, Thomas	B 1721, m 1729, p and br
Davies, James II	app 1704, B 1721, p and br, s. of James I
Felton, John II	b 1694, app 1711, B 1721, d 1758, p and br, s. of James I (of Oswestry, q.v.)
Davies, Sarah	m 1704, br
Burges, Thomas	m 1714, d 1758, p and br
Foster, Thomas II	app 1708, B 1721, p, s. of Thomas I
Reynolds, Michael	app 1706, B 1734, d 1740, p and br
Chively, Richard	m 1705–20, br
Roberts, Thomas	m 1711–28, d 1730, br
Price, Samuel	B 1721, br
Fothergale, William Best	m 1731, br
Phillips, Thomas	app 1722, d 1785, p and br
Harrop, Samuel	app 1727, B 1750, d 1779, p and br
Lee, Joseph	m 1738, br
Reynolds, Martha	m 1740s, p and br, w. of Michael
Plummer, Richard	B 1753 (? formerly of Ludlow)
Burges, Ralph	m 1758, d 1773, p, br. of Thomas
Cooke, White	m 1760, d 1785, p and br, s.-in-law of Samuel Harrop
Clarke, Thomas	app 1750, m 1774, p and br
Phillips, William	m 1774, br
Winstanley, John	B 1779, m 1790, br
Davies, John	m 1781, p
Bryan, Joseph	m 1786, br
Cooke, Mrs.	m 1786, br
Phillips, Edward	app *c.* 1760, B 1796, m 1835, br
Vincent, W.	m 1786–90, br
Barrow, Thomas	m 1795, p
Ball, Thomas	B 1796, br
Basnett, Edward	B 1796, br
Bryan, John	B 1796, br
Collier, Joseph	B 1796, br (of Wellington)
Corfield, John	b 1796, br
Davies, Richard	B 1796, br
Harwood, Edward	B 1796, br
Fewtrill, Samuel	B 1796, br
Phillips, Richard	B 1796, br (of Welshpool)
Tovey, Joseph	B 1796, br
Winstanley, John	B 1796, br
Bevan, Joseph	B 1796, p
Crump, James	B 1796, p
Farmer, Thomas	B 1796, p
Jones, Thomas	B 1796, p
Purslow, Thomas I	B 1796, p
Basnett, Mrs.	m 1803, br
Bryan, Thomas	B 1806, br
Jarratt, Stephen	B 1806, br
Jones, Charles	B 1806, br
Schofield, George	B 1806, m 1835

Brain (Brayne), William	B 1809, br
Newling, T.	m 1809, br
Price (Pryce), Robert	B 1812, br
Parry, Edward	B 1814, br
Lloyd, John	Admitted B 1796, sworn 1826
Purslow, Thomas II	B 1848, p, s. of Thomas I

Shrewsbury Apprentices

This list contains details of Shrewsbury apprentices who have not been subsequently identified as working craftsmen.

Under the Mercers' Company

Apprentice	Master	Date
Wylson, John	Wylmot, Katherine	1473–4
Reignold, Robert	Kensall, Christopher	1506–7
ap Ric' ap John, Edward	Nycolls, Thomas	1556–7
Spark, Nicholas	Rosengrove, John	1594–5
Evans, Benjamin	Collins, Rowland	1656

Under the Smiths' Company

Apprentice	Master	Date
Tanat, Thomas	Felton, John	1676
Walton, William	Felton, John	1677
Carpenter (?), Benjamin	Sherwin, Humphrey	1678
Vaughan, Richard	Felton, John	1680
Kinaston, Samuel	Felton, John	1681
Wright, Joseph	Sherwin, Humphrey	1684
Gregg, Francis	Felton, John	1685
Smith, John	Felton, John	1687–8
Foster, William	Foster, Thomas	1688
Evans (?), William	Felton, John	1691–2
Jones, Jonathan	Davis, James	1698
Lloyd, John	Browne, Samuel	1698
Jones, John	Felton, John	1699
Browne, Samuel	Browne, Samuel	1707–8
Browne, James	Browne, Samuel	1708
Corbett, Adam	Foster, Thomas	1709
Norton, John	Browne, Samuel	1712
Davies, David	Davies, James	1717
Jones, John	Felton, Jeremiah	1718
Baxter, Samuel	Browne, Samuel	1719
Gittins, Edmund	Churchyard, Thomas	1722–3
Pepley, Joseph	Davies, Thomas	1722–3
Hill, John	Reynolds, Michael	1723

Apprentice	Master	Date
Conyers, Thomas	Clemson, William	1724
Baxter, Samuel	Reynolds, Michael	1725–6
Roberts, John	Robert, Thomas	1728
Llewellyn, Richard	Reynolds, Michael	1729
Burgess, William	Price, Samuel	1731 (?)
Norton, Samuel	Fothergale, William B.	1731
Deuxall (?), Adrian	Phillips, Thomas	1731
Lomax, William	Phillips, Thomas	1731
Holland, Gilbert	Burgess, Thomas	1731
Pugh, Edward	Phillips, Thomas	1734–5
Parker, Thomas	Reynolds, Michael	1734–5
Davies, William	Burgess, Thomas	1737
Reynolds, Andrew	Reynolds, Michael	1738
Lee, John	Lee, Joseph	1739
Mackannos (?), Edward	Harrop, Samuel	1741–2
Milton, Thomas	(illeg.), Samuel	1741
	(brazier of Whitechapel, London)	
Phillips, Thomas	Phillips, Thomas	1745
Burgess, Thomas	Burgess, Thomas	1745
Reynolds, Michael	Reynolds, Mrs. Martha	1747–8
Strang, Thomas	Phillips, Thomas	1747 (?)
Dalliman (?), Richard	Reynolds, Mrs. Martha	1749
Kendrick, William	Harrop, Samuel	1748–9
Hopkins, Richard	Harrop, Samuel	1748–9
Lee, William	Burgess, Thomas	1751
Tovey, Thomas	Harrop, Samuel	1751

NOTES AND REFERENCES

Shrewsbury

1. 'Indenture of Apprenticeship 1414', *Transactions of the Shropshire Archaeological Society*, vol. 8 (1884–5), p. 411.
2. Forrest, H. E. (ed.), *The Shrewsbury Burgess Roll* (1924) and 'The Shrewsbury Burgesses 16th–17th Century', *Transactions of the Shropshire Archaeological Society*, vol. 48 (1934–5).
3. Leighton, W. A., 'The Guilds of Shrewsbury — Mercers, Ironmongers and Goldsmiths' Company', *Transactions of the Shropshire Archaeological Society*, vol. 8 (1884–5).
4. *The Shrewsbury Smiths' Company Book*, Shrewsbury Local Studies Library, MS. 4583.
5. 'The Ancient Guilds, Trading Companies and the Origin of Shrewsbury', *Transactions of the Shropshire Archaeological Society*, vol. 6 (1883).
6. *The Parish Registers of St Chad*, Shropshire Parish Register Society.
7. *The Parish Registers of Oswestry*, Shropshire Parish Register Society. *See also* the chapter *Oswestry and Ludlow*.
8. Lloyd, J. D. K., *Montgomeryshire Collections*, vol. 66 (1978), pp. 61–3 and vol. 12, pp. 325, 330.
9. *Shropshire Nonconformist Registers*, Shropshire Parish Register Society.

General

Parish Registers of the Church of the Holy Cross (Abbey Church), Shrewsbury Local Studies Library MS.

Calendar of Deeds and Charters, Shrewsbury Local Studies Library MS.

Morries, Joseph, *Shropshire Genealogies*, Shrewsbury Local Studies Library MS.

Leighton, W. A., 'The Guilds of Shrewsbury', *Transactions of the Shropshire Archaeological Society*, vol. 6 (1883).

Shrewsbury Chronicle, 'List of the Burgesses and Freemen who voted in the Election of 11–14 October 1774' (1774).

Transactions of the Shropshire Archaeological Society. Various volumes but particularly vol. 10 (1886–7), pp. 157–348 and vol. 50 (1939), p. 11.

Trades Directories, Minshull 1786; Universal British 1798; Minshull 1803; Newling 1809; Tibnam & Co. 1828.

OSWESTRY AND LUDLOW

THE COUNTY of Shropshire, recently renamed after a short spell as Salop, contains a number of historic market towns in addition to Shrewsbury. Although none of these was of the same significance as the county town, many of them included amongst their tradesmen and craftsmen pewterers and braziers. Two of these towns, Oswestry and Ludlow, seemed to be of particular interest and have therefore been selected for more detailed study.

Oswestry, which is only 17 miles from Shrewsbury, has always been overshadowed by the larger town, but despite economic subservience it has a distinct character of its own as the border town par excellence. Today the visitor is more likely to hear Welsh spoken in the streets of Oswestry than in many towns in Wales. A study of the registers of the parish church indicates that this is nothing new, as Welsh surnames are to be found in considerable numbers at all periods. Located as it is so near to the political boundary between England and Wales it could not be other than a point of contact, whether of a military, political, social or economic nature. As at Shrewsbury, with the end of the centuries of military conflict, economic opportunities opened up and the town played for some decades a significant part in the Welsh wool trade. The producers brought their cloth to Oswestry where a market was held, at which they met and dealt with the Shrewsbury Drapers. Eventually in the early 1620s conflict over this trade arose between Oswestry and Shrewsbury in which perhaps inevitably the former suffered defeat at the hands of its larger and more powerful neighbour. Despite this set-back the town continued to perform the function of a place of exchange, contact and trade between the Welsh and the English. In addition, during the late 17th and 18th centuries the development of coal production nearby introduced a new strand to the economic life of the town.

As far as records are concerned Oswestry has municipal records which should be of significance to this study but which in fact do not offer much that is worthwhile. Charters were granted to the borough by James I in 1617 and again in 1674 by Charles II. After the confirmation of the second charter a new book for recording the admission of burgesses was started and continued in use with some gaps until 1834, but this book regrettably includes no pewterers or braziers.[1] Apparently a number of guilds existed but none of their documents or papers have survived; so the main source of information which has been used is therefore the registers of the parish church, supplemented by information contained in the Shrewsbury records. The parish registers have been transcribed and printed.[2]

The earliest mentioned pewterer in the registers is Edward Baker or Bakere who first appears in 1595 and his death is noted in September 1608. If this was all the information which had survived about Edward Baker he would indeed be a shadowy figure. His will however exists at the Public Record Office among the probate records of the Archdiocese of Canterbury and this shows him to have been a man of some substance, owning for example 12 silver spoons, and he was the holder of a burghal tenement in Middle Street. His will clearly describes him as a pewterer, but gives little further information about the nature and scale of his business. It includes a list of 45 people who owed him money including the names of minor figures in the local gentry, fellow tradesmen and others, none however can be identified as a fellow pewterer. The implication of this list is that Edward Baker was engaged in other business activities and that some of his wealth may have been due as much to these activities as to the making of pewter. Indeed he had loaned money to various individuals on goods as diverse as a feather bed, a lady's gown, a pair of scales, and six pewter platters suggesting that he was a pawn-broker. A son and heir, Richard, is mentioned in this document and several daughters, but no evidence has been found to suggest that Richard followed his father as a pewterer.

During the next four decades two braziers are mentioned in the parish registers. David ap Richard, who was Welsh, and Richard Lankeshire. Then, in the 1650s we find the first reference to the Felton family who have already been discussed in connection with Shrewsbury. This family, as has already been seen, is an example of the provincial pewterer and brazier prospering in the high noon of pewter production. Thomas Felton, the founder of the family business, is first mentioned in Oswestry parish registers in 1654 and continues to appear until his death in 1675 in a variety of different contexts. It would appear that he was a nonconformist and a supporter of the Commonwealth. In 1660 he is listed as a malignant and an enemy of the King and in 1673, when appointed a Common Councilman under the new Borough Charter, he disqualified himself from taking office by refusing to take the oath against the Solemn League and Covenant.[3] He died in 1675 and his probate inventory and will are held by the National Library of Wales. The inventory of his movables indicates total property to the value of £300 12s. 8d. This includes two horses, furniture and fittings, good and bad debts, money, tools, scales and weights, new and old brass to the value of £131 and pewter worth £54 but no details are given of the items of pewter and brass in stock. Coal is mentioned as fuel which must relate to the development of mining in the area.

Thomas was followed briefly in his pewtering business in Oswestry by his widow Gwen who died in 1678. She is mentioned in the London Company Search Book for 1677 with the following entry:

> Spoons by Felton of Shrewsbury; Saucers by Felton of Shrewsbury; Porringers made by him; Candlesticks made by him; Dishes 3 lb made by Tho. Ford [Wigan]; Dishes 1 lb made by him; Dishes ½ lb made by William Ford [Wigan]; Porringers made by I.B. Wigan; Flagon made by J. Ford [Wigan]; Porringer marked IF (possibly John or James Felton); Chamber pots by Williams of Shrewsbury; Chamber pots by IF; Other Chamber pots by Williams.

There is no indication in the above list that Mrs. Felton was making any pewter of her own although, unlikely though it seems, it could be that all her own products passed the assay. The inventory of her movables does seem to support the idea that following her husband's death she had reduced her pewtering activities. The inventory which was taken on 18 July 1678 by Hugh Price and Gwen's son John (the Shrewsbury pewterer) lists the following items:

3 horses with their implements valued at	£10	0s. 0d.
In old and new pewter	£42	2s. 10d.
All the brass new and old	£178	19s. 1d.
In hay and compost	£5	0s. 0d.
In iron potts and all other iron ware with all the working tools	£29	9s. 9d.
In debts owing	£5	0s. 0d.
Money in the house	£18	0s. 0d.
If anything be forgotten and not mentioned	£10	0s. 0d.
Total	£343	10s. 8d.

Although this inventory shows an increase in the value of the goods listed by over £40 compared with that of her husband, the value of the pewter has fallen from £54 to £42 and the corresponding figure for brass has risen substantially to nearly £179.

At this time James Felton, who would follow his mother in Oswestry, had not completed his apprenticeship in Shrewsbury, to his elder brother John, which he had begun in 1670. James Felton was born in 1654 and died in 1716. He settled in Oswestry and was a prominent citizen of that town although he appears not to have taken any part in municipal government, probably for the same reason as his father, that is, he was a dissenter. The one document which gives a picture of his life and work in his will which shows that his assets at that time included land in Montgomeryshire and at 'Porkinton' (= Brongynton) in Shropshire, property in Shrewsbury, and in three different parts of Oswestry, Bailey Street, Willow Street and Legg Street. James lived in Bailey Street where he apparently had his business premises, whilst his other Oswestry properties were occupied by various tenants. The Shrewsbury property was occupied by his son Jeremiah in August 1716 and these premises were in all probability those occupied previously by John Felton.

James Felton had a sizeable family all of whom were provided for in his will, but initially all the property was bequeathed to his wife Elizabeth, née Jones. His widow carried on with the business after James' death until her sons grew to an age to take over and she is mentioned in John Duncumb's day book as a customer from 1720–4. Quite what the extent of James Felton's business was has not been established, although described as a brazier, he sold a bell to the Wrexham Churchwardens in 1706 for which they paid him £3 13s. 6d., suggesting that he was also a founder.[4] In view of his apprenticeship it is almost certain that he made pewter and hall-marks and a touch mark with the name 'Felton', dating from about 1700 have been recorded (Cott. 1469A) which can only be those of either James or his brother John, with the former being more likely.

Of James' and Elizabeth's many children a number of those born in the early days of their marriage died young. Of those who survived, five sons followed the trade of pewterer and/or brazier; James was apprenticed to his uncle John, and Thomas, Jeremiah and Philip were apprenticed in turn to their father. Only Samuel does not seem to have been apprenticed to the trade. John and Thomas became burgesses of Shrewsbury in 1721 when they were described as being pewterers of Oswestry.[5] John and Philip were admitted as burgesses of the nearby Welsh market town of Welshpool in 1717. Jeremiah died in 1720, Philip in 1731, John in 1758 and Thomas in 1765.

With the death of the last of James' sons this successful and extensive family firm seems to have disappeared. Feltons are however found in Ludlow later in the 18th century and William Felton, ironmonger, was a steward of Ludlow Hammermen's Company in 1795.

Felton of Oswestry and Shrewsbury

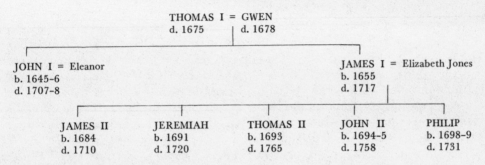

Note: Pewterers/braziers only shown.

Two other contemporary braziers are mentioned in the Oswestry parish registers, Robert Boulton and his son, another Robert. Robert the elder first appears in 1692 and his death is noted in 1708. His son who was born in 1702, died in 1786. The registers cannot, of course, tell us whether the Boultons were independent craftsmen or whether they were employees of the Felton family.

No evidence survives that after the death of the last of the Thomas Felton's grandchildren any pewter was made in Oswestry, however a number of braziers are recorded in the last years of the 18th century and the early years of the 19th century including William Bickerton, Lewis Gwyn or Gwynne and Edward Howell. These men belong to that large group who in the first two or three decades of the 19th century are described as braziers. Their function as far as pewter is concerned seems to have been to retail goods made by others and to repair damaged items. Lewis Gwyn is recorded as a customer of the Ingram and Hunt partnership of Bewdley.

LUDLOW

Ludlow, lying about half way between Shrewsbury and Hereford, is perhaps the most attractive of the Welsh border towns and its surviving old buildings give proof of its previous wealth and prosperity. Ludlow's history is quite exceptional for the area and the town was for many years an important administrative centre. Firstly the powerful Mortimer family, then the House of York and finally the Council of the Marches established themselves there. This council was the governing body for Wales and the Marches from the 1470s until 1689 with a break during the Commonwealth period when it was dissolved. Obviously the Council brought to what would otherwise have been only an ordinary market town, major political figures, judges, lawyers and administrators and the local English and Welsh gentry. Such people would offer a welcome and substantial market to the local merchants, shopkeepers and artisans. The town clearly attracted Welsh as well as English craftsmen as is evidenced by the names appearing in the records, Morgan Tyler and Griffiths Smythe in 1510 and the pewterer Edward ap Owen in 1577-8. Even after the Council of the Marches ceased to exist, the town remained a social centre for the gentry who kept houses there or rented them for the season.

The records of the Craft Guild of Ludlow are extensive and well preserved and cover the period from 1510 to 1848.[6] As well as the guild's minute books, ordinances of 1510 and charters of 1576 and 1715 survive, together with admission certificates for the period 1597 to 1797 and other documents. Cotterell, in *Old Pewter its Makers and Marks*, summarised the history of the guild and recorded a number of Ludlow pewterers extracted from these papers. A new study of this source of information has led to the identification of additional pewterers who worked in the town, has provided more information on the organisation of the craft, and has allowed the correction of certain of Cotterell's observations. A study of the parish registers has helped to fill out the picture, though these seldom give occupations.

John West, in *Town Records*,[7] refers to a Palmers' Guild (a fraternity of pilgrims) in Ludlow from the 13th century, and the town's charter of 1461 mentions a merchant guild. The earliest reference to the craft guild in Ludlow appears to be in certain ordinances promulgated by Richard Duke of York, which survive in a later copy, probably of early 16th century date. These prohibit the employment of any 'foreigner' in any craft in the town on penalty of the very large sum of £40 (not £10 as given by Cotterell), and must date from before 1460 when the duke died. The charter of 1576 claims that the guild long predated an Act of 19 Henry VII (1503-4).

Whether the guild included pewterers in the 15th century is unknown and the earliest reference to this craft is in the ordinances of 1510. This commences as follows:

> To all christian men (etc) we Robert Tenche, Thomas Cutler, Hughe Goldsmythe, William Wele, Thomas Hunt, William Hop(er), John Russell, Thomas Mordyford, John Sadeler, Thomas Llose, Hugh ? Deyas, Hughe Marrs — smythe, John Halpeny, Thomas Cuppar, Morgan Tyler, Thomas Foxe — tyler, Thomas Meyrek, Griffiths Smythe, William Tyler the elder, Thomas (illeg), William Tyler the younger, John Cle, John Smythe, John ? Acke — carpenter and Richard ? Cyth — carpenter, masters of the crafte of smythes, ironmongers, sadelers, brasiers, pewterers, sporyers, buckel makers, brygand iron makers, armorers, masons, cardmakers, and coupers of the town of Ludlow sende greetings . . .

Regrettably only four names are followed by occupations and none of those named can so far be identified as a pewterer.

The guild at that time held its meeting in St Lawrence's Church (and indeed continued to do so until 1848) and it clearly had religious as well as well as secular purposes. Thus in these ordinances the members of the guild undertake 'the keeping, susteynynge and mayntenyaunce of the light yerely from henceforth for evermore in the howse of all mighty God . . .'. At a practical level the guild was to be supervised by two stewards and 'six of the most honest and saddest men to be called by the name of the vi men', all of whom were to be elected. A master apprenticed in Ludlow was to pay 6s. 8d. for his freedom and any apprenticed outside the town, 13s. 4d. Any master summoned to a meeting who did not attend was 'to present to the said light at every default half-a-pound of wax', and the same penalty was imposed on any journeyman who rebuked a master.

Assuming those subscribing to this document constituted the total membership, the guild then had 25 members. By 1647 it seems to have reached 39; by 1665, 48; and by 1739 just over a hundred. Its monetary resources in the last-named year totalled £37 10s. 0d., and about that time a resolution was passed not to allow them to fall below £20. The fines payable on admission in 1539 were 10s. 8d. for a townsman and £2 0s. 8d. for a stranger. Although the sums changed in later years, the differential was maintained and it is thus possible to determine whether a freeman was or was not a native of the town by the amount he paid for his freedom.

The churchwardens' accounts, published from 1540 to 1600,[8] give us perhaps the earliest identifiable brazier, Philip Tynker, who is recorded in 1540 when he was paid 4d. for 'brassynge of a kandylstyke'. He also supplied solder to the church and was therefore presumably also a plumber or pewterer. From 1541 to 1543 a general metal-worker, Philip Jokes, was paid various sums for supplying solder, mending the parish cross, mending the clock, casting a new lead weight for the clock and 'mendynge of the irone that the barelles of the chymes do the goo in'. There does not appear to be any specific mention of pewter or pewterers, or of the guild in these accounts.

The earliest recorded pewterer in the guild records is William Bradshaw, who was free in 1544-5. He is mentioned in the churchwardens' accounts in 1548 when he paid 24 shillings for 'iiii standards weynge a C and d and xxvi li' which were among much 'popish' furnishings then being disposed of. There is then a long gap before Edward ap Owen, pewterer, was made free in 1577-8. He was clearly of Welsh origin, though he chose to work in England, and he was prominent in the guild's affairs until after 1600. He was followed by Roger Baylys, free in 1588-9, and by Robert Ellice, free in 1593, neither of whom are noted by Cotterell. Robert Ellice is recorded as having been apprenticed to Edward Bowen, pewterer of Ludlow, also previously unrecorded.

There is something of a mystery about another 16th century Ludlow pewterer, Martin Cropper. In an article on the Hammermen of Ludlow[9] it is said that in 1575, after he had been working as a pewterer in the town for some twenty years without joining the Guild, despite suits against him, he was finally allowed by the authorities to continue in the trade unhindered. His name does not appear among the freemen of the guild and it is somewhat chastening to the historian to realise that at the height of guild control, and in the face of apparently stiff penalties, a craftsman could escape being enrolled as a member.

Five pewterers were admitted between 1600 and 1660, one being Roger Tomkyns who was a stranger, paying £2 for his freedom, and who later moved to Leominster where he founded a family business which is described in a later chapter of this book. Two others, Henry Barber (1633) and Henry Nicholls (1659), were also strangers indicating that the town's pewter craft was not self-sustaining at this time. For some reason which is not given Roger Norton, who was made free as a pewterer in 1660, was disenfranchised along with nine others of various trades in 1665. In the mid-17th century there appear the first members of two families who were to dominate the Ludlow pewter trade for the next hundred years. Thomas Deuxhall (also Duksell, Dewxell and variants) and Richard Plummer. No relationship of the former to Henry Deuxell of London (Cott. 1365, c. 1600) has been found, but it seems likely in view of the uncommon name they shared.

The shops of both were visited by the London searchers in 1677. As well as tankards, polished cans, porringers, standishes and chamber pots of his own making, Thomas Deuxhall stocked wares made by Sampson Bourne and Job Wareing of Worcester, by Edward Williams of Shrewsbury and by widow Tompkins of Leominster. Richard Plummer made his own spoons, flagons, candlesticks, porringers and chamber pots, and also stocked a range of wares by Sampson Bourne and others.

Thomas Deuxhall, himself free in 1661, was followed by two sons, Robert in 1693 and Richard in 1700. Robert died in 1741. Richard Plummer was a stranger paying £5 for his freedom as a pewterer in 1664 and a further 16s. 8d. a few months later to be admitted additionally as a brazier. He was followed in 1693 by his son, in 1717 by his grandson and in 1749 by his great-grandson, all of whom bore the name Richard. From the Hereford diocesan records, the will and inventory of the first Richard Plummer has been recovered; this is dated 1689 and was proved in 1692. The probate inventory gives comprehensive details of Richard's tools and stock and also evidence of his other property and goods, the total monetary value of which was £417 13s. 8d. Below is an extract from this inventory giving details of working tools, stock in trade and other items relevant to the practice of his craft.

Inventory of Richard Plummer of Ludlow

	£	s.	d.
1 hundred of pewter dishes sadware etc	4	4	0
1 cwt more of sadware at 9d./lb	4	4	0
1 cwt more of hollow ware at 10d./lb	4	13	4
1 cwt more of hollow ware	4	13	4
1 cwt more of hollow ware	4	13	4
1 cwt more of hollow ware	4	13	4
3 quarters of chamber pots lay at 7d./lb	2	9	0
1 cwt of (illeg) cettles at 7 li 8s.	7	8	0

	£	s.	d.
1 cwt of (illeg) cettles)			
1 cwt more of (illeg) cettles)	11	4	0
1 of skilletts and kan [?] cettles and pott cettles	7	0	0
5 warming pans and shafts		15	0
14 pounds of brass candlesticks		18	8
1 lb [sic] of new brass potts	2	16	0
3 quarters and 15 pounds of new brass and potts . . .	3	6	0
1 cwt of cast pewter at 7d./lb	3	5	4
1 cwt of old pewter)			
1 cwt more of old pewter) at 7d./lb	9	16	0
1 cwt more of ould pewter)			
2 qrs of fine shearings at 6d./lb	1	8	0
10 pounds of skimeers		12	0
1 cwt of yellow brass at 9d./lb	4	4	0
1 close stole & coales in the shop and led [lead]		10	0
40 lbs of lay in the say [?] at 7d./lb	1	3	3
40 lbs of trifles shearings at 6d./lb	1	0	0
	£80	16	8

In the warehouse

		£	s.	d.
1 cwt and 4 pounds of sadware moulds)				
1 cwt & 8 pounds more of sadware moulds)				
1 cwt & 11 pounds more) at 10d./lb		24	5	0
1 cwt 1 qr & 13 pounds more)				
2 qr & 14 pounds more of sadware moulds)				

		£	s.	d.
1 cwt of hollow ware moulds)				
1 cwt more)				
1 cwt more)				
1 cwt & 8 pounds more) at 12d./lb		34	0	0
1 cwt more)				
1 cwt more)				
2 [cwt?] of working tools)		3	17	0
3 qrs of hambers and other tools)				
2 wheels and the materials		3	0	0
2 marments [?]		1	0	0
		£66	2	0

The Plummers disappear from Ludlow in the middle of the 18th century when the family may have moved to Shrewsbury, a Richard Plummer, brazier, being recorded there in 1753.

In 1711 the guild began to consider applying for a new charter and appointed one representative of each craft to form a committee to advise on this. The representative for the pewterers and braziers was one John Dipple who died at the end of 1713. The new charter was granted in 1715 and added to the existing trades, which had already been extended by the charter of 1576, those of silversmith, clock and watch maker, glazier, tinplate worker, chairmaker and cabinet maker. The upsurge of one of these trades, that of tinplate worker, is apparent from the considerable number of Ludlow craftsmen plying this trade in the early 1700s. It also apparently tempted some pewterers to diversify, an activity which brought down the wrath of the stewards upon them. Thus we read the following under the date 2 October 1722.

> 'Notice to Hopkin Bowen that if he do not leave off working of tin work and withdraw all his tin work out of his shop he will be forthwith sued by the Company and upon the complaint of Mr. Jacob Davies to the contrary the said stewards do summon a private meeting.

Hopkin Bowen had been admitted as a pewterer in 1720 and another Hopkin Bowen was made free as a pewterer in 1738 after serving an apprenticeship with Richard Plummer. He was the son of John Bowen of Bishops Castle, not the son of the elder Hopkin.

Another trade which was combined with that of pewterer and brazier was that of plumber. Edward Wood was admitted as a pewterer and brazier in 1704 and 11 years later was also admitted as a plumber on payment of an additional 6s. 8d. His eldest son, another Edward, was made free in 1752 as a pewterer and brazier and also as a plumber 'his father having been one'.

A later family of some prominence was that of Collier. There were three named Edward, free in 1754, 1785 and 1820 respectively. The first was a pewterer, but his son and grandson were described as braziers and tinplate workers. One James Collier, son of an Edward, was also made free in 1785 as a tinplate worker, though he is described in the *Universal British Directory* in 1798 as a brazier. He is also found mentioned as a customer of Ingram & Hunt from whom he purchased a wide range of pewterware for resale. A Samuel Collier, brazier, was admitted in 1816, he also was the son of an Edward, presumably Edward II.

As well as its more serious trade responsibilities the guild, which at some uncertain date began to call itself 'The Company (or Society) of Hammermen', undertook festive activities. For example on 9 October 1746 it was ordered that all the company 'assemble in the Market House at 10 in the morning with their streamers' and form a procession of thanksgiving for the victory at Culloden. Those not appearing would be deemed 'disobedient to the Company and disloyal to the government'. The streamers, which are described by Cotterell, were made in 1734 of embroidered silk and are about fifteen feet long. Two survive and bear the arms of 16 different crafts. The pewterers, presumably without any authority, used the arms, crest, mantling and motto of the London Company.

By 1831 the Society of Hammermen found their authority eroded to the point of impotence. They consulted counsel in that year for an opinion on whether they could do anything about a score of tradesmen who had been in business in Ludlow for many years without membership of the Society. The opinion was not encouraging. The Society continued, no doubt as a social club, for a few years longer and held its last meeting on 8 August 1848 in St Lawrence's Church and afterwards the members repaired to *The Feathers* for refreshment, and no doubt solace.

Over a period of 300 years some thirty-four pewterers and braziers practised their craft in Ludlow, a number which illustrates the importance of this comparatively small town as a market and trading centre in the border region of England and Wales. The number who continued into the late 18th century perhaps indicates also the comparative isolation of the town from the main commercial centres and the need for self-sufficiency.

Oswestry Pewterers and Braziers

Baker(e), Edward	m 1595, d 1608, p
Richard, David ap	m 1619, br
Lankeshire, Richard	m 1637, br
Felton, Thomas I	m 1654, d 1675, p and br
Felton, Gwen	m 1675, d 1678, p, w. of Thomas I
Felton, James	b 1655, app 1670 in Shrewsbury, d 1717, p and br (*see also* under Shrewsbury)
Felton, James II	b 1684, app 1698–9 in Shrewsbury, d 1710, p and br (*see also* under Shrewsbury), s. of James I
Felton, John II	b 1694, app 1711 in Oswestry, d 1758, p and br, s. of James I
Felton, Jeremiah	b 1691, app 1711 in Oswestry, d 1720, p and br, s. of James I
Felton, Thomas	b 1693, app 1708 in Oswestry, d 1765, p and br, s. of James I

Felton, Philip	b 1698–9, app 1714 in Oswestry, d 1731, p and br, s. of James I
Ford, Hugh	m 1683–87, br
Boulton, Robert I	m 1692, br
Boulton, Robert II	b 1702, d 1786, br, s. of Robert I
Bickerton, William	m 1806, br
Gwyn(ne), Lewis	m 1784, br
Howell, Edward	m 1807, br

Note: Reference should be made to the chapter on Shrewsbury for additional members of the Felton family.

Ludlow Pewterers and Braziers

Note: f = free of the Company of Hammermen

Tynker, Philip	m 1540, br (and plumber/pewterer?)
Jokes, Philip	m 1541–3, ?p
Bradshaw, William	f 1544–5, p
Cropper, Martin	m 1575, p, Cott, 1226
Owen, Edward ap	f 1577–8, p. Cott. 3469
Baylys, Roger	f 1588–9, p
Ellice, Robert	f 1593, p
Bowen, Edward	m 1593, p
Taylor, Roger	m 1600, p, Cott. 4671
Tomkyns, Roger	f 1603, p (recorded later at Leominster) Cott. 4765
Barber, Henry	f 1633, p, Cott 246
Crafte, Henry	f 1637, m 1642, p, Cott. 1194
Nicholls, Henry	f 1659, m 1667, p and br, Cott. 3390
Norton, Roger	f 1660, p and br, disenfranchised in 1665, Cott. 3421
Deuxhall, Thomas	f 1662, m 1677, p and br, Cott. 1364
Plummer, Richard I	f 1668, m 1677, d 1692, p, Cott. 3705
Deuxhall, Robert	f 1693, d 1741, p and br, s. of Thomas, Cott. 1363
Plummer, Richard II	b 1672, f 1693, p and br, s. of Richard I, Cott. 3706
Draper, Martin	m 1693, p
Deuxhall, Richard	f 1700, p and br, s. of Thomas, Cott. 1362 (who erroneously gives him as the son of Robert)
Lugg, John	f 1701, p and br, Cott. 3015
Wood, Edward I	f 1704, m 1715, p, br and plumber, Cott. 5255
Dipple, John	m 1711, d 1713, p and br
Plummer, Richard III	b 1695, f 1717, dead by 1749, p and br, s. of Richard II, Cott. 3707
Bowen, Hopkin I	f 1720, m 1722, p and br, Cott. 527
Bowen, Hopkin II	f 1738, p and br, *not* the s. of Hopkin I
Plummer, Richard IV	b 1718, f 1749, p and br, s. of Richard III, Cott. 3708
Wood, Edward II	b 1706, f 1753, d 1776, p, br and plumber, s. of Edward I, Cott. 5256
Collier, Edward I	b 1729, f 1754, d 1770, p and br, Cott. 1033
Scarlett, Anthony	f 1771, p and br, Cott. 4133
Collier, James	f 1785, tinplate worker and br, s. of Edward I
Collier, Edward II	f 1785, dead by 1820, br and tinplate worker, s. of Edward I
Cross, William	f 1819, br
Smith, John	f 1819, br and tinplate worker
Collier, Samuel	f 1816, br, s. of Edward II
Collier, Edward III	f 1820, br, s. of Edward II

NOTES AND REFERENCES

Oswestry and Ludlow

1. *Oswestry Burgess Book*, MS. at Oswestry Public Library.
2. *Oswestry Parish Register* (Shropshire Parish Register Society).
3. Watkin, Isaac, *Oswestry* (1920), pp. 200-2.
4. Palmer, A. N., *History of the Parish Church of Wrexham*, p. 140.
5. Forrest, H. E. (ed.), *The Shrewsbury Burgess Roll* (1924).
6. *Record Books, Ordinances, Charters and Admissions of the Ludlow Guild of Hammermen*, Shropshire County Record Office, 352/1 — 335, 356.
7. West, John, *Town Records* (1983), p. 126.
8. Wright, Thomas (ed.). *Ludlow Church Wardens' Accounts* (Camden Society, 1869).
9. Jones, L., 'The Hammermen of Ludlow', *Shropshire Archaeological and Natural History Society Transactions* (1888).

General

Register of St Lawrence's Church, Ludlow, Shropshire County Record Office.
Universal British Directory (1798).
For further information on the Felton family and additional bibliography *see* Hall, D. W., and Homer, R. F., 'A Family of Braziers', *The Montgomeryshire Collection*, vol. 71 (1983), pp. 42-7.

WORCESTER AND HEREFORD

HAVING LOOKED at Shropshire in some depth, we shall now turn our attention to two other major centres in the West Midlands, Hereford and Worcester. These two cities have many superficial similarities; both stand on the banks of major rivers and both were significant ecclesiastical and urban centres in Saxon times. Worcester is of Roman origin and the Severn was bridged there at that time. A surviving monastic charter of the late ninth century shows that the town then had a market and that it was also fortified. Hereford and Worcester in medieval times were centres of the woollen cloth trade, and Hereford's position on the frontier with Wales gave it great strategic importance as a military base and bastion. From the poll tax returns of 1377 Hereford appears to have been somewhat the larger with 1902 tax-paying citizens compared with 1057 for Worcester. By the close of the first quarter of the 16th century the position was reversed and the lay subsidy returns for that period show £312 to have been paid by Worcester whereas Hereford returned only £273. This change in status, stemming from the decrease in the military importance of Hereford and its waning position in the cloth trade, accelerated during the ensuing centuries and by comparison Hereford became economically stagnant. In contrast Worcester benefited as an entrepôt for the manufacturing trades which became established to its north and its population in 1750, estimated at 10,300, was double that of Hereford.

A number of crafts were well established in Worcester by the 13th century. These included metal working and there were at least three goldsmiths in the city by the mid-13th century. Simon the bell-founder is mentioned as early as 1226 and copper-smiths were active by 1333. The main commercial activity of the city at this time was, however, in shoes, gloves and other garments which find frequent mention in the records from the 13th century onwards.

While Worcester has many ancient records these are held in the city's Guildhall and though accessible to students, little has been published and the absence of a comprehensive index makes research more difficult than at Shrewsbury. The Hereford city archives are held by the County Record Office, but it is a considerable disappointment that they are incomplete. The records of the admission of freemen survive only from 1709 and an apprentice list exists for the first few decades of the 18th century but apparently relates only to apprentices whose indentures were partly or wholly paid for from charitable funds controlled by the City Corporation. Other sources are however available and much information has been gleaned from parish registers, probate proceedings and 18th century poll books.

In view of the early establishment of metal-working trades in Worcester one might expect pewterers to have been at work in the city in the late 14th century,* as they

---

* A pilgrim souvenir of the second quarter of the 13th century in the form of a pewter ampulla bearing the image of St Wulfstan and the inscription 'IN HONORE SANTI WULSTANI', which was made at Worcester (presumably in the abbey), has recently been described. Spencer, Brian, *Worcestershire Archaeological Society Transactions* (1984), pp. 7-11.

1. The will of Agnes, widow of Thomas Charlement of Worcester, 1536. (Hereford and Worcester Record Office)

were in Coventry. This may indeed have been the case, but the earliest reference to a Worcester pewterer which has so far been traced is to Thomas Charlement who, with many others, was required to present himself before the city's justices in 1502. He was dead by 1536 when his widow, Agnes, made her will. Another early 16th century pewterer was Nicholas Green. *The Journal of Prior William More* records as follows,

1519 'payd to Nicholas grene for ye changyng of olde pewter disshes to ye lords kychion ... 6s. 8d.

He died in 1541.

William More records other purchases of pewter. In 1518 'ii garnes (garnishes) of pewter Dysshes', in 1523 'ii quarte pewter pootts', and in 1532 he records having spent 46s. 9d. on pewter vessels and the 'rennying' of the same during the previous year.[1] John Matthews, pewterer, figures in the accounts of St Michael Bedwardine in 1542 when the churchwardens paid him twenty shillings for unspecified goods. He appears a few years earlier in a lease of 1539. From 1643 the pewterers of Worcester were entitled to membership of the Glovers' Company,[2] which received a charter in 1497, and which also embraced whittawers, tanners, pursers, saddlers, braziers and 'hammers'. Although the records of the Glovers survive for the period 1571 to 1662 it has not been possible to identify any of the there recorded apprentices or freemen as pewterers or braziers. Nevertheless between 1502 and the end of the 16th century a

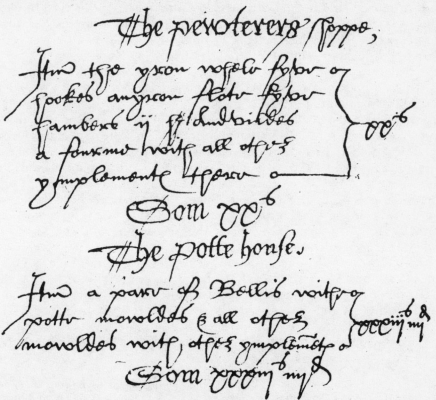

2. Extract from the inventory of Margery Green of Worcester, widow of Henry Green, 1570.
(Hereford and Worcester Record Office)

total of 13 Worcester pewterers have been identified from various sources. Chief among them during the 16th century appear to have been the Greens and the Basies. Henry Green, died in 1569, has appeared previously in print, e.g., in Hatcher and Barker, *A History of British Pewter*, where his inventory is reproduced.[3] He was worth the considerable sum of £112 and was a bell-founder as well as a pewterer. His father, Nicholas, who has already been mentioned, was also a bell-founder and was even more prosperous, being worth £155 on his death in 1541. Henry had a sizeable establishment with a warehouse, a bell-house, a sadware shop, a casting chamber, a working chamber and a pot-house. Bell-founding appears to have been only a minor part of his activities and when his widow died in 1570 it seems to have been no longer part of the business.

Three members of the Baysie family have been found. John I, his brother George and John I's son John II, all pewterers. The will of John I bequeaths to his son,

> half my sad ware moulds and tools, a pair of clamps, a great ladle, a sad ware wheel fully and wholly, a set of hammers, an anvil and a swage, a rapping hammer, a tower hammer and half a flat salt mould in brass.

His brother George was to have the use of these items until John II came of age. The mention of half a salt mould implies that this was something which John Baysie shared with another pewterer. Appended to the will is a list of 23 debtors, most for small sums of money, and none identifiable as contemporary pewterers. However, two at least appear to be trade debts, 'Thomas Williams for v pounds of brass' and 'Heritage the tinker'. Others included are Thomas Taylor of Stoke, Bragger of Malvern, Kemmerson of Bridgnorth and a Welshman, Richard ap Thomas, indicating a quite broad geographical spread of contacts. His inventory shows his stock-in-trade to have included sadware, hollow-ware, kettles and candlesticks. Out of a total of £41 10s. 5d. his stock and tools amounted to £25 10s. 0d.

Pewter then was being made in Worcester on a significant scale in the 16th century and those responsible for its production seem to have had the opportunity to prosper. The information for the period is however fragmentary and the picture which we can offer is therefore sketchy. For the Stuart period more information is available and it is now apparent that Worcester was a much more significant pewtering centre than has hitherto been recognised or imagined. Some fifty pewterers have been discovered who were active before the end of the reign of Queen Anne and four families dominate the period; those of Letsome, Greenbank, Bourne and Trapp. The searches of the Pewterers' Company are revealing; in 1677 they note no less than nine pewterers, a figure surpassed by only the largest provincial centres of the craft such as York, Wigan and Bristol. This must in part reflect the growing prosperity of Worcester as a city and also its central position as a trading centre with ready communications up and down the river Severn.[4] As will be seen shortly the river trade with Gloucester included pewter as early as 1636. In that year, and again in 1640, the searchers visited Worcester and recorded the outcome of their searches in some detail. Thus they record for 21 May 1636,

> Search mayd at Thomas Nicholas of Woster in the County of Woster and ther was wine potes of his own making being worse than the Seay [assay] of London by 2 graines and they wayre all defaced and wee fined hime for it at five shillings but wee received of hime but the some of three shillings.

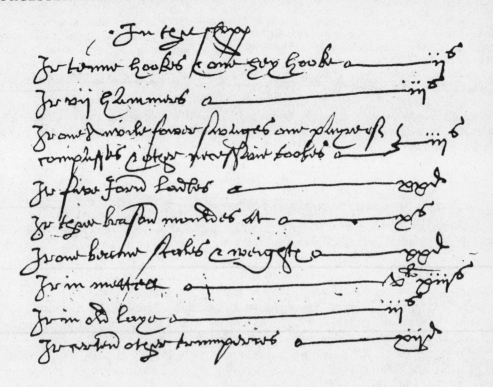

3. Extract from the inventory of William Hopkins of Worcester, 1602.
(Hereford and Worcester Record Office)

In 1636 they also visited Sampson Bourne 'and ther found lay of his own making [which we] defaced and broke', and he was fined five shillings. However from a subsequent visit to the same craftsman in 1640 it is apparent that he was by then running a much larger business and the wares seized included flagons, ephraim pints, hooped quarts, saucers, potingers, candlesticks and salts. He was fined seven pounds, which was abated five shillings 'for cutting of some wares of his which we found quite good being one still head and other things'. Much pewter made by Sampson Bourne was discovered at Gloucester in the searches of 1640 and 1641. Thus at one William Browne's 'there was of one Sampson Bourne of Woster chamberpotts, flagons, half pound dishes, pound dishes, turned trencher plates, candlesticks and a bereboul'. His wares were also found on the premises of three other Gloucester pewterers. In the same searches ware by Thomas Nicols (Nichols, Nicholas) of Worcester was found at Gloucester and it is clear that he was in the habit of shipping pewterware to Gloucester by river, as is seen from the following extract from the Gloucester search of August 1636; an extract which sheds considerable light on the powers of the searchers.

Searched and the goodes and chateles of one Thomas Nicholes of Woster in the County of Woster his wayres being in a barge at Gloster the sheriffs of Gloster caused the Barill which this wayre was packed up in to be brought to the Kinges wairehouse and there they caused it to be broke open and when it was broke open they desired us for to search, and so we did, and found there 8 houped quartes and they wayre worse than the seay of London by 26 graines And three wine pintes being worse than the seay of London by 10 graines and one barberes pottell and it was worse than the seay of London by 12 graines and seven midell chamber potes and they wayre worse than the seay of London 3 graines and 4 graines and broke all of them waied three score poundes wayigh praised at sixpence the pound comes to the some of one pound ten shillings. Receaved our part being fifteen shillings and left the other fifteen shillings being the Kinges parte in the towne.

Sampson Bourne had been made free of the city of Worcester in 1634 'by composition' suggesting that he may not have been a native of the city, and he died in 1674.[5] His son, Sampson II, who succeeded him died unmarried and intestate in 1689. His inventory survives in the Public Record Office and this shows him to have been by far the wealthiest pewterer of the 17th century for whom we have an inventory. His goods and chattels, plus debts owing to him, are valued at no less than £3,275. His house, which he inherited from his father and which we know from a deed of 1671 to have been in Foregate Street, had 12 rooms plus a cellar and stables.[6] His personal belongings included a silver sword, silver shoe buckles, silver shirt buttons, a watch 'with a silver studded case', three gold rings, one copper and one nutshell tobacco box, and 40 ounces of plate. Only one book is noted however, a copy of Foxe's *Book of Martyrs*. Also numbered among his effects is a bird cage. His stock-in-trade was very substantial and included 18 cwt. of brass kettles, pots and skillets; 27 cwt. of brass metal (plus 19 cwt. of 'old mould metal' and 12 cwt. of 'new mould metal'); 25½ cwt. of pewterware, and about three tons of pewter metal as fine, lay and trifle. In addition there was no less than 75 cwt. of 'blowed metal' valued at only 3d.–3½d. per pound and thus presumably some inferior pewter alloy. (The *O.E.D.* gives a 17th century definition of 'blown' as 'stale or tainted').

It is however the list of creditors under the heading 'Bonds upon Trade' which is the most informative part of the inventory. This includes the 21 individuals listed below, of whom those whose names are marked with an asterisk have been identified as pewterers and will be found elsewhere in this book.

*Edward Williams, Salop	£50
*Mr. Trapp, Hereford	£372 15s. 4d.
*Charles Maries, Gloucester	£40
*John Tompkins, Leominster	£60
*John Bradshaw, Wellington	£80 8s. 7d.
*John Perks, Stratford-on-Avon	£28 16s. 0d.
Thomas Groyn [?], gent	£3 6s. 0d.
*Thomas Harries, Kidderminster	£50
Ditto	£20
Ditto	£20
Edward Oten, Coventry[7]	£20
*Abraham Deakin, Walsall	£32
*Edward Williams, Salop	£22 11s. 8d.
Thomas Deakin & Jane Hopkins	£2
John Hodgkinson, Walsall	£15
*Walter Hill	£11
*Thomas Arundell, Kington	£25
Thomas Birch	£20
Thomas Harries, Kidderminster	£100
Robert Gower	£4 19s. 6d.
Ditto	£4

*Dewxell, Ludlow	£10
Bridgett Scruby	£10 4s. 4d.
John Griffiths	£5
*Philip Newcombe	£30 5s. 9d.
Mr. Longden	£5

Of those not positively identified, Bridgett Scruby may have been the widow of John Scruby (or Scroby) who was a pewterer in Shipston-on-Stour in 1663, and John Griffiths may have been related to Richard Griffiths who is mentioned as a Shrewsbury pewterer about 1703.

This list is remarkable in indicating the extent of the credit extended to some customers; £372 to Francis Trapp of Hereford (who was related to the Worcester Trapps) and a total of £190 to Thomas Harries of Kidderminater. More important still it shows the geographical extent of Sampson Bourne's business which covered most of the area with which this study is concerned. Interestingly one of the rooms in his house is styled 'the chapman's chamber' and was furnished with beds, chests and a side cupboard. Clearly it was a room for living in, and this could be interpreted as meaning that Sampson Bourne had a resident salesman who made the rounds of his customers. In Sampson Bourne we can perhaps discern the beginning of a movement away from the parochialism of the past and the emergence of the businessman with a broader outlook and wide geographical contacts; an outlook which was to come to maturity with John Duncumb of Birmingham and Bewdley about forty years later.[8]

The appraisers to the inventory were John Greenbank, Ben Shepperd and Walter Hill. Greenbank was a well-known pewterer and we may assume that Walter Hill was the Worcester pewterer who is otherwise recorded only as 'Mr. Hill'. The inventory of Sampson Bourne II's father, Sampson I, has not been found but his will suggests that he too was of some considerable wealth. Not only did he own the house in which he, and subsequently his son lived, but the monetary bequests in his will total a little over £500. Regrettably Sampson II died intestate, which appears strange to modern eyes for a man of his wealth, so that we do not know what became of his business. It may however have passed to his brother Joshua Bourne who was free in 1689–90. Pewter by Sampson Bourne II survives in some quantity and chargers made by him may be seen at the *Fleece Inn*, Bretforton, Worcestershire (National Trust) and at Henley-in-Arden guildhall. Sampson I's marks are recorded, along with those of his son, in Cotterell as numbers 5463 and 5464 respectively. The hall marks shown under 5462 are also to be attributed to one of these two pewterers. In MPM.5464 Sampson II's marks are seen with the touch mark of another Worcester craftsman, John Trapp, who was his brother-in-law.

Mention of John Greenbank leads us to consider the family which was a part of the Worcester pewtering scene for over one hundred and sixty years. We shall see later, in the chapter on Bewdley and Birmingham, that a James Greenbank is recorded as a brazier who paid for a stall in Bewdley market in 1570. A man of the same name was paid for repairs to the lead of the church steeple and for mending the conduit in Bewdley in 1578 and his son William Greenbank was similarly employed in 1613. Presumably the James Greenbank recorded in Bewdley in 1570 and 1578 is the same individual who died in Worcester in 1603 and whose inventory shows him to have worked in pewter as well as brass and lead. His birth has not been found, but he was

4. Worcester freedom entries for Sampson Bourne I (1634), Francis Greenbank (1647) and William Huntpatch (1682), from 'Liber Recordum'. (Worcester City Council)

the James Greenbank who is recorded in St Swithin's registers in Worcester as having fathered several children between 1578 and 1585. James Greenbank was succeeded in Worcester by his son William Greenbank who was free of the city in 1629. When he died in 1639 the family's business had prospered and expanded and William's will (dated 1637) describes him variously as pewterer, plumber and brazier. He held property in Worcester itself and in a number of places outside including Loosemore, 'Ledberye' and Tidbury and was clearly of some substance.

William Greenbank appears to have fathered at least fifteen children, two of whom certainly became pewterers in Worcester and one, another William, is of the right age to be identified with the William Greenbank of Worcester who moved to Shrewsbury in 1629. The two who remained in Worcester, John and Francis, became free in 1643–4 and 1647 respectively, the latter having been apprenticed to Thomas Nicholls. John died in 1680[9] and Francis in 1689. John had a son, John II, and Francis was father of Dickenson Greenbank. Both were pewterers and John II rose to the rank of alderman in 1683. Each fathered yet another generation of pewterers. John II was father to a William who was born in 1674 and to a John born in 1678. William was probably owner of the touch mark illustrated by Cotterell (No. 1992) and John II owner of those shown at No. 5619. These latter marks are found on pewter chargers with multiple reeded rims at the *Fleece Inn* in Bretforton. Dickenson Greenbank was father of another Francis Greenbank, pewterer, who was alive in 1733. John II's son John III was apprenticed to an apothecary, but he appears also to have been a pewterer, as that is the occupation given against his name in the entry of his burial in St Swithin's Church in 1723. Two of his children, Elizabeth (b. 1704) and John (b. 1705) were baptised at St Thomas's Church, Dudley, suggesting that he lived there for a time after his marriage. John II also had a daughter, Elizabeth, who married Thomas Harper and their son, Hopwood Harper, became another pewterer. We can therefore trace the craft of pewterer through at least six generations of the Greenbank family. Most of the family is recorded in the parish registers of St Swithin with occasional entries at other churches, from these records and with the aid of wills the family tree which follows can be constructed. This shows 11 members of family who were pewterers and braziers between 1570 and the 1730s.

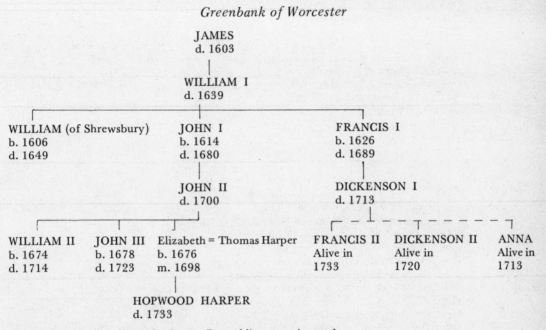

Greenbank of Worcester

JAMES
d. 1603

WILLIAM I
d. 1639

WILLIAM (of Shrewsbury)	JOHN I	FRANCIS I
b. 1606	b. 1614	b. 1626
d. 1649	d. 1680	d. 1689

JOHN II
d. 1700

DICKENSON I
d. 1713

WILLIAM II	JOHN III	Elizabeth = Thomas Harper	FRANCIS II	DICKENSON II	ANNA
b. 1674	b. 1678	b. 1676	Alive in	Alive in	Alive in
d. 1714	d. 1723	m. 1698	1733	1720	1713

HOPWOOD HARPER
d. 1733

Note: Pewterers/braziers only shown. Dotted line = conjectural.

The Trapp family, like the Greenbanks, provide us with several generations of pewterers and interesting and comprehensive probate inventories survive for two members of the family. These give full details of the tools, equipment and stock-in-trade of the master craftsmen concerned and help to provide a fuller picture of the technical and practical aspects of the production of pewter in Worcester. The first of these inventories is that of Francis Trapp who died in 1633 and the relevant sections of this document are reproduced below.

In the shop

Four hundred and xxii pounds of sadware
In bowles and basons five score and seven pounds
More two sortinge basons and ewers
Three hundred and a half and xv pounds of new lay
More six and twenty pounds of stoole panns
A hundred and a half and fifty pounds of new flaggons and trifles
Spoons dishes and sosers [saucers]
In old fine two hundred less x pounds
In old lay half a hundred and 25 pounds

Weights
In old spoons xl pounds
One hundred and a half of shroffe
In old brass candlesticks five score pounds
Two hundred and forty four pounds of plate
Wyer one hundred and forty four pounds
Old iron one hundred pounds
More wyer half a hundred pounds
Eighteen hundred and a half and thirteen pounds of cettells
One hundred three quarters and two pounds of kettells unwyred
Forty one pounds of skilletts
Skilletts frames
Potts Mill brass mortars and posnetts four hundred and a half and xi pounds
In old brass potts three hundred pounds
In brass weights xxxi pounds
One dozen and a half of brasen bastinge spoons
Two cast skimers
viii pounds of skimers
xxxviii pounds of brass candlesticks
Three warming panns
Four drippinge panns
Six bastinge spoons

In the working chamber

Thirty pounds of pewter garnish moulds
Four hundred and viii pounds of hollow and trifill moulds
Fifteen score and seven pounds of sadware moulds
Five hundred and four score and xiiii pounds of ledd
One sadware whele with a tower and fifteen hooks
Two anvells seven hammers and three swaggs
One other wheele with a tower and mandrills and other things to the same
One vice
Eight and forty screwe pinns
One other wheele with a tower the mandrills belonging to the same whele
Four flots [*sic*]
Three other floats
Two raspes
Thirty hooks and burnishes
Twenty four other hooks
Another vice
Two pairs of sheres
Nine sowdringe irons and ladles
One casting forme with other things in the working chamber
Two ladles
One grinding stone
Three brass potts
One brasse possenett
Two kettells one pann two dobnetts
One iron pan two frying pans and two dripping pans
One pair of cobbornes one gridiron one tynn dripping-pan with other old things
     about the house
Two pairs of bellish trenchers, dishes a chopping knife, one axe, one hatchett
Two barrells of metal ashes
Three pairs of (blank)
More one whele

Three pairs of beames and skalls
Two hundred and thirteen pounds of fine wrote [wrought?]
Nine score pounds wrought lay
One hundred pounds of fine
In fine thirty one pounds
One hundred of lay
Three hundred thirty and five pounds of ledd
One hundred of —emell [?]

Francis had the necessary resources to keep several journeymen and apprentices gainfully occupied. Three lathes, two anvils, two vices, soldering irons and ladles, and 745 pounds weight of moulds; all the material and equipment needed to manufacture a whole range of pewter products. The substantial nature of his operations is confirmed by the amount of money he had tied up in working capital, that is, invested in tools and equipment, goods ready for sale and old metal and scrap. This totalled one penny short of £310 — a very large sum of money for the early 1630s. As with the Shrewsbury pewterers, there is clear evidence of trade in brazen goods as well as pewter at this early date, although it cannot be proved that he was actually making items in brass rather than retailing the products of others.

Francis Trapp's son John (born 1622) followed his father in the family business and when he died in 1675 he appears to have been briefly succeeded by his widow, Anne. She however died in 1677 and John II, nephew of John I, continued the family trade until his own death in 1713. The very detailed 'True and perfect Inventory of all and singular the goods chattels and credits of John Trapp', was taken on 20 November 1713 by Henry Whittington, John Greenbank and Sampson Letsom. An extract from this inventory, which deals with his stock-in-trade, is reproduced below:

In the Shop	Cwts:	qts:	lbs	£	s.	d.
Kettle Potts	1	00	23	7	17	6
Raw Kettles	1	01	25	10	6	3
Wired Kettles	3	00	18	14	15	0
One Copper Furnace	0	02	08	4	5	4
One Brass Furnace	0	02	02	3	7	8
Sadware	02	03	08	11	17	0
Plates	00	03	06	3	11	3
New Triffles	06	03	05	5	7	4
New Lay	01	02	10	4	9	0
Copper sawespannes	00	03	14	7	7	0
Putty	00	00	02		2	0
Wiggan Kettles) Candlesticks)	01	00	14	6	6	0
Plate Mettle	01	02	22	6	5	8
Hard Plates	00	01	26	2	9	6
Soop Plates	00	01	08	1	10	0
Triffle Mettle	01	02	00	4	18	0
Old Lay	00	01	02		12	6
Copper Nayles	00	01	08	2	2	0
Millbrass & Mortars	01	00	20	3	17	5
Pott Brass	01	00	09	2	10	0
Brass Shruff	01	00	24	4	10	9
Spelter	00	01	12	3	6	8

In the shop	Cwts:	qts:	lbs	£	s.	d.
Tin Glass	00	01	12	1	13	4
Warming Pan Covers	00	00	08		13	4
34 Brass Cocks	00	00	00	1	19	8
Working tools and other lumber in the shop				5	0	0

In the Workshop						
Old Moulds	10	1	20	24	6	8
Platter Mettle	1	00	00	3	14	8
Lay	00	02	20	1	18	8
Triffle Mettle	00	03	08	2	13	8
One Wheel and Block, Pitt, Ladles) Pewter ashes and other odd lumber)				6	10	0

In the Entry						
Five potts, five kettles, five) potts . . . and other things)				1	10	0

In the Cellar						
Old Copper Plates	00	02	00	2	16	0
Old Brass plates and Shruff	01	02	00	7	0	0
Old iron with a large pair of shears	3	00	00	1	8	0
Four tuns of Coles				1	4	0
Lard	10	0	00	1	0	0

In the Pantry	Cwts:	qrs:	lbs	£	s.	d.
Old Pewter		1	00	00	3	14	8

Unfortunately, this inventory has been prepared and compiled in such manner as does not make it always clear whether certain items are part of the pewterers stock-in-trade or part of his domestic goods.

In many ways the inventory gives the impression of a similar operation to that of his ancestor of 80 years earlier, there is however, one major difference, the emphasis is on stock rather than on manufacture. Working tools and equipment are mentioned in a casual way, almost as an afterthought, and the only mention of those essential requirements for the manufacturing process, moulds, is prefixed 'old' and gives a valuation which implies scrap value. The emphasis is on stock rather than production. Provincial pewterers had always trade with one another, but by 1713 a fundamental change was under way. Some pewterers' operations were growing while others were beginning to concentrate more on retail sales or on an even broader range of products, made of copper and brass. This will become clearer when the Bewdley pewterers are discussed in a later chapter. Interestingly, in this context, the whole style of this late Trapp inventory is reminiscent of John Duncumb's business records.

The death of John Trapp II was not, however, the end of the Trapp pewtering business. John II's two sons, John III and Edward continued as pewterers until well into the 18th century, the latter being alive in 1753. The marks of 'IT', recorded by Cotterell under No. 5977 and shown by Peal in *More Pewter Marks* under No. 5464 in conjunction with the hall marks of Sampson Bourne, are now identified as those of John Trapp II. Again they are to be found on pewter at the *Fleece*, Bretforton.

As there is a probable link with Bewdley for the early members of the Greenbank family, so there is a possible one for the Trapps. The Ribbesford (Bewdley) parish registers record a Francis Trapp born there, the son of Richard Trapp, tawer (?tanner), on 29 August 1596. The Francis of Worcester who died in 1633 was married in Worcester at All Saints to Eleanor Holborrow on 11 June 1621; he could well therefore have been born in 1596. Bearing in mind that no Trapps have been found in the Worcester registers before 1625, and that there was frequent commerce between the two towns, the link is at least possible. There may also have been a family connection with the London pewterer, John Trapp (Cott. No. 4803) whose apprenticeship details show him to have been from Stratford-on-Avon. Two other members of the family, perhaps the son and grandson of Francis, are later found in Hereford.

Trapp of Worcester and Hereford

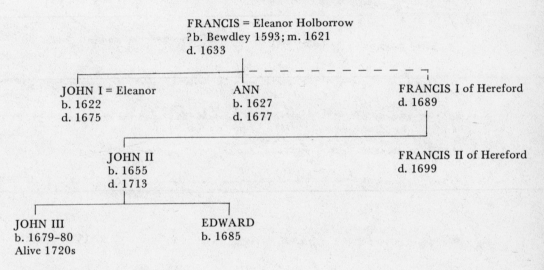

Note: Dotted line = unconfirmed.

Before moving on to the later phases of pewtering in Worcester we should mention the remaining important 17th century family who practised the craft, the Letsams. The name is found spelt in many ways, Lettsom, Ledsham and Ledsome being but a few. It is an uncommon name and one must postulate a relationship with the Roger Ledesham and Richard Ledsham who are recorded as Chester pewterers and who received their freedoms in 1536-7 and 1558-9 respectively. The earliest mention of the name recorded in Worcester is Henry or Harry Ledsam who died in 1593, who is described as a brazier in his inventory. (*See* page 50).

Again there is a link with Bewdley, for one Henry Letson appears as a brazier in the Bewdley Bridgewardens' Account Book in the years between 1574 and 1625. Obviously these Bewdley entries cannot all relate to the Henry who died in 1593, but the registers of All Saints, Worcester, record also a Henry Letsom who was fathering children between 1607 and 1631, who could have been the elder Henry's son, thus explaining the later Bewdley references. The younger Henry's son, Thomas, was also a

Itm three of mowldes — iij[s]
Itm one paier of bellowes — v[s]
Itm tooles belonginge to the occupation — [...]
Itm three hundred wayght of brasse — [...]li
Itm twenty ware — iij[s] iiij[d]
Itm tow paier of andirons on [...] one bar of iron three paier of tonges one fier shouell tow paier of tobyeans on [...] & tow paier of [...] — [...]li [...]d
Itm mowldes belonginge to the occupation & tooles belonginge to the same — v[s]
Itm he ware in [...] — [...]li [...]
Itm one man — [...]
Itm clothes belonginge to the standinge — viij[s] iiij[d]
[...]

5. Extract from the inventory of Henry Ledsam of Worcester, 1593. The last entry refers to 'clothes belonging to the standinge': a reference to Bewdley Fair, *see* p. 76. This inventory illustrates the handwriting problems facing the researcher. (Hereford and Worcester Record Office).

pewterer and brazier (born 1608) and Thomas was the uncle of Sampson Letsome I whose son in turn, Sampson II (born 1673), carried on the trade of pewterer and brazier until his death in 1737. Sampson II's inventory is incredibly detailed listing many hundred items over its closely-written pages. It seems likely that Henry's son Richard, father of Sampson I, was also a pewterer and he may be the 'Lettson senior' mentioned in the 1677 Pewterers' Company search.

Letsome (Letsam) of Worcester

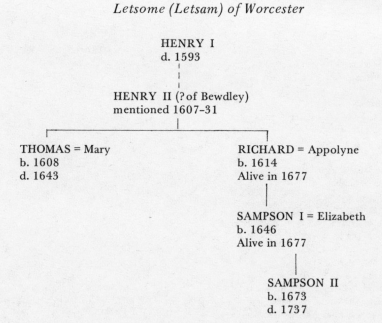

HENRY I
d. 1593

HENRY II (? of Bewdley)
mentioned 1607–31

THOMAS = Mary   RICHARD = Appolyne
b. 1608   b. 1614
d. 1643   Alive in 1677

                       SAMPSON I = Elizabeth
                       b. 1646
                       Alive in 1677

                       SAMPSON II
                       b. 1673
                       d. 1737

Note: Pewterers/braziers only shown. Dotted line = unconfirmed.

We have seen that the Trapps, the Letsams and the Greenbanks provided continuity of the pewtering trade in the city well into the 18th century. Another Worcester pewterer of the first half of the 18th century was Russell Laugher, whose touch mark (Cott. 4077) has been known for many years, if mistakenly, as that of a mythical partnership of Russell and Laugher of London. Information from a colateral descendant of the family reveals that Russell Laugher, grandfather of the pewterer, died in 1698 and that his inventory showed large quantities of both pewter and brass in his chandler's shop. His goods were valued at over £1,000 at his death. The business passed to his son Henry and thence to Russell Laugher the pewterer who was born in 1696 and was baptised at St Swithin's church on 28 October. He was buried in the same church in 1751 where there is a plaque to be seen in his memory. He was a man of substance, with agricultural land at Cleveland and he owned at least two properties in the city. His will, however, does not contain any suggestion or implication that either of his sons would follow him in his stated trade of pewterer.

A contemporary of Russell Laugher whose career was less successful was Francis King, who died in 1730, and who was described as a pewterer and brazier. His probate inventory dated 21 December is an itemised and lengthy list of his domestic and working possessions. Part of this is reproduced below:

	Cwts:	qts:	lbs		£	s.	d.
Item Old Iron	02	2	14 at 1½d.		1	2	9
50 Blocks						6	8
More Old Iron	0	2	23 at 1½d.			9	10½
An old barrel						2	0
A wheel head & tower bench						10	0
A bacon rack						6	0
Cast Iron to be judged 100 lbs						2	1
Brass and Coper	10	2	0 at 9d.		9	9	0
Old Brass and Iron with potts,)							
cans and a pewter still head)					3	14	8
Yellow brass	0	2	14 at 7d.		2	0	10
Pott Brass	1	2	0 at 6d.		4	4	0
A Brass Pott and other things —)							
90 lbs at 9d.)					2	12	6
A still and worm						3	00
A Lyon						5	0
Cocks and Beams						12	0
A pair of scales						4	0
Chest and shelves						5	0
Old pewter in the chest						9	0
Window grates and Iron Potts and)							
Slow grates)						15	0
Old Iron in the Chest						4	0
A pewter standish						2	6
Working Tools in the Backshop					1	10	0
Old lead, a Grindle Stone & odd things						5	0
An old watch and buckles					1	5	0
In the upper workshop, a wheel)							
Jack, bedstead and other things)					1	0	0
Hard brass candlesticks 37 etc.					1	16	0

Such inventories, which include itemised lists of all the deceased's possessions, are not common, at least in the West Midlands, at this late date. Francis King's inventory confirms the impression that the small provincial masters were having to change the nature of their business. In 1719 he described himself as a pewterer and brazier. His stock at the time of his death was mostly brass, copper and iron and very, very little pewter. He had been producing pewter at one time, but had ceased to do so. This is underlined by the final entry which reads as follows: 'Item Moulds lent to Mr. John Duncombe of Wribbenhall and valued by Mr. Banks of Bewdley amounted to the value of £6 7s. 4½d.'

Richard Green, whose touch has now been identified and attributed, was also of this period. He was free in 1717 and died in 1730. Another name familiar to collectors, John Underhill (MPM.4856a) is now also known to have been a Worcester pewterer who was free of the city in 1733. It is noted that his hall-marks appear with the touch of William Greenbank to whom he may perhaps have been apprenticed. Yet another Worcester mark has long been recorded without its provenance being recognised, that of John Brain (Cott. 555, MPM.555). There were two Worcester craftsmen of this name, father and son, in the second quarter of the 18th century.

It has always been believed that the dramatic growth in the use of pewter in the 17th century did not continue in the 18th century, and that as the 18th century proceeded, there was an actual contraction in the use of pewter. This does appear to be the case, but as with Shrewsbury, the evidence from Worcester suggests also a change in the trade's character. Some substantial pewterers were prospering and even extending their production, while smaller craftsmen were by stages, possibly in some cases painful stages, changing from pewterers to braziers. How far this was a forced change and how far because the growing supply of copper and brass made the change possible and profitable is not clear. The change of emphasis is clearly seen by reference to the 1747 Worcester Poll Book[10] which lists 10 resident braziers and only three

6. Extract from the inventory of Edmund Leeth of Worcester, 1746–7.
(Hereford and Worcester Record Office)

pewterers as well as several non-resident who also cast their votes. One of the pewterers was Russell Laugher, the others being Edward Goode and John Underhill. Edward Goode incidentally is recorded in deeds of 1731–5 as then being resident in Droitwich. The strength of Worcester as a centre for the non-ferrous metal crafts is still apparent but the change from the tin-based alloys to copper-based alloys is clear. No doubt some of the braziers were still making pewter; Giles Redding for instance had been apprenticed to Francis King in the second decade of the century, and many more will have been retailing the product of local pewterers such as Laugher and Duncumb of Wribbenhall

The Redding family, who are first noticed with the mention of Giles (Egidius) in 1722 as a pewterer and brazier, provide an example of a late family business. While the relationships are not all clear we find Giles' son Samuel in the mid-18th century as a pewterer and brazier and at the same time Thomas and James were also in the trade. A Thomas Redding is found as a brazier in the 1790s, having been admitted to the freedom of the city in 1789. Between that date and 1837 we find a further 10 braziers, including another James Redding, but by then pewtering appears to have been dead and indeed is not mentioned after the 1750s. No doubt it had been by then swamped by Bewdley and Birmingham.

It has been possible to reconstruct the history of the pewter trade of Worcester in some detail over a period of three centuries and to recover the names of 96 pewterers and braziers during that period. The marks of a number of them have been identified and will be found reproduced later in this book. As with Shrewsbury the city provides a microcosm of the growth and decline of the craft as economic factors led to the abandonment of pewterware in general domestic use in the face of competition from other cheaper and more practicable alternatives during the 18th century.

HEREFORD

The picture we have been able to produce for Hereford is much less complete. The indications are strong that it was never a major pewtering centre, but the craft was carried on in the city from the early 16th century at least. The earliest reference, which we have unfortunately not been able to confirm, is in a card index at Pewterers' Hall which briefly records that one Thomas Grainger, pewterer, is mentioned in Hereford city archives in 1514. Twenty years later an intriguing and somewhat bizarre passage is to be found in *Letters Foreign and Domestic of the Reign of Henry VIII*[11] which is here reproduced in full, and summarises the contents of a letter from Thomas Gebons, mayor of Hereford, to Thomas Cromwell. It is dated 6 June 1534.

> On Monday next after the feast of Pentecost late past, Robert Stopar *alias* Robert Pewterer of Hereford asked me, 'What tidings?'. I said I had none. He replied 'I trust to see queen Katherine's banner spread again, and she shall be queen of England in her old place, by the grace of God'. For these words I brought the said Robert before Sir Jas. Baskervyle, John Scudamore, John Guilliams, Ric. Warmecombe and John Buryton, justices of the county . . . On this Stopar was strictly examined on his words and what he had to say in that cause, when he not only confirmed what he had said but spake divers other opprobious words, which I send.

The tactless Stopar, on being brought before the justices, confessed as follows:

> He said that he himself was king, that he was of the name of Henry, the eldest son of Henry late earl of Wiltshire, and that he was proclaimed king of England on Lowe Easter Even last at Charing Cross, by the name of Henry king of England. He trusts that queen Katherine's banner shall be spread again, and that she shall be queen of England in her old place, by the grace of God.

Whether he was deranged, or just clever, is not clear, and neither, regrettably, is his fate disclosed!

These fragments are all that has so far been discovered about the craft in Hereford in the 1500s; it is perhaps significant that pewterers do not figure among the 17 trades represented in 1562 in the city's Smiths' Company.[12] Nor does any further information emerge until a century later when Cotterell records, under No. 3384, that Brian Newton is mentioned as a pewterer in Hereford in 1641; a William Lea is also mentioned at about the same time. That there was little pewtering in the city at this time is probably indicated by the fact that the London Company's searchers did not visit it in the period 1635-47, though as we have seen they were very active in Worcester during that time. Their sole visit appears to have been in 1677 when they found only one pewterer, and one with a name that is familiar to us, Francis Trapp. Although the relationship is not certain, he was of the Worcester family of that name and he appears to have been used by Sampson Bourne as an outlet for his pewter in Hereford, so explaining the large sum owed to Bourne by Trapp which has previously been commented upon. Thus candlesticks, flagons, porringers and chamberpots of Bourne's were seized, as were wares by pewterers from Gloucester, Walsall and Shipston-on-Stour. The only items which are recorded as of Trapp's own making were spoons. Since it is unlikely that all his own wares passed the assay, we must conclude that he was a retailer more than a maker. He died in 1689 and his son Francis followed him in the trade until 1699.

Much more information is available from the 18th century, but by then the tradesmen who obtained their freedoms are almost all described as braziers. One of these, Randolph Phillips, appears to have made pewter in a small way since he advertised in the *Ludlow Post Man* in 1719 that he cast old pewter into spoons. The other pewterer and brazier was John Hopkins who voted in 1734, 1741 and 1747 and he also, like Francis Trapp, was an immigrant from Worcester.

Although 26 tradesmen described as braziers have been found for the period 1719–1810, and the trade was associated with the families of Gowler, Homiatt and Haywood for much of the century, there is no indication that any of them were pewter makers or factors. The contrast between the two cities of Hereford and Worcester is therefore a total one. Worcester was among the more significant of provincial pewtering centres for some two hundred and fifty years while Hereford appears to have played a negligible part, comparable with that of towns of far less apparent standing.

Worcester Pewterers and Braziers

Note: f = free of the city of Worcester

Charlement, Thomas	m 1502, dead by 1536, p
Green, Nicholas	m 1519, d, 1541, p and bellfounder
Mathews, John	m 1539–42, p
Jerman, Henry	d 1558, p and plumber

Green, Henry	d 1568, p and bellfounder, s. of Nicholas
Green, Margery	d 1570, p, w. of Henry
Baysie, John I	d 1585, p
Baysie, John II	m 1585, p, s. of John I
Baysie, George	m 1585, p, b. of John I
Clare, Gilbert	m 1584, d 1589, p
Letsam, Henry I	d 1593, br
Hopkins, William	m 1588, d 1602, p and br
Greenbank, James	d 1603, p and br
Letsam, Henry II	m 1607-31, p and br, ? s. of Henry I
Trapp, Francis	? b. 1596, d 1633, p
Greenbank, William I	d 1639, p, br and plumber, s. of James
Nichol(a)s, Thomas	f 1629-30, p
Bourne, Sampson I	f 1634, d 1674, p (Cott. 5463)
Ten, . . .	m 1640, p
Greenbank, John I	b 1614, d 1680, p, s. of William I
Letsam, Thomas	b 1608, d 1643, p, s. of Henry II
Woodward, William	d 1644, p
Addison, Richard	f 1648, p
Greenbank, Francis	f 1647, d. 1689, p, s. of William I
Harvey, Godfrey	m 1667, br
Crump, Philip	f 1669-70, m 1677, p
Greenbank, John II	f 1675, d 1700, p, s. of John I (Cott. 5619)
Trapp, John I	b 1622 d 1675, p, s. of Francis
Trapp, Anne	d 1677, p
Bourne, Sampson II	m 1677, d 1689, p, s. of Sampson I (Cott. 5464)
Baker, John	m 1677-1702, p
Hill, Walter	m 1677-89, p
Nicholls, Richard	m 1647-77, p
Letsam, Richard	b 1614, m 1677, p, s. of Henry II
Letsam, Sampson I	b 1646, f 1669-70, m 1677, p, s. of Richard
Wareing, Job	m 1677, p
Bray, Thomas	f 1679, p
Wheeler, John	f 1680-81, p
Huntpatch, William	f 1682, m 1689, p
Greenbank, Dickenson I	f 1685-6, d 1713, s. of Francis
Bowen, Edward	f 1686, n. 1702, p
Wheeler, Benjamin	f 1687-8, p
Rowe, Samuel	m 1689, p
Bourne, Joshua	f 1689-90, p
Bond (Bounds), Edward	m 1689, p
Greenbank, William II	b 1674, m 1714, p, s. of John II (Cott. 1992)
Greenbank, John III	b 1678, d 1723, p, s. of John II (Cott. 5619)
Letsam, Sampson II	b 1673, f 1696, p and br, s. of Sampson I
Smith, Samuel	f 1697, p
Trapp, John II	b 1655, d 1713, p, n. of John I (Cott. 5977)
Greenbank, Ann(a)	f 1713, p (a spinster)
Prosser, Charles	f 1714, p and br
Greenbank, Dickenson II	m 1720s, p
Leeth, Edmund	m 1715, d 1746-7, br
Bond, Richard	f 1717, m 1747, p
Green, Richard	f 1717, d. 1730, p
Greenbank, Francis II	f 1720, m 1733, p, ? s. of Dickenson I
Hows, Thomas	f 1720, br
Trapp, Edward	b 1685, m 1717, p, s. of John II

King, Francis	d 1730, p and br
Redding, Giles (Egidius)	f 1722, m 1747, p and br
Goode, Edward	f 1720, m 1747, p
Trapp, John III	b 1679-80, m 1720s, p, s. of John II
Brain, John I	m 1725, p (Cott. 555, MPM 555)
Child, Thomas	f 1723, p and br
Southall, William	f 1722-3, m 1747, br
Redding, William	f 1734, p and br
Harper, Hopwood	d 1733, p and br, n. of John Greenbank III
Dun, William	f 1734, br
Baylis, Thomas	f 1737, p and br
Redding, Samuel	app. 1741-2, p and br, s. of Giles
Redding, Thomas	app. 1744, p and br
Redding, James	app. 1745, m 1798, br
Brain, John II	f 1746, p, s. of John I
Dineley, Thomas	m 1747, br
Smith, Richard	f 1734, m 1747, br
George, Richard	m 1747, br
Noxon, Joshua	m 1747, br
Reeves, Robert	m 1747, br
Greenhill, William	m 1747, br
Rae, James	m 1747, br
Laugher, Russell	b 1696, d. 1751, p (Cott. 4077)
Elcocks, Robert	b 1715, m 1747, br
Underhill, John	f 1733, m 1747, p and br (MPM 4856a)
Baylis, Thomas	f 1739, m 1750, p and br
Field, Joseph	f 1755, p and br
Redding, Thomas	f 1789, m 1798, br
Elcox, Henry	f 1775, m 1798, br
Garmaston, Thomas	m 1793-1800, br
Knight, Stephen	f 1780, m 1793, br
Williams, Robert	m 1798, br
Stephens, William	m 1798, br
Barnett, George	m 1815, br
Coley, William	f 1811, m 1827, br
Coley, Henry	m 1828, br
Lane, Henry	m 1837, br

Hereford Pewterers and Braziers

Note: f = free of the city of Hereford

Grainger, Thomas	m 1514, p
Stoper (*alias* Pewterer), Robert	m 1534, p
Lea (Lee), William	m 1640, p
Newton, Brian	m 1641, p (Cott. 3384)
Trapp, Francis I	m 1677, d 1689, p (from Worcester)
Trapp, Francis II	d 1699, p, s. of Francis I
Poole, Francis	f 1694, br
Haywood, Philip	m 1716-34, br
Mathews, John	m 1716, br
Parkhouse, William	m 1716, br

Gwatkin, Richard	f 1722, br
Haywood, James	f 1723, m 1747, br
Prosser, Barnaby	f 1715, br
Gowler, Samuel	m 1734–44, br
Hopkins, John	m 1734–47, p and br
Peat(e), John	m 1734–41, br
Philips, Randolphus	m 1734, p and br
Price, Thomas	m 1733–47, br
Bradford, Thomas	m 1736, br
Floyd, Thomas	f 1749, br
Homiatt, Thomas	f 1753, br
Papps, George	f 1753, br
Gowler, Samuel	f 1757, br
Colloe, Christopher	f 1761, br
Gowler, John	f 1764, m 1784, br
Webb, Sergent	f 1767, br
Gowler, Richard	f 1784, br
Haywood, Francis	f 1784, br
Haywood, Thomas	m 1784, br
Homiatt, Thomas	f 1784, br
Spencer, Richard	f 1784, br
Tully, William	f 1784, br
Homiatt, Charles	f 1810, br
Downie, Richard	f 1826, br

NOTES AND REFERENCES

Worcester and Hereford

Note: WHS = Worcestershire Historical Society

1. Fegan, Ethen, S. (ed.), *The Journal of Prior William More* (WHS 1914), pp. 73, 110, 169 and 356 respectively.
2. Noakes, John, *Worcester in Olden Times* (n.d., *c.* 1860).
3. Hatcher, J., and Barker, T. C., *A History of British Pewter* (1974) pp. 215-6.
4. Davis, S. W., *The Economic History of Bewdley to 1700*, London Ph.D. thesis (1981), p. 247 for tabulated data on the river trade for several towns and p. 253 for data from the Gloucester Port Books.
5. A Sampson Burne for whom no occupation is given is included in the Walsall Ship Money returns for 1636. It is tempting to speculate that he is identical with the Sampson Bourne of Worcester.
6. *Deed* of 1671 at Worcester guildhall.
7. Edward Outen of Coventry, brazier, died in 1699. A brief inventory of his goods survives.
8. Hatcher and Barker, *op. cit.*, pp. 261-2 show the distribution of pewter by Samuel [*sic*] Bourne throughout the whole of the Midlands from information in the searches of 1676 and 1677.
9. John Greenbank is described as a plumber in his inventory but as a pewterer in a deed of 1657 at Worcester guildhall.
10. *Alphabetical Copy of the Poll taken at the City of Worcester 1747* (1747).
11. *Letters Foreign and Domestic of the Reign of Henry VIII*, 26 Hen. VIII, entry No. 802, p. 306.
12. Fisher, F. J., *Provincial Guilds*, London M.A. thesis (1931), appendix.

General

Liber Recordum (Worcester), MSS at Worcester guildhall.
Chamber Order Book (Worcester), MSS at Worcester guildhall; also Bond, Shelagh, *Chamber Order Book 1602-50* (WHS 1974).
Freeman Book (Worcester), MSS at Worcester guildhall.
Parish Registers of St Swithin and of St Nicholas (Worcester), HWRO.
Hereford Poll Books, 1716, 1734, 1741, 1747 and 1784, Hereford Public Libraries.
Hereford City Records (various) at HWRO.
Amphlett, John (ed.), *Churchwardens' Accounts of St Michael in Bedwardine* (WHS 1896).
Bloom, J. Harvey (ed.), *Original Charters Relating to Worcester* (WHS 1909).
Carver, M. O. H. (ed.), 'Mediaeval Worcester, an Archaeological Framework', *Transactions of the Worcestershire Archaeological Society*, 3rd Series, vol. 7 (1980).
Dyer, Alan, *The City of Worcester in the Sixteenth Century* (1973).
International Genealogical Index, Worcester(City).

BIRMINGHAM TO c. 1790, BEWDLEY AND KIDDERMINSTER

IN THE CITIES and county towns surrounding Birmingham there were numerous pewterers plying their craft in the 16th and early 17th centuries. We have already seen that in Coventry, which then had a population of about six thousand, there were two pewterers, Robert Burnett and John Yalle, in 1474 when the Pewterers' Company, intent on exercising the rights of search granted to them under their first charter, carried out their first country search. However, from other sources, it is known that pewtering was carried on there as early as the 14th century. There is a record of a pewterer in Walsall in 1438, and an indication that the trade may have been practised there in 1399. The inventory of Richard Parker of Walsall who died in 1534 records pewter valued at £7, and weighing five hundredweights. This represents a significant business and indicates a considerable demand for pewter among the local populace. Other early Walsall inventories reveal a similar state of affairs.

In 1546 Birmingham is estimated to have had a population of fifteen hundred to two thousand which had risen to about five thousand by 1680. The manorial influence of Birmingham waned with the departure of the manorial family in 1530 and the town, free of merchant and craft guilds, provided an environment during the 16th and 17th centuries in which new trades could flourish unimpeded. This encouraged an influx of entrepreneurial craftsmen and merchants from cities such as Coventry, Warwick and Worcester where the restrictive guild practices inhibited departure from tradition. By the end of the 16th century Birmingham was a flourishing market town with an expanding manufacturing industry which enjoyed considerable social and economic freedom. During the 17th century the availability of local iron and coal encouraged nail making, edge-tool and weapon manufacture, gun smithing, buckle making and general metal-working and it would be surprising if pewterers were not attracted to the town as early as the 16th century. No occupations are given in St Martin's parish registers and the absence of a guild system and lack of borough status means a corresponding lack of other records. However, the position in the late 17th century is indicated by two searches made by the Pewterers' Company, the first in 1676 and the second in the early 1690s. In 1676 the searchers visited several midland towns and searched the premises of pewterers in Stafford, Walsall, Henley-in-Arden, Stratford-on-Avon, Warwick, Banbury and Birmingham. In the later search the itinerary included Evesham, Alcester, Walsall, Birmingham, Stratford-on-Avon, Shipston-on-Stour and Banbury.

In 1676 the searchers visited the shops of four Birmingham pewterers, Thomas Gorton, William Wood, Benjamin Wood, and William Hall, and they also found pewter spoons made by a J. Gorton on the premises of Thomas Gorton. It is likely that this is the John Gorton, relationship unknown, whose name appears in a deed of 1663. They were both members of a family of Birmingham metal-workers other members of which, Edward and Michael, were recorded as paying hearth tax[1] in the 1660s

60

and '70s. Michael is also mentioned in a document of 1673 as a coppersmith; he died in 1722 when he was described as a brassfounder.

Pewter by Thomas Gorton was found by the Company's searchers in Warwick, Stratford-on-Avon, Stafford, Walsall and Kidderminster. The range of ware seized is wide and includes flagons, chamber-pots, salts, porringers, plates, saucers, spoons, candlesticks and aqua vitae bottles. Thomas Gorton's will and inventory survives. He died in 1683 worth £185 and was quite well-to-do with the comforts of a bed with curtains and valences, and luxuries of a looking glass and four silver spoons. The part of his inventory concerned with his trade and his pewter reads as follows:

In the house . . . 19 pewter dishes, 19 plates, 2 flagons, 4 pints, 12 spoons, 4 kettles, 3 pots, 23 porringers, 4 chamber pots, 3 basins, 12 trenchers, 1 salt . . .

In the garret . . . twenty four dozen of shovelboard pieces, twenty six dozen of ladles, five score and one pounds of quarter pints and small measures; of gunnes flagons, cans and candlesticks six score and one pounds; of new chamber pots 28 pounds . . .

In the shop . . . one vice, 2 steadies, 2 bright hammers, one bickorn, one iron pot, soldering irons, bellows, beams and scales, stamp hammer, shavers, 3 patterns, lead weights. Lay 74 pounds and 8 dozen of bells.
Moulds 30 score pounds weight.
Moulds 30 score pounds more.
One wheel, mandrels and hooks, burnishers, one spindle.
Pot ears 63 pounds, old copper 29 pounds.
Three mill brasses 30 pounds, 4 dozen of melting pots.
Old brass ware, four saddlers rasps and files.
Three box moulds, 8 ordinary moulds, 4 pairs of screws, one vice bench, nine old files, one brass screw, one pair of bellows, one moulding trough . . . ".

The appraisers to the inventory are his father-in-law Edward Beck and William Wood, a fellow pewterer. It is possible that Edward Beck was also a pewterer as one George Beck (location unknown) was a customer for John Duncumb's pewter in 1718.

Thomas Gorton died a comparatively young man leaving two infant children and a widow, Lydia, who briefly inherited his business. She married, shortly after her husband's death, another Birmingham pewterer, John Sorrell, whose pewter was found elsewhere in the midlands in a search of 1689, and on the premises of a further Birmingham pewterer, James Acton, who is listed in the 1690s Birmingham search. He was related to Edward Acton and several other Actons who were pewterers in Bridgnorth. Curiously the shop of John Sorrell was not itself visited but the wares he made included saucers, porringers, flagons, chamber pots and cups. He was probably the John Sorrell (also Sorrill) of 'Sawford in the County of Warwick' who was apprenticed in London on 6 November 1676 to John Emes, a well-known London pewterer, and made free of the London Company on 20 December 1683.

William Hall is found in the hearth tax returns for 1662 and was certainly a member of the London Company. His name appears, endorsed 'Bremigem', in their records for 1665, and later, William Hall 'of Bermingham' took as apprentice one Thomas Harres of Warwick who was later established in Kidderminster as a customer of Sampson Bourne II of Worcester. Unfortunately several William Halls were members of the London Company in the latter part of the 17th century and other mentions of the name cannot be unambiguously attributed to the Birmingham pewterer. However, it seems likely that he was the William Hall who also took as apprentice in 1667–8 Ephraim Acton, who later practised the craft in Bridgnorth. William Hall the pewterer died in Birmingham in 1702; his son William, a brazier died in 1723.

Another 17th century Birmingham pewterer whose will and inventory survive was Joseph Bradnock who died in 1684 worth £265. His house was furnished with mirrors, carpets and curtains and he left his tools and wearing apparel in the custody of his mother, Joyce Blackham [sic], for the benefit of his son John. Although he describes himself as 'pewterer' his tools are referred to both in his will and inventory as 'Tools used in the working of brass', indicating a dual trade as both pewterer and brazier; they are valued in his inventory at only £1. His stock of both metals was however substantial, 'Pewter, Brass and Tin wares' being valued at £98 5s. 2½d., about three thousand pounds in weight.

It is however the Wood family which throw most light on the 17th century Birmingham scene and enable us to go back to the earliest years of the century. The grandfather of the William Wood who is recorded in 1676 and in the early 1690s search was Robert Wood, pewterer, who died in 1637, having fathered several children between 1602 and 1615 by his wife Alice. His inventory discloses goods worth £136 1s. 0d., including pewter and brass to the value of some £80 and tools valued at £2. His pewtering business passed to his wife, and thence to his eldest son, William I, who married a Dorothy Vaughton in 1630 and sired seven children by 1650. In the hearth tax returns of 1663 William I was living in Corn Cheaping (now the Bullring) next door to the *Red Lion Inn* and in addition to his smith's hearth in the 'hallhouse' he had a grate and hearth in the 'chamber over the hall'. He was clearly of some standing in the trade since, in 1664, he was appointed at Warwick quarter sessions, with five fellow pewterers from Coventry, Warwick and Alcester, as a 'person expert and skilfull in the art and mystery of pewterers . . . to make search in the said county of Warwick for all and all manner of pewter . . . not being lawful pewter . . . or of such goodness and fineness or not so sufficiently wrought, mixed or marked . . .'. The others appointed with him were Lovell Smith, Joseph Seeley and John Dowell of Coventry; Richard Comberlidge of Warwick and Richard Pershouse of Alcester.

In 1665 he died, leaving his pewtering and brazing business to his son William II, and desiring that his younger son Benjamin be apprenticed to William II. In 1671 the hearth tax returns show both William and Benjamin to have had forges in Digbeth. His inventory valued his goods at £219 13s. 0d. including some 334 lbs. of old and new pewter in the shop, together with 200 lbs. of platter moulds. However, his more significant business seems to have been in brass since he had a stock of no less than 840 lbs. of new kettles and 320 lbs. of other new brassware. His tools were valued at £2 10s. 0d.

William Wood II, who lived until 1726 when he died aged 81, was the father of nine children. His sons Thomas and Samuel established themselves as brassfounders, John was a tallow chandler and Joseph continued the pewtering business which was bequeathed to him in William's will. His will also bade Joseph bind his grandson William Smallwood apprentice to him for seven years. Joseph was alive in 1745, but his death has not been found. The seal on William Wood II's will is of a classical bust and this confirms that he is the 'WW' listed by Cotterell under Numbers 6028 and 6031 and by Peal (MPM, 6032).

William Wood II's chief claim to recognition lies in the marriage of his daughter Elizabeth to John Duncombe or Duncumb,[2] founder of the most significant 18th century pewter business. John Duncumb was a younger son of a landed Surrey family who had purchased the manor of Weston Gumshalve in Albury, near Guildford, in 1610, and who were a collateral line of the Duncombe's who became Earls of Feversham. The Surrey family were well connected by marriage to a number of titled families in Surrey and elsewhere and owned estates which extended to over three thousand acres in the late 17th century.[3] John's father, Stynt Duncumb, died in 1690 at the early age of 35, leaving John fatherless at the age of six or seven. Under his will Stynt left £600 to provide for his sons, William, John's elder brother, and John to be bound apprentice to such trade as might be thought fit by his widow, Elizabeth.

Stynt Duncumb had a London residence in the parish of St Clement Danes[4] and in the adjoining parish of St Martin in the Fields there lived, in 1726, a William Wood, seedsman, who at that date was concerned with Thomas Wood, son of William Wood II, in proving a codicil to William II's will. Clearly William the seedsman was a relative of William the pewterer and it appears very likely that he was his nephew, son of William II's brother Joseph, who was born in Birmingham in 1641. The rather unlikely apprenticing of John Duncumb to a Birmingham master is then explained through this link with the London seedsman, who may well have supplied seeds for the Duncumb estates in Surrey. Be that as it may, by about 1702 John Duncumb had become William Wood II's son-in-law, and shortly thereafter he was in business on his own account as a pewterer in Birmingham. John Duncumb was the father of 13 children whose baptisms are record in St Martin's Church, Birmingham, between 1703 and 1720.

No doubt because of his London connections, and the standing of the family, John Duncumb applied in 1706–7 to be admitted as a freeman of the Worshipful Company of Pewterers, being sponsored by a Mr. Cumberland, of whom nothing more is known. He journeyed to London in 1706–7 and appeared personally before the Court of the Company on 20 March, but for reasons unknown his application was refused. The Court book of the Company all too briefly notes 'John Duncombe of Birmingham appeared at this Court and desired to be admitted a Freeman of the Company by Redemption. After some debate it is agreed upon the question that he should not be admitted a Freeman of this Company.'

He continued to work in Birmingham and a deed of 1719 describes him as of that town. A later deed of 1730 describes him as of Kidderminster,[5] but it is clear that he moved to Wribbenhall in 1720 since, by a remarkable chance, his day book[6] for the period 1718–24 survives and refers for the first time to goods being sent from Bewdley on 3 August 1720. It seems likely that he, and later his son, lived at Wribbenhall House, an apparently William and Mary building which was demolished some forty years ago, and which stood adjacent to the still existing lane named Pewterers Alley. The reason for this move may well lie in his fortunes as a member of the Duncumb family. Although, as a younger son of a younger son, John had no expectation of inheriting the Surrey estates, the two male heirs who had precedence over him, a cousin, George, and his own elder brother William, both died young without male issue. Thus, in 1719, under a settlement made by his uncle, the holder of the estates, who was to die in the following year, John found himself possessed of a considerable fortune.[7] Some of this he appears to have invested in setting up a new pewterering business in Wribbenhall, a thriving river port.

The town of Bewdley and the hamlet of Wribbenhall on the opposite bank of the River Severn were first linked by bridge in 1447. The watermen of Bewdley navigated the river as early as the 14th century, the town was granted a charter in 1472, and for several hundred years many tradesmen and merchants of the town shipped their produce up the river to Shrewsbury and down the river to Worcester, Gloucester and Bristol from wharves on both banks of the River Severn near to the bridge. During the 17th and 18th centuries hundreds of packhorses were quartered in the town to provide communication between the river wharves and the surrounding towns, including Birmingham via the turnpike road through Stourbridge and Dudley. In 1746 Bewdley was described as 'a place of a considerable trade for by means of the Severn great quantities of salt, iron, glass and Manchester goods etc., are put on barges which render this town a populous thriving place'. The attraction of Bewdley as a commercial base for his activities must have been very apparent to John Duncumb. He was already, before his move, dispatching goods to the Bewdley pewterer Christopher Banks who had moved there from Wigan in 1697 and who had a thriving business in the town, and to William Mountford, no doubt related to the William Mountford who is known from a trade token to have been a Kidderminster pewterer as early as 1666. As we shall see later, numerous braziers and pewterers were working in Bewdley as early as the 16th century.

From the surviving day book of John Duncumb, which covers the period from July 1718 to December 1724, it is possible to get a very good picture of his business at that time. This remained at a steady level, generating a turnover of about £2,000 per annum, and serving some sixty-five customers at any one time, though a total of 124 are named over the five-year period and are listed in Appendix I to this chapter. The locations of about a third of them are indicated and others have now been identified with pewterers known from other sources of information. Most of them are situated in towns within a thirty to forty mile radius of Bewdley with Shrewsbury predominating, but a few consignments were made to places further afield such as Chester, Grantham and Burton-on-Trent. Goods were packed for carriage either in baskets or in (pack) clothes. At the price of 9d. to 1s. 0d. per pound weight, some twenty tons of pewterware was produced each year, the equivalent of about fifty thousand common plates of 9½ in. diameter. Although a little scrap pewter was purchased the quantity of this was only a fraction of that needed for the business and much new tin from Cornwall must have been imported via the Severn to the wharves at Wribbenhall. Practically all sales were of sadware, mainly plates and dishes, but with a proportion of basins, bedpans, chamber pots and a very little hollow-ware, often not separately itemised. In addition very large numbers of spoons were produced. Those present-day firms which continue to produce pewterware by traditional methods employ at least one craftsman for every ton of ware produced annually. Since we can hardly suppose that early 18th century workers were significantly more efficient, even though they may have worked longer hours, we can deduce that John Duncumb employed some twenty workers or so. (see Table II on facing page).

As an example of a typical sales pattern the consignments of John Duncumb to his father-in-law William Wood over the period November 1718 to July 1722 when they cease, show that the four-and-a-half tons of pewterware sold to him over that period consisted of 4,285 lbs. of sadware, 2,120 lbs. of ordinary plates, 1,045 lbs. of hard

TABLE II

August (year)	No. of customers	Pewterware sold (lbs.)	Value of Pewterware (£)	Old pewter bought (lbs.)	Additional sales of spoons (doz.)
1718	24	3,477	222	324	37
1719	32	4,536	256	495	60
1720	23	2,610	145	105	12
1721	26	4,286	165	968	—
1722	24	4,350	199	522	111
1723	27	2,790	127	573	48
1724	22	3,137	189	1,031	8

Sales of pewter by John Duncumb for the month of August in successive years (from his day book).

plates, 1,047 lbs. of ordinary dishes and only 276 lbs. of hollow-ware. In addition there were 183 dozen of various spoons, but only 26 lbs. of pint pots. It is clear that the expression 'ordinary plates' describes items weighing 11 lbs. per dozen and that corresponding 'hard plates' weighed 12 lbs. per dozen, i.e., common 9½ in. plates in both cases. Other sizes of plates are included in the general description 'sadware'. As well as supplying finished goods, 'rough plates' were supplied to Edward Box (of Banbury) at the cost of the metal 65s. 0d. to 70s. 0d. a hundredweight, plus a charge for casting. Presumably Box finished these himself and added his touch mark (Cott. 538). The location of Edward Box at Banbury is shown by an advertisement in *Aris' Birmingham Gazette* for 20 April 1752 noting the sale 'of the stock in trade and all sorts of moulds and brazier's tools' of Edward Box, pewterer and brazier, and offering the lease of his house and shop at Market Street, Banbury.

An entry of this type from Duncumb's day book reads:

23rd April 1720

	£	s.	d.
Mr. Ed. Box Dr.			
To ord[inary] rufe dishes wt 1:1:06	00	05	09
rufe hard plates wt 1:0:08 casting	00	12	10
[metal] 2:1:14 at 66/- [per cwt]	07	16	09
for carriage and cording	00	05	01½
	09	00	05½

A few non-pewter items were supplied, copper nails, brass and iron candlesticks, copper cans and brass cocks. Also a small amount of bar tin and 'tin glass' (bismuth).

It is apparent that John Duncumb supplied many midland pewterers, braziers and wholesale ironmongers with their requirements, and known pewterers among his customers include:

Ephraim Acton, Bridgnorth
Abraham Archesden, Warwick
Christopher Banks, Bewdley
Edward Box, Banbury
Thomas Brock, Chester
Samuel Browne, Shrewsbury
Thomas Churchyard, Shrewsbury
Stephen Cumberlidge, Warwick

Humphrey Hollin(g)s, Ashby-de-la-Zouche
Francis King, Worcester
Jonathan Lugg, Ludlow
William Mountford, Kidderminster
Richard Plummer, Ludlow
Joseph, Robert and William Seney, Walsall
Thomas Smith, Bridgnorth
Edward Trapp, Worcester

James Davies, Shrewsbury   Samuel Turnpenny, Birmingham
Elizabeth Felton, Oswestry   Edward Wood, Ludlow
Thomas Forster, Shrewsbury   Joseph Wood, Birmingham
Richard Green, Worcester   William Wood, Birmingham
William Hall, Birmingham

A typical entry from John Duncumb's day book is that comprising orders destined
for his father-in-law William Wood during September 1719.

		£	s.	d.
Sept. 8th	Sadware 0:1:27 at 8¾	2	0	1½
9th	Hard plates 0:1:17 at 11½d	2	3	4
	18 doz of ord R spoons 0:0:27 work		4	6
12th	Ord plates 0:1:24:10 at 9¾d	2	3	4
	Sadware 0:0:10:4 at 8¾d		7	0
	Hollow^r 1:0:09 work	1	5	2½
18th	Sadware 1:3:08 at 8¾d	7	8	9
	Ord plates 0:3:3:8 at 8¾d	3	11	1
	12 doz of hard spoons at 22	1	2	0
19th	4 prs brass candlesticks		9	8
24th	1 barbers basin, one pott		5	0
	Sadware 0:0:24 at 8¾d		17	6
	ditto 2:1:06:04 at 8¾d	9	8	3½
	Ord plates 0:2:16:12	2	19	1
	Hard plates 0:0:26:4	1	5	2
	6 doz of L hard spoons at 22		11	0
	7 doz of R spoons 10:14 work		1	9
30th	Sadware 0:0:16:6 at 8¾d		11	0
	6 pair of brass candlesticks		16	0
		37	10	11

The items with the entry 'work' against them must be assumed to relate to fabricating or finishing ware from starting material provided. Quantities are to be interpreted
as hundredweights, quarters, pounds and ounces; or hundredweights, quarters and
pounds as appropriate.

John Duncumb died in 1745, in his early sixties, and was buried on 8 November at
Kidderminster.[8] His will, made on 7 June 1739, bequeathed his estate as follows:

> To his eldest son George his land etc. in Surrey
> To his daughters Ann and Sarah £1,000 each
> To his son Stent [sic] all his household goods, stock in trade and personal effects together
>   with his buildings at Wribbenhall
> To his son Joseph £500
> To his grand-daughter Mary Ingram £500 on attaining 21 years
> To his grandson John Ingram junior £200 on attaining 21 years
> Witnesses were Christopher Banks, Edward Burlton and John Ingram senior, his son-in-law

His son Stynt (Stent, Staint), who was baptised Staint at St Martin's, Birmingham on
22 May 1712, is clearly the pewterer well known to collectors as 'Samuel Duncombe'.
Possibly he preferred to be so known, but the reason for Cotterell's use of this name
has not been traced, and his touch gives only the initial 'S'. This appears with labels

reading 'London' and 'Bewdley' and Cotterell's attribution to Birmingham may well rest on a misidentification with the Duncombe of Duncombe, Davis and Ingram, a Birmingham merchant partnership which flourished in the late 18th century and which appears in many Birmingham trade directories. It is however apparent from the will of Stynt Duncumb that it was his brother Joseph who was the merchant of Birmingham, and this is confirmed by the fact that a Joseph Duncombe paid rates on a property in Digbeth from 1736-53 and later, from 1753-69, on property in The Square, Bull Street quarter. The rate for the latter was 1s. 8d. plus 2d. or 3d. for a shop. Joseph had previously inherited, at the early age of 18 under the will of Thomas Wood, son of William Wood II, the former's house and brassfounding business in 1734. He resided later, until his death in 1793, in Sutton Coldfield. A memorial tablet in Sutton Coldfield church is inscribed 'Joseph Duncombe Esq., died 1793, aged 76, descendant of the family of Duncomb, of Beds'.[9]

From the amount of surviving pewter bearing his touch mark it is clear that the business continued to flourish and probably grow under Stynt's control, though no contemporary details of it have been discovered. He died in 1767, apparently unmarried, and was buried at Kidderminster on 3 May. His will provided for the passage of his business to his nephew, John Ingram junior, son of John Ingram senior and his second wife Mary Duncumb, sister of Stynt. Other bequests provide as follows:

> To his sister Ann his household effects at Wribbenhall
> To his brother George of Kidderminster £500
> To his niece Elizabeth Ingram £400 at the age of 18 or on her earlier marriage
> To his servant Mary Davis the younger £400
> To his brother Joseph, Merchant of Birmingham, his property at Edgbaston [Birmingham]
>   leased from Sir Henry Gough, together with the residue of his estate.

The will is sealed with a seal bearing the well-known Duncumb crest of a horse's jamb rising from a coronet. The crest was confirmed to the Surrey Duncumbs by the Herald's Visitation of Surrey in 1623.

John Ingram junior came of a distinguished family, being descended from John Ingram of Upper House, Clifton-on-Teme, who was granted the arms 'Ermine on a fesse gules three escallops or', in 1614. These arms appear in one of the shields of the hall-marks found on John Ingram's pewter (Cott. 5725). His father, John senior, was Gentleman Remembrancer of the Exchequer and a flourishing Bewdley attorney. Through his first wife, Anne Winnington, daughter of Sir Francis Winnington, John senior had acquired the lease of the ancient Royal Manor of Tickenhill. Tickenhill House was originally the residence of the Mortimer family and was acquired as a royal residence by Edward IV. It was a meeting place of the court of the Marches of Wales until the reign of Charles I and the body of Prince Arthur, son of Henry VII lay there. After the restoration it fell into disrepair and was restored and cased in brick by John Ingram in 1738. However this property eventually passed to the son of John's first marriage, Francis Ingram. John junior, the pewterer, was born in 1731 the son of his father's second marriage to Mary Duncumb (which must have taken place after 1724, the date of Francis' birth) and it is likely that he resided at River House, a Charles II town house which still stands on Riverside South and was for long an Ingram family home. John Ingram junior also had a younger brother Thomas, who died in 1817 aged 75 and was probably the Ingram of the Birmingham merchant partnership. A Thomas Ingram 'of Birmingham' paid tax on a male servant in 1780.

Wood, Duncumb and Ingram

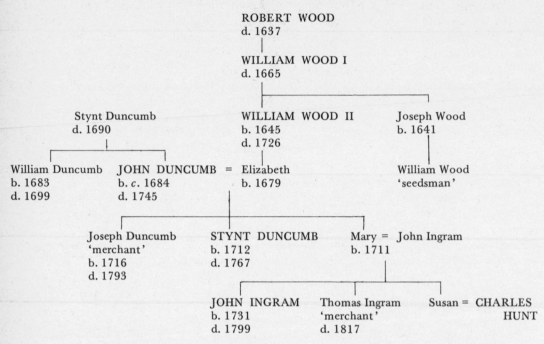

Note: Only those individuals mentioned in the text are shown. Pewteres shown in capital letters.

It seems very likely that John Ingram was apprenticed to his uncle and he must have worked for some time for him. However he would have been 37 years old at the time of Stynt Duncumb's death and he could well have been in business on his own account before that date. There is an indication of this in a news item in *Aris' Birmingham Gazette* for 28 December 1767 which reports the committal of one Gilbert Holland at Worcester for stealing a quantity of pewter from the shop of John Ingram at Kidderminster. Further he was made a burgess of Bridgnorth on 18 October 1768, when he was described as a brassfounder. John Ingram junior went into partnership some time before 1778 with his brother-in-law Charles Hunt, husband of his sister Susan, and continued to run a very large pewtering business, the accounts of which survive from 1769 onwards into the early 1800s.[10] The names of some seven hundred customers are recorded in these for the period 1769 to 1790. Included are the well-known Birmingham pewterers, Birch and Villers, the merchant partnership of Duncombe, Davis and Ingram, James Yates (not to be confused with the later James Yates of the mid-19th century), William Tutin (inventor of the alloy tutania) and such notables as Matthew Boulton. Locations of all the customers are given and these cover most of England and Wales north to Gainsborough and Doncaster, east to Yarmouth and Norwich and west to Penzance and Haverfordwest. There was considerable dealing with London traders but only one recorded London pewterer, Richard Jones (Cott. 2671), appears; and with many individuals and firms identifiable as ironmongers and hardware suppliers from local trade directories of the period. From the amount of Ingram and Hunt pewter found in the U.S.A. it is apparent that they had a large export trade to America. Unfortunately no record of this appears to survive. One export order only, to George Gustav Peterson of Hamburg, appears during the period 1769–90. Regrettably the entries for this period are tantalisingly brief and for the most part refer only to 'goods' or 'metal'. John Ingram, then described as 'of Warshill' (a neighbouring district) died in 1799.

Two later volumes for the period 1800 to 1805 give very detailed descriptions of the ware supplied. The list of items if formidable and is printed in Appendix II to this chapter.

Various types of drinking vessel appear twice, once with the appellation 'full' and again with 'short'. It can only be supposed that this refers to the measure! Ingram and Hunt produced well over a hundred thousand spoons a year at the beginning of the 19th century, an incredible number, none of which appear so far to be identified, compared with an annual output of some two and a half thousand pint tavern pots and about half that number each of quarts and half-pints. They advertised in *Aris' Birmingham Gazette* in 1783 for two men to work at their spoon branch in Bewdley, suggesting that this was a separate part of the business. Most of the types of spoons are referred to by pattern numbers, of which there are over fifty.

The name Stinton appears frequently in these later books. Sometimes as a customer in Worcester and at other times orders are endorsed 'per Stinton' or 'per J.S.'. This indicates that Stinton was an agent for Ingram and Hunt seeking business for them; a suggestion confirmed by the study of entries so endorsed which form clear geographical patterns representing Stinton's excursions as a 'traveller' for Ingram and Hunt. Thus for example 26 consecutive Stinton orders relate (in order) to the towns Ludlow, Leominster, Hereford, Ross, Gloucester, Stroud, Wotten-under-Edge, Bath and Bristol. Elsewhere seven cover Bridgewater, Exeter, Plymouth Dock and Plymouth, and again another 22 cover Dudley, Walsall, Burton-on-Trent, Derby, Nottingham, Lutterworth, Hinckley, Nuneaton, Coventry, Warwick, Alcester and Bromsgrove. Similar patters are repeated many times.

By 1800 much of the trade passed through major wholesalers in the large cities. The turnover of the firm was about £6,000 per annum at that time, representing about fifty-five tons of ware at the average price of 1s. 0d. per pound. William Wallis of Birmingham took over 10 per cent. of Ingram and Hunt's output in 1805–6 and a further 10 per cent. was taken by five other wholesalers in Birmingham, Manchester and Limerick. Few items appear at that time to have been supplied from stock and large orders took two to six weeks to fill. A typical large order to William Wallis in August 1805 comprised over fifty-three hundredweights of plates, dishes and basins packed in 10 casks — equivalent to some six thousand nine-inch plates. An order for over fifty gross of spoons was despatched to Smyrna in August 1806 and thirty gross and ten dozen of spoons to Jonathan Trotter of London in December 1805. The era of mass production had begun. (*See* Fig. 7 overleaf).

A fascinating but enigmatic early 19th century account book in the Hereford and Worcester Record Office,[11] which is unattributed, but which appears to belong to the same series as the Ingram and Hunt ledgers, records the purchase of various assorted materials. Some of these were bought-in accessories and fittings for pewterware and include teapot handles, teapot buttons, wood buttons (the last two presumably being

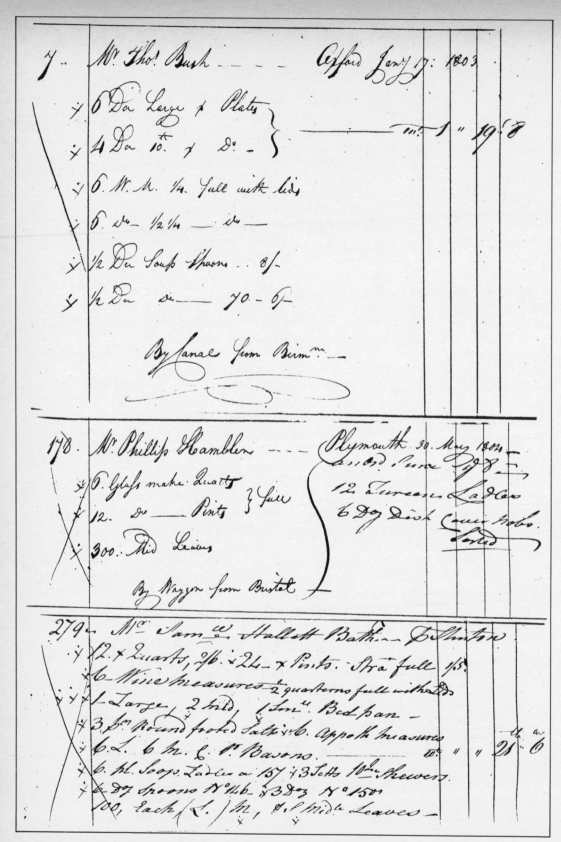

7. Three extracts from the order books of Ingram and Hunt for 1803 and 1804. Note the endorsement 'per Stinton' in the last entry and the instructions for carriage in the other two. (Messrs. Hemingways, Bewdley).

handle insulators) green baize (for candlestick bases?) and glass bottoms. Very large quantities of 'grease', presumably animal fat from the kitchen, were purchased at 4d. a pound in small quantities at a time from various local residents, from 'Ticknell House' and from 'the house' – possibly Wribbenhall House. Named suppliers of grease on a regular basis are Cotterell, Dovey and Greaves, individuals who are known from other sources to have lived in premises adjacent to Wribbenhall House in the Pewterers' Alley area.[12] They were probably employees of Ingram and Hunt. Monthly purchases of grease varied between nine-and-a-half pounds and ninety pounds and averaged fifty-three pounds during the period September 1805 to October 1806. It can be supposed that this grease was used for lubricating the 'wheels' used for finishing the pewter articles and perhaps for flux. During this same period 12 tons of coal was delivered in September, and a further 10 tons in April 1806.

The use to which many other purchases were put can only be conjectured. Eggs, turpentine, nut oil, gum arabic, verdigrease and white lead could perhaps all have found application for coating moulds to improve the flow of the molten metal and prevent sticking. Resin was used as a flux for soldering and for tinning brass. Emery and pumice have self-evident use for polishing the pewter and some purchases were clearly of general cleaning materials, for example soap, washing cloths and besoms. Other items include files, glue, corks, nails, flax and a cask 'for packing'. Not infrequent purchases were made of 'hatts', but the cost of any one purchase under this heading was only a few pence. A still-working master pewterer, asked if he could shed light on this entry, remarked that old felt hats were very useful for handling hot moulds and that he recalled their use for this purpose many years ago! Hat making was a local Bewdley trade.

Miscellaneous payments include a shilling to one Taynton for mixing solder, and eight pence for 'carrying up 4 block of tin'. Entries also appear for postage, carriage, bridge tolls and 'expenses for taking stock' (6s. 0d. on 30 December 1805).

The entries for August 1805, a typical month, are as follows:

1805		£	s.	d.
Aug. 9	Rosin			4
	Eggs at Sundries [sic]		1	0
	Northall for turning wood buttons		1	0
Aug. 20	3 lbs grease Mrs. Breadney		1	0
	40 lbs do. Mrs. Brasier		13	4
Aug. 23	7¾ lbs do. Cotterills girl		2	7
	Turpentine			1
	Hatts			3
	2 cards, B Crane			6
Aug. 24	Owner Pealing, a basket from Charlwood			7
	Tachenend*			2
Aug. 30	Cranes girl, 6 lbs grease		2	0
	To post, letters in the month	2	6	0
		3	8	10

* Perhaps a reference to the junction on the Kidderminster road at Catchem's End where tolls could have been payable

Weekly entries also appear in this account book under the heading 'Sundries paid to the men' which vary widely and average some £11 a week. Thus in the same month we find:

		£	s.	d.
Aug 3	To sundries paid the men	23	4	8
Aug 10	To do.	7	18	4
Aug 17	To do.	8	11	7½
Aug 24	To do.	9	6	10
Aug 31	To do.	19	7	5½
		68	8	11

Unfortunately no satisfactory explanation can be given for these entries. If they referred to wages one would have expected this to have been stated. Possibly they are 'piece-work' payments to outworkers, or perhaps the value of materials supplied to outworkers for them to finish in their own homes. Over the course of a year, August 1805 to July 1806, these payments totalled the very considerable sum of £650. During the same year the turnover of Ingram and Hunt's business was £5,620.

Some time before 1811, and probably in 1807, the business passed to Crane and Stinton who are noticed in Holden's *London and County Directory* for 1811 as pewterers in Bewdley. They owned a lease on workshops adjoining Wribbenhall House in the Pewterers' Alley area of Wribbenhall from 1807.[12] The Crane family is an old established Bewdley one and several members of it appear in 18th century Bewdley records. Four Cranes held the office of Bailiff of Bewdley on 10 occasions between 1747 and 1804, but little else has been discovered about Stinton, apart from his earlier activities as a 'traveller'. However a William Stinton of Birmingham was a customer of Ingram and Hunt in 1785. The touch mark 'C & S' found on typical Bewdley pots of the early 19th century can now be attributed to this partnership.

From Crane and Stinton the firm passed, before 1822, to John Carruthers Crane who retired in 1838. Since the lease of Crane and Stinton ran for 14 years from 1807 it seems likely that John Carruthers Crane took it over when the lease expired in 1821, since he is first mentioned in a trade directory of 1822. On his retirement in 1838 his moulds are said by Cotterell to have passed to James Yates of Birmingham and the business then returned to the city where it had been founded a century and a half earlier by John Duncumb. By various subsequent changes of ownership it passed into the hands of James Smellie of Birmingham who produced traditional pewterware until 1983.

Returning now to the earlier period of Bewdley pewtering a well known contemporary of John Duncumb in that town was the ex-Wigan pewterer Christopher Bank(e)s who migrated to Bewdley in 1697. The Banks family can be traced back as pewterers in Wigan to Adam Banks who flourished *c.* 1539 and died in 1559, and the family continued as pewterers in Wigan until the mid-18th century.[13] Christopher Banks arrived in Bewdley with a letter of introduction from the mayor of Wigan certifying that 'Mr. Christopher Bancks is a real worker and maker of all sorts of pewter, and that he has served a lawful apprenticeship in the art, mystery and calling of pewterer, and that he is well disposed towards the Government and towards the Church of England as by law established'. It has previously been assumed that Christopher Banks was the first of that family to settle in Bewdley. However, in 1702 the Pewterer's Company searchers visited the town for the first and only time and the record of their activities shows that this was not so. The visit to Christopher Banks is headed 'At

X'pher Banks's' but 'X'pher' is written above 'Robert', which has been crossed out and there is a marginal note reading 'Robt. Banks of Ribbenhall in Kidderminster parish, dead'. Here is something of a mystery which has yet to be solved. Christopher's father was a Robert, but he died in Wigan in 1692. Another Robert was alive in 1716 when he signed certain documents concerned with the estate of Christopher's uncle, Adam Banks, a Wigan pewterer, but no Robert has yet been found who can be identified with the Bewdley pewterer of that name.

8. Pewterers Company search of Bewdley in 1702 showing the amended entry for Christopher Banks and the marginal reference to the death of Robert Banks. (The Worshipful Company of Pewterers).

The family business in Bewdley continued in the pewter and later the brassfounding trade until the middle of the 19th century. Of Christopher's business there is little detailed information. He was a modest customer of John Duncumb during the period 1718-24. By his wife Margaret Anderton he had a son Robert who was born *c*. 1695 and who was drowned at Bewdley in 1748.[14] Robert had two sons, Christopher II (b. 1721) and William (b. 1728) who carried on an extensive pewtering, iron and brassfounding business, at one time in partnership and later separately, until *c*. 1790. It was then taken over by another Christopher, son to William, who was born in 1755 and died in 1834. The Banks' business became a partnership, Banks and Stokes in the early 1830s and was later acquired by Messrs. William Stokes and John Smith, under which name it continued until the late 19th century.

Banks of Bewdley

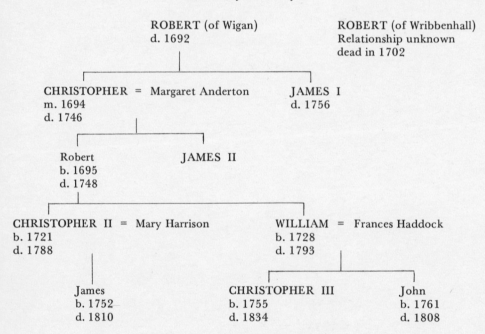

Note: Pewterers in capital letters.

Our attention was drawn to the existence of James I and James II late in the preparation of this book through the will of the former, brazier of Bewdley, died 1756. He left his brass moulds 'now in the hands of John Undrill' (presumably John Underhill of Worcester) to his nephew James and both were thus apparently pewterers. (Private communication from the Bewdley Research Group *per* Rhoda Murray). The mark 'I. Bancks & Co.' (Cott. 227) thus appears to be that of James II and the hall-marks shown with it are those of Christopher II.

Various notices and advertisements in *Aris' Birmingham Gazette* in the period 1741 to 1799 provide the following information on the Banks's business.

6 August 1764: John Baron apprentice to Messrs. Banks Pewterers and Brass founders in Bewdley has absconded.

27 April 1767: The partnership between Christopher and William Banks is being dissolved . . . The business will be carried on in all its branches separately.

4 October 1784: Christopher Banks of Bewdley requires a journeyman pewterer.

28 April 1788: Christopher Banks, Iron and brass founder, pewterer and brazier has deceased. The business is to be carried on by his son Thomas. [A memorial to this Christopher is to be found in Ribbesford Church].

17 June 1793: William Banks, brazier of Bewdley, died. [Curiously, in his will he describes himself as a 'horner'].

From an index to apprentices and apprentice masters for 1710–62 it is possible to recover the names of two of Christopher Banks' apprentices. In 1712 he had apprenticed to him Charles Acton, son of Ephraim Acton of Bridgnorth, pewterer; and in 1736, Peter Neale of whom there is no more information given. Almost certainly he must have had many more apprentices but presumably, to save the tax then payable, they were not registered. Probably for the same reason, no record has been found of any apprentices bound to John Duncumb or to Stynt Duncumb.

Robert and Christopher Banks were not by any means the first pewterers in Bewdley. The names of the earliest recorded Bewdley braziers and pewterers are to be found listed in the *Bewdley Bridgewardens' Account Book*[15] which contains details of market stall holders at the various fairs in the town from 1569 to 1662. The first name which appears is that of James Greenbank(e), brazier, who paid for a 'standing' at St Andrew's Fair in 1570. He must certainly have been related to the Greenbank family of Worcester who flourished there as pewterers and braziers for a century. He was paid ten shillings in 1578 for 'mending the lead of the steeple and the conduit and bringing water to the cistern'. A later namesake was similarly employed in 1616, as was his son, William, in 1613.

9. Receipts from pewterers for standings at St Andrew's Fair, Bewdley, in 1588.
(Bewdley Museum)

In 1574 Harry Wydsam and Richard Worthynton paid respectively for the 'uppermost' and the 'second' pewterers' standings at St Andrew's Fair, and from the lists of stall holders for 1573–88 we can recover the names of 18 pewterers and braziers (the terms seem to have been used with no particular distinction of trade) trading in the town at that time. Among these are some undoubted Worcester pewterers who had travelled to Bewdley for the fair. One, William Hopkins, is stated to be 'of Worcester', but the names also appear of Gilbert Clare and Harry (sometimes Henry) Ledsom(e). The former died at Worcester in 1589, and the latter (or someone of the same name), in the same city in 1593. His inventory (*see* p. 50) records 'clothes belonging to the standing . . . xiiis ivd'. Members of the Redding and Trapp families also appear, though they are different members of the families from those which have been identified in Worcester. The record in the Ribbesford (Bewdley) registers of the baptism of Francis Trapp on 29 August 1596, the son of Richard Trapp, tanner, raises the interesting possibility that he is the Frances Trapp who died in Worcester in 1633, a very wealthy pewterer, and who sired two further generations of Worcester pewterers and braziers. Richard Worthynton whose name appears from 1573 to 1588, may well have been related to John Worthynton who is recorded in Shrewsbury in 1550 as the son of Robert Worthyngton, pewterer of Walsall.

Later entries in the Bridgewardens' Book are generally less informative.

> 1608;   Received at St Andrew's Fair for five pewterers' standings for the whole
>   year . . . . xxs
> 1629;   Received for brasiers' standings at St Andrew's Fair . . . . 12s. 6d.
> 1642;   Received at St Andrew's Fair for braziers . . . . 8s.

However a few later individuals are named including a Harry Ledsome in 1614. Either he was a second generation of the same name, or the Bewdley Harry Ledsome was after all a different individual from the Worcester one who died in 1593.

In 1584 a 'citherminster' (Kidderminster) brazier, Richard Morries rented a standing for 16 pence. This, together with the presence of Worcester pewterers, indicates that St Andrew's Fair was an important one which attracted sellers from other nearby towns and cities. Clearly, as early as 1570, Bewdley was an important pewtering and brazing town in its own right and it is likely that it had been one for some time previously.

Unfortunately there is a gap of some fifty years before the next Bewdley pewterer can be identified. He was Thomas Smyth 'of Bewdley' who was made free of the Bridgnorth Smiths' Company in 1672. Shortly after, the Pewterers' Company search of 1677 refers to William Mountford 'of Kidderminster'. He is presumably the issuer of the 1666 trade token referred to earlier and the 'Mr. Mountford' who is recorded in the registers of St Mary's, Kidderminster, as being buried 'in the woollen' on 26 January 1680. In the same 1677 search flagons were seized elsewhere which had been made by a Mrs. Mumford 'of Kidderminster'. A Mr. Mumford figures among John Duncumb's customers as does a later William Mountford who is recorded in the 1702 search. Possibly there were earlier Mountfords working as pewterers or braziers in Bewdley for the name of Howard Mounford [*sic*] appears in 1614 as a market stall holder, though his occupation is not given, and one Edward Mountford was a burgess in 1661.

Apart from the Banks' family, the Duncumbs and Ingrams, there are a few scattered references to other later Bewdley pewterers. The 1702 search shows that Thomas Smith was still working at that date, and Thomas Hill and John Wine are jointly named as owners of another shop. The death of Henry Goode 'pewgerer' is recorded in the Dowles registers in 1725, but his inventory shows him to have been worth only £19 10s. 6d., and the only entry relevant to his trade is to 'Brass, pewter and iron materials' valued at £1 18s. 6d. Clearly he can only have been a journeyman. The Worcester Poll Book for 1747[16] names a Thomas White, pewterer, and in 1759 an advertisement in *Aris' Birmingham Gazette* reads 'Joseph Field, tinplate worker, Bewdley, provides all sorts of brass, copper, pewter, cutlery and ironmongery and tin goods wholesale and retail. Requires a journeyman in the tinplate way'. Finally mention should be made of Thomas Ravenhill who is recorded by Cotterell (No. 3843) as being listed as a pewterer from Bewdley in a Bristol Poll Book of country voters in 1784. However no other reference to him has been found and it seems doubtful whether he was a separate individual from the Bristol pewterer (Cott. 3842) of the same name.

A 16th or 17th century timber-framed building, which was removed by Lord Sandys from Wribbenhall to the nearby village of Ombersley in 1841, was the Bewdley Pewterers' Guildhall and stood adjacent to Pewterers' Alley. It now stands opposite to the *Crown* in the main street of Ombersley.

Picking up the story again of the Birmingham pewterers we find that there are few records for the earlier part of the 18th century and the first trade directory appears only in 1767. (*See* Fig. 10, p. 78).

The search of 1702 adds one name, that of Samuel Turnpenny who was a customer of John Duncumb in the 1720s. For the period from 1741 *Aris' Birmingham Gazette* indicates that the trade did continue there, apparently at a low level, though this impression may be due to the lack of records. Additional information can be gleaned from the rate books and other sources. Thus the *London Gazette* for 14 September 1731 notes the bankruptcy of the Birmingham pewterer Edward Linthwaite. In August 1750 a fire took place 'at the pewterers adjoining Lady Parsons' brewhouse' (perhaps the shop of William Durnell who was active from 1736 to 1756), and in September 1766 Richard Brett, who is recorded from 1736, advertised his intention 'to give up the braziery business' and offered for sale his premises near the Old Cross with 'all his stock of furnaces, pot kettle, warming pans, tea kettles, coffee pots, saucepans, candlesticks, pewter dishes, plates, quarts, pints, and all sorts of braziery goods and cast metal pots etc.' He was however still paying rates on a shop in 1780. In March 1770 William Simpson, 'pewterer and tin plate worker' proclaimed that 'he had fitted up the late shop of Mr. Durnell at the sign of *The Bell and Two Candlesticks*, Bull Street, Birmingham, and makes and sells 'all sorts of goods in this manner'.

George Birch, apparently related to the Birch's who were braziers in Wolverhampton, Stafford and Uttoxeter, was a brazier between 1754 and his death in 1772 and advertised for sale Joseph Spackman's patent oval pewter plates in 1765. Spackman's patent, No. 821 of 1764, is concerned with a lathe for 'Turning ovals in pewter, English china, and all other Earthen Wares'. This business passed on his death to Joseph Garrison who is recorded as a brazier and tin plate worker in 1772 and who appears as a customer of Ingram and Hunt. In November 1784 Elizabeth Garrison 'brazier, pewterer and tin plate worker' took over her father's business which was then at 140 Digbeth.

Edward Durnell (son of William), who was in Litchfield Street from 1759, advertised in November 1766 that he had opened shop at *The Bell and Two Candlesticks* in Bull Street, 'selling all sorts of brass, copper, pewter and cast iron goods' and proclaiming that 'he has also made an entire new set of brass candlesticks of the most elegant

Mr.
Davis
ffrith

At Birmingham   23 July

At Wm Wood

J.S. bellied porringer at — 1
J.S. upright chamberpott — 1½
J.S. Round brim chamb pott — 1½
T.S. of Candlestick at — 2½
Rugby
J.S. Flaggon at — 5
Bed pan handle at — 3
An old wine ½ pint — ½
Wm Wood Round handle spoon at — ½
J.S. Another round brim chamb pot — 2
                        Recd — 2.5

At Wm Hall
ij de...
Do Wigan — Saltseller — 4
Do one handle cupp — 4½
W.B Wigan — Spoon flatt handle at — 1
The Smith of Rugby His bellied flow — 3
                        20 d — 1·5

idem p
Mr Frith
At Sam Turnpenny
M.B. Bellied porringer at — 3
J.S. — A tankard at — 5½
W.W. Spoon flatt handles at — 1½
                        Recd — 15::

10. Pewterers Company search of Birmingham in 1702 with entries for
William Wood II, William Hall and Samuel Turnpenny. (The Worshipful
Company of Pewterers).

pattern'. Although, as seen above, he gave up this shop to William Simpson in 1770 he remained in business at other addresses until at least 1796. Although he advertised from time to time for scrap pewter it is not clear whether in fact he made pewterware. Other names from the latter half of the 18th century include John Darbyshire, Richard Goolden, Joseph Blunt, Robert Mercer and Francis Ratcliffe.

Soon after 1770 the first recorded major firm of Birmingham pewterers, John Birch (son of George Birch) and William Villers, came into being and moved from their original home in Digbeth to Moor Street in 1772. In that year they advertised for 'a hammerman and two or three spoon makers, a maker of hollow-ware and a sadware man' for their 'pewter manufactury'. The firm also dealt in brassware and advertised for warming pan makers in 1772. In 1775 and 1776 they had for sale, 'tile, sheet and bar copper, copper shruff, pot metal, ingots of brass, spelter and lead, and black, bar and grain tin'. At the same time they sought two or three journeymen braziers. In 1782, from their warehouse in Moor Street they offered 'a quantity of metal bars very near the quality of tin at a price considerably under that of tin'. The final mention of them is in 1786 when, in January, the partnership was dissolved. William Villers continued in business under his own name advertising shruff and manufactured copper in 1787. He remained at Moor Street until 1808 when the partnership of Villers and Wilkes appears.

William Tutin, inventor of the Britannia type alloy 'tutania' also set up in the 18th century and was purchasing pewter from Ingram and Hunt in 1785. He remained in business until about 1825 in Coleshill Street. Trades directories afford a few more 18th century names, Robert Rowley, a spoonmaker of Snowhill from 1783 and Sarah Rowley, also a spoonmaker, in 1791. Thomas Schofield from 1781 to 1811 and Thomas Mannison, a spoonmaker, from 1790. Schofield entered into a partnership with Edward Whitfield who is recorded alone from 1781. The vast expansion of the pewter industry in Birmingham during the 19th century which involved some fifty different manufacturers — excluding those who appear to have been solely concerned with Britannia metal — is the subject of a separate chapter.

As for Bewdley, the retirement of John Carruthers Crane in 1838 and the acquisition of the Banks' business in 1835 by William Stokes marked the end of major pewtering there, though Cotterell records a few spoon makers who remained active until perhaps 1850.

Birmingham Pewterers and Braziers to c. 1796

Wood, Robert	m 1602, d 1637, p
Wood, Alice	m 1637, p, widow of Robert
Wood, William I	m 1630, d 1665, p
Hall, William I	m 1662, d 1702, p
Wood, William II	m 1665, d 1726, p, s. of William I
Gorton, Thomas	m 1676, d 1683, p
Gorton, John	m 1676, p
Wood, Benjamin	m 1672, p, s. of William I
Bradnock, Joseph	d 1684, p
Gorton, Lydia	m 1683, p, widow of Thomas

Sorrell, John	app 1676, m 1689, p
Hall, William II	d 1723, p and br
Bradnock, John	m 1684, p, s. of Joseph
Acton, James	m 1690, p and br
Turnpenny, Samuel	m 1702–24, p
Duncumb, John	c. 1702–20 when he moved to Bewdley, p
Wood, Joseph	m 1710–49, p and br, s. of William II
Linthwaite, Edward	m 1731, p
Brett, Richard	m 1736–88, br
Durnell, William	m 1736–56, br
Birch, George	m 1754, d 1772, p and br
Darbyshire, John	m 1750–64, br, succeeded Joseph Wood
Durnell, Elizabeth	m 1756–71, br, widow of William
Simpson, William	m 1770, br
Durnell, Edward	m 1759–96, br
Garrison, Joseph	m 1772–84, br
Garrison, Elizabeth	m 1776–88, p and br, widow of Joseph
Blunt, Joseph	m 1767–93, br
Mercer, Robert	m 1773, br
Ratcliffe, Francis	m 1767, br
Stringer, Thomas	m 1771, br
Goolden, Richard	m 1764, br
Simpson, William	m 1770, br
Birch, John	m 1765–72, p, s. of George
Birch, John and Villers, Wm.	m 1772–86, p and br, Cott. 430
Villers, William (later Villers and Wilkes)	1786–1827, p, Cott. 4867
Grove, Abel I	1773–1809, p (toymaker)
Meeson, Aaron	1774–1807, p
Schofield, Thomas	1781–1811, p, Cott. 4144A
Whitfield, Edward	1781–, p, cf. Cott. 5118A
Dyatt, John	m 1783, p (spoonmaker)
Tutin, William	1783–1825, p
Garrison, Ann	d 1788, p, d. of Joseph
Rowley, Robert	m 1783, p (spoonmaker)
Mannison, Thomas	m 1790, p (spoonmaker)
Rowley, Sarah	m 1791, p (spoonmaker) succeeded Robert, Cott. 4051A
Milward, Thomas	m 1791, p

Bewdley and Kidderminster Pewterers and Braziers

Greenbank(e), James	m 1570–1616, br (? two generations)
Gilson, William	m 1572, br
Doteson, Henry	m 1573, br
Worthynton, Richard	m 1573–88, p
Redding, Hugh	m 1573, br (perhaps of Worcester)
Wydsam, Harry	m 1574, p
Letson, Harry (Henry)	m 1584–1625, br (? two generations)
Wether(s)by, Thomas	m 1584, br
Wigfalle, Rafe	m 1584, br
Morries, Richard	m 1584, br ('of Kidderminster')
Best, John	m 1584, br
Morries, Thomas	m 1584, br

Raynoles (Rainolls), Henry	m 1584, br
Towstance (?), George	m 1588, p
Cradley, William	m 1588, p
Mounford, Howard	m 1614)
Glover, John	m 1617) No occupations are given for these five
Trapp, William	m 1625) individuals but it seems probable that some
Glover, William	m 1625) or all were pewterers or braziers.
Trapp, Widow	m 1630)

Note: All the above are from the Bewdley Bridgewardens' Account Book.

Mountford, William I	m 1666, d 1680, p ('of Kidderminster')
Smyth, Thomas	m 1672, d 1719, p
Harries, Thomas	app 1672-3, m 1689, p (of Kidderminster)
Mumford, Mrs.	m 1677, p ('of Kidderminster')
Banks, Robert	d 1702, p
Banks, Christopher I	m 1697-1746, p
Hill, Thomas	m 1702, p
Wine, John	m 1702, p
Hill, Stephen	d 1700, br
Duncumb, John	1720, d 1745, p, Cott. 1465
Mountford, William II	m 1702-20, p (of Kidderminster)
Goode, Henry	d 1725, p
Banks, James I	d 1756, p and br, b. of Christopher I
Duncumb, Stynt	b 1712, d 1767, p, s. of John, Cott. 1466
White, Thomas	m 1747, p
Field, Joseph	m 1759, p and br
Banks, Christopher II	b 1721, d 1788, p and br, grands. of Christopher I
Banks, William	b 1728, d 1793, p and br, grands. of Christopher I
Banks, James II	m 1756, p, n. of James I
Banks, Christopher III	b 1755, d 1834, p and br, s. of William
Banks, Thomas	Succeeded Christopher II in 1788
Ravenhill, Thomas	m 1784, p, Cott. 3843
Ingram, John	b 1731, d 1799, p, nephew of S. Duncumb, Cott. 5708
Ingram and Hunt	before 1788-1807, p
Crane and Stinton	1807-1821, p
Crane, John Carruthers	1821-1838, d 1845, p, Cott. 1197
*Nest, Robert	c. 1820, p (spoonmaker), Cott. 3362
Timmins, John	c. 1840, p (spoonmaker), Cott. 4749
Wheeler, James	m 1820-50, p (spoonmaker), Cott. 5078
Cotterell, Henry	c. 1800, p, Cott. 1131
Cotterell, Mary	d c. 1840, p, Cott. 1132
Cotterell, Samuel	d c. 1820, p, Cott. 1133
Vickers, I. (or L.)	c. 1830, p, Cott. 4874
Stokes, William	Succeeded to Banks's business in 1835.

*Cotterell's source for this and the next six entries has not been found.

NOTES AND REFERENCES

Birmingham to c. 1790, Bewdley and Kidderminster

1. *Hearth Tax Returns*, Birmingham Reference Library.
2. Both John and Stynt used the spelling 'Duncumb' as did the Surrey branch of the family. The form 'Duncombe' was used by Stynt's brother Joseph and by the Feversham branch. An extensive family tree of the Duncumbs, showing the Wood connection and the Ingram link, is to be found in Manning and Bray, *History and Antiquities of the County of Surrey* (1809), p. 126.
3. *Duncumb papers* at Guildford Muniment Room (Surrey Record Office).
4. Chester's *London Marriage Licences*, p. 428
5. *Deeds* at Guildford Muniment Room.
6. *Day book of John Duncumb*, HWRO 4600 b 705:550/316.
7. *Duncumb papers* at Guildford Muniment Room.
8. *Parish register of St. Mary's, Kidderminster*, HWRO 8426/2(ii).
9. Hill, J. and Dent, R. K., *Memorials of Old Square* (1897), p. 100.
10. *Ingram and Hunt Ledgers*, HWRO 4600 b 705:550/1060; /559; /96; /357; /316.
11. *Account book*, HWRO 4600 705:550/393.
12. *Title to Wribbenhall House 1807-*, County Secretary and Solicitor's Office, Worcester.
13. Shelley, R. J. A., 'Wigan and Liverpool Pewterers', *Transactions of the Historic Society of Lancashire and Cheshire* (1946).
14. *Banks Family Tree*, Bewdley Museum.
15. *Bewdley Bridgewardens' Account Book*, HWRO 498 BA: 8681/236(i).
16. *Alphabetical Copy of the Poll taken at the City of Worcester 1747* (1747), Worcester Public Library.

General

Pelham, R. A., 'The Growth and Settlement of Industry *c.*, 1100-1700', *Birmingham and its Regional Setting* (British Association for the Advancement of Science, 1950), pp. 135-58.
Aris' Birmingham Gazette (1741-), Birmingham Reference Library. A card index abstracting mentions of metalworkers is housed in the Faculty of Commerce and Social Science, University of Birmingham.
Burton, J. R., *A History of Bewdley* (1883).
Burton, J. R., *A History of Kidderminster* (1890).
Davis, S., *Bewdley as it was* (1979).
Trades Directories for Birmingham, Sketchley 1767 etc.: Swinney 1773 etc.; Pearson and Rollason 1777 etc.; Bailey 1783; Pye 1781 etc.; for Bewdley, Bailey's Western and Midland 1783; Universal British 1793; Holden's Annual London and Country 1811; Pigott's London and Provincial 1822.
Parish registers of St Martin's, Birmingham, Birmingham Reference Library.
Parish registers of Dowles, Ribbesford and St Mary's Kidderminster, HWRO.
Birmingham Rate Books, Birmingham Reference Library.
Bewdley Borough Rate Book 1818, HWRO.
Law, A. S., 'Birmingham Pewterers of the Seventeenth Century', *Journal of the Pewter Society*, Autumn 1982, pp. 128-32.

APPENDIX I

The Customers of John Duncumb

The following names are extracted from the day book of John Duncumb for the period August 1718 to December 1724. The day book (with two exceptions) gives no locations, but in some cases indicates this by noting the town to which carriage was paid. Where this appears it is given in quotation marks in the list. Other locations have been deduced during the course of this work. Some appear certain; others, as indicated by a question mark, are conjectural.

Acton, Ephraim; pewterer of Bridgnorth
Archesden, Abraham; pewterer of Warwick
Ashwill, William; brassfounder of Birmingham
Ashworth, William
Astley, Margaret
Badger, Thomas; 'carriage to Henley'; pewterer of Stratford-on-Avon
Bankes, Christopher; 'of Bewdley'; pewterer
Beck, George; ? Birmingham
Blackway, Thomas; 'carriage to Charnhill'; 'carriage to Salop'
Bond, Richard; ? Worcester
Box, Edward; pewterer of Banbury
Box, William; ? Banbury
Brindley, James
Brock, Thomas; 'carriage to Chester', 'carriage to Salop'; pewterer of Chester
Brosley, Jac [sic]
Browne, Samuel; 'carriage to Salop'; pewterer of Shrewsbury
Brown, William; ? Birmingham
Browne, Mrs.
Bullock, Elizabeth; ? Warwick
Burges, Thomas; pewterer of Shrewsbury
Canning, William
Carver, Henry; brassfounder of Birmingham
Churchyard, Thomas; 'carriage to Salop'; pewterer of Shrewsbury
Collins, Edward
Cottrill (Cottrell), John
Cradock, Samuel
Cromwell, William
Cumberlidge, Steven; Warwick
Davis, James; pewterer of Shrewsbury
Davis, Thomas; 'carriage to Salop'; pewterer of Shrewsbury
Deane, Richard; 'carriage to Salop'
Dickison (Dickenson), Samuel, 'carriage to Hampton', 'carriage to Bridge(north?)'
Dodd, Edward; 'carriage to Newport'
Ebb, Robert; 'carriage to Stafford'; brazier of Stafford
Faulchner, Thomas; Thomas Falconer, brazier of Coventry
Faulkingham, Thomas
Faulkingham, William
Felton, Elizabeth; 'carriage to Salop'; of Shrewsbury or Oswestry
Felton, Jeremiah; of Shrewsbury or Oswestry
Forster, Margaret
Forster, Thomas, of Shrewsbury
Fothergill, William; of Bristol (? Cott. 1743)

Gamble, John; ? Coventry
Grace, Sylvester
Green, Richard; pewterer of Worcester
Griffis, Richard; 'carriage to Salop'; brazier of Shrewsbury
Grookock, John
Hall, William; pewterer of Birmingham
Harrison, Lewis
Harrison, Richard
Hassall (Haswell), Peter
Hollier, Isaac
Hollin(g)s, Humphrey; 'carriage to Bir(mingham?)'; pewterer of Ashby-de-la-Zouche
Hughes, Thomas
Hunt, William; ? Birmingham
Ikin, Jonathan; gentleman, of Draycott in Hales
Jesson, John; ? merchant of West Bromwich
Jones, John
Ke(e)mp, Bridget, 'carriage to Whitchurch'
Kilby, Jonathan, 'carriage to Lichfield'; pewterer of Lichfield
King, Francis; pewterer of Worcester
Letsom, Samuel (also Sampson); pewterer of Worcester
Linthwaite, George; ? Grantham, *see* next entry
Linthwaite, Richard; 'carriage to Grantham'
Littlefear (-fare, -fire), Garvis; 'carriage to Burton'
Littlefare, Jeremiah
Lloyde, Sampson; ironmaster of Birmingham
Lucas (Luckus), Thomas; ? Coventry
Lugg, Jonathan; pewterer of Ludlow
Merry, Joseph; ? Birmingham
Molinex, Thomas; ? a Molineux of Wolverhampton; ironmasters
Moss, Richard; 'carriage to Salop'
Mountford, William; pewterer of Kidderminster
Mumford, Mr.; ? Kidderminster
Nichols, Harry
Norris, Thomas
Osborne, Mr. Charles; ironmonger of Wolverhampton
Peet, John; brazier of Hereford
Pershouse, Richard; ? Alcester
Pershouse, Thomas; ? Alcester
Plummer, Richard; pewterer of Ludlow
Prise, Samuel; 'carriage to Salop'; brazier of Shrewsbury
Roberts, Thomas; brazier of Shrewsbury
Robinson, James
Roome, John; 'carriage to Burton'; brazier of Lichfield
Saunders, Richard
Seney, Joseph; pewterer and brazier of Walsall
Seney, Robert; pewterer and brazier of Walsall
Seney, William; pewterer and brazier of Walsall
Shaw, Robert; 'carriage to Salop'
Shaw, William
Smith, Joseph
Smith, Samuel
Smith, Thomas; ? Coventry
Stanton, Moses; 'carriage to Coventry'
Stripling, William
Swanwick, Mary; 'carriage to Salop'

Taylor, Thomas
Trapp, Edward; pewterer of Worcester
Turner, Philip; 'carriage to Salop'
Turnpenny, Samuel; pewterer of Birmingham
Turnpenny, Mrs.
W(h)ebl(e)y, Mr.
Weymont (Wyment), John; 'carriage to Coventry'
Wathall, John; 'carriage to Coventry'
Whates (Watts), Mary; 'of Gloucester'
Wheler, Edward
Whyle, Samuel; 'carriage to Salop'
Williams, Andrew
Wills, George
Willson, Margaret
Winnan, Jonathan
Winn(e)s, Elizabeth
Winns, Moses
Wood, Edward; brazier of Ludlow
Wood, Joseph; 'brother', i.e. brother-in-law, of Birmingham
Wood, Thomas; ditto
Wood, Samuel; ditto
Wood, William; referred to as 'father Wood', of Birmingham
Wood, Mr. William; a different man from 'father'
Wright, Charles
Wright, Lawrence; ? Coventry

APPENDIX II

Items of Pewterware Listed in an Ingram and Hunt's Order Book 1803–5

This list is compiled from a sample of *c.* 10 per cent. of the entries in HWRO 7600 705:550 96 which comprises some 160 leaves in total and is incomplete at the end. The range of wares is formidable.

Plates and dishes
Shallow dishes, 2 lb, 2½ lb, 4 lb, 5 lb, 6 lb
Common shallow dishes, 2 lb, 2½ lb, 3 lb, 5 lb
Common P.B. dishes, 3 lb, 4 lb
Deep dishes, 5 lb
Common dishes 15 in. very narrow rim and
    deeper than common
27 in. oval dish, 13 lb 8 oz
Oval water venison dishes, no bridge before
    well, 18 in. and 21 in.
Small x plates 9 in.
Small x soup plates 9 in.
Middle plates
Large plates
*10 lb plates
*11 lb common P.B. plates
*12 lb common P.B. plates
Plates 12 in. (2 lb), 13 in, 14 in, 16 in., 16½ in.
    (4 lb), 18 in., 20 in., 22 in. (10 lb), 23 in.
Plates 24 in. oval (11 lb 2 oz)
Common plates
Large water plates
New fashioned water plates
*These figures believed to be lbs/dozen

Basins
Small common piece basins
Middle common piece basins
Large common piece basins
Extra large basin with lid, say 32 (lb?)
Small wash hand basins with feet
Large wash hand basins with feet
Piece basin 12½ in. over the top inside, a little
    deeper than usual, say two courses of the
    hammer

Tureens etc.
Mid oval tureens 6 lb 8 oz
Soup linings — no covers
Soup linings with covers
Large soup linings
Mid tureens

Porringers
Pint porringers
Small common porringers
Middle common porringers

Sanitary ware
Middle common chamber pots
Common chamber pots
Large common chamber pots
Large x chamber pots
Small bed pans
Middle bed pans
Small stool pans
Middle stool pans
Large stool pans
Child's chair pans
Urinals

Funnels
Quart funnels
Pint funnels
Half pint funnels
Phial funnels

Tea pots
1 pint round tea pots
1½ pint round tea pots
Tea pots, largest of the old shape
Oval 1½ pint tea pots
Oval quart tea pots
Oval 3 pint tea pots
3 pint bellied tea pots

Drinking vessels
Quarts, pints, ½ pints, bellied full
Quarts, pints, ½ pints, bellied short
Quarts, pints, ½ pints, full with rings round
Quarts, pints, ½ pints, straight full
Quarts, pints, ½ pints, straight short
Pints, ½ pints, straight short, wide bottom
Quarts, pints, straight short, wine
Common quarts, pints
Common straight full ½ pints
Small tavern pots
Quarts, pints, straight with lip
Glass bottom quarts, pints
Glass make quarts, pints

Drinking vessels — continued
Quarts, pints, ½ pints, straight short with the
    foot cut lower
Glass bottom tankards
Quarts at 2 lb

Measures
Wine measures, short, with lids, ½ quartern,
    quartern, ½ pint, pint, quart
Wine measures, full, with lids, ¼ pint, ½ pint,
    quart, gallon
Common straight quart wine measures
Full quart liquor measures
Pint liquor measures, wine, with lids
Apothecary measures

Candle moulds and candlesticks
Candle moulds, 4 lb, 5 lb, 6 lb
Short candle moulds, 6 lb
Hand candlesticks
Bracket candlesticks

Ink stands
Ink stands small size
Ink stands large size
Small round inks, no caps
Large round inks, no caps
Small round inks, with caps
Large round inks, with caps
Medium chest inks
Medium loggerhead inks

Syringes
Small French syringe pipes
Small ear syringes
Middle ear syringes
Large ear syringes
Small female syringes
Middle female syringes
Half pint syringes with pipes
Pint syringes with pipes

Spoons
    Spoons are in the main identified only by
numbers, over fifty different ones being listed.
The following few have some description:
Basting ladles No. 106, 107, 108
x teas No. 26
Teas No. 141
Teas plain 70
Teas flow'd (flowered?) 70
Brit. table No. 69

Brit. tea No. 60
Tutane plain tea No. 60
Pap, lowest price, No. 62
Gravy spoons, No. 46
Soup ladles No. 109
Five sizes of soup spoons, 6/-, 8/-, 9/-, 10/-,
    12/-, [per doz.?]
Three sizes of ladles, 12/-, 15/-, 18/- [per doz.?]
    There are indications that many were sup-
plied both in common and in 'x' qualities.
There is also mention of a 'pattern card of
pewter spoons'. Some tinned iron spoons
were made.

Miscellaneous items
Small common cullenders
Middle cullenders
Large cullenders
Butter boats
Pepper boxes
Pepper casters
Mustard pots with glass linings
Mustard pots 12/-, of a larger size and a joint
    to the lid, Wt. 8 oz
Salts round, 3 legs, with glass linings
Round foot salts
Tooth powder boxes
Shaving cans
Limbecks (Alembics) middle size
Diddy bottles
Dram bottles
Child's boats
4½ in. crumb [?] combs
Wine strainers
Dish cover knobs
Scolloped ice moulds to hold rather more
    than ½ a pint
Ice pots or churns assorted; 3 lb, 7/-; 2 lb 6 oz,
    4/6; 1 lb 12 oz, 3/6
Grained tin
Grain tin shavings
*Leaves, extra large
Leaves, large
Leaves, middle
Leaves, small middle
Leaves, seconds
Leaves, small

*Leaves appear to have been small thin sheets of
tin or pewter used for tinning copper and brass
articles.

BIRMINGHAM IN THE NINETEENTH CENTURY

WE HAVE SEEN that with the coming of the canals linking Birmingham and the Midlands with the Severn in the last third of the 18th century, the advantages of Bewdley as an entrepôt waned, and by the end of the 1700s Birmingham had become a more attractive centre for pewter production. The brass trade had already begun to concentrate there in 1740 with the establishment of Turner's Brasshouse and 1761 saw the founding of Matthew Boulton's Soho Manufactory. No fewer than 66 firms of merchants and factors were established in the town by 1781 to handle the output of what had by then become the hardware centre of the country. Birmingham's proximity to abundant sources of coal, iron and water, together with its central position led to a rapid growth of population. From about fifteen thousand in 1700 it had grown to 70,000 by 1800 and 300,000 by 1861. As well as supplying manufactured goods it became for a while an intellectual centre and attracted many famous scientists, engineers and entrepreneurs to the Lunar Society, which had been founded about 1766 by Matthew Boulton, Erasmus Darwin and William Small.

Particularly important in the first half of the 19th century were Birmingham's four staple trades, guns, jewellery, buttons and brassware. The last named employed 1,785 persons in the town in 1785 which had risen to 8,334 by 1831.[1] Besides this the pewter industry of Birmingham becomes insignificant in terms of the town's economy, only 21 pewterers are listed in the 1841 census; nevertheless in terms of the overall supply of pewter Birmingham was probably as significant as London during much of the 19th century. The local concentration of industry in the industrial midlands was certainly a factor in this for the local labourers and the workers in the heavy iron and steel industry and in coal mining in the adjacent industrial towns had an insatiable thirst; it was nothing for an iron puddler to consumer 16 pints of beer a day. The Beer House Act of 1830 led to 45,000 new public houses and beershops coming into existence in the following eight years. As an example of what this proliferation meant, the nearby town of Dudley had no fewer than 252 taverns and beershops in 1842 to serve a population of 31,000 inhabitants! We can assume that most of these establishments would have been equipped with pewter pots and measures and this local market for tavern pewter must have been a profitable and continuing one. Already the introduction of Imperial Measure, only four years earlier in 1826, had rendered many existing pewter measures illegal, and the replacement of these had provided a stimulus to that sector of the pewter trade.

Thus, as the household and domestic market for pewter disappeared, a new market opened up and numerous new businesses were established to meet it. Some were small and transient, others lasted for many years and their products, hithero rather neglected by collectors, still exist in large quantities. Not only was pewter in demand for drinking vessels and measures but bar tops, ale-house plumbing and 'beer-engines' were made from it, and several specialised makers of pewter beer engines and bar fittings are to be found in 19th-century Birmingham.

Thomas Yates, writing in 1866[2] states,

'There is scarcely any business, not actually obsolete, which has been more changed by fashion than this. Plates and dishes, which were at one time the staple production, are now made only in small quantities for a few foreign markets, and latterly the trade had been chiefly engaged in the manufacture of ale and wine measures, drinking cups, and other requisites for hotel purposes. A very considerable branch is now employed in fitting up refreshment stores with beer engines, liquor fountains, and other conveniences belonging to those establishments; the mechanical contrivances employed to facilitate despatch of business being not more remarkable than the elegance and style with which the improvements are carried out'.

Yates later comments,

'There are but few, if any, improvements in the process of manufacture since its first establishment. The article is cast in a mould made of brass or iron, as nearly as possible of the ultimate shape required. It is then placed in a lathe and turned to the pattern, size and weight required. The finishing is done by burnishing. No females are employed in any department.'

He later continues,

'In addition to the articles already mentioned, there are a variety of others made by the pewterers, although the demand is somewhat limited, such as syringes, inkstands, hot water bottles, funnels, soup tureens, hot water plates and dishes, freezing pots and other requisites for the use of confectioners, jugs, basins, and chamber services for hospital and ships' use. A teapot is also made by them, called Dutch pattern, which being formed in one piece by casting is of great strength and very durable; and although the shape has been copied in a lighter article made from rolled metal, there are some markets in which it still holds pre-eminence, although of the most primitive design . . . a very considerable trade was carried out in the manufacture of moulds for the production of candles . . of late years this demand has fallen off; a few sets are occasionally made for the Australian market.'

The Australian market was clearly of some significance at this time for Yates relates that the discovery of gold there had considerable influence in promoting the pewter trade, which was then increasing, particularly in respect of ale and wine measures and drinking cups. He then writes at some length about Britannia metal which was fabricated in abundance in Birmingham and approximately one hundred makers, compared with some three hundred for Sheffield, have been noted in the city.[3] Though Britannia metal is a pewter alloy, its method of construction by rolling or by spinning is clearly distinguishable from traditional pewter casting. Its manufacture was in the main identified as a separate trade in the 19th century trade directories, and though it represents an important aspect of metal working it has been excluded from the scope of this chapter. Let it be said, however, that spoons (and indeed other items) were made from *cast* Britannia metal and also from tutania, a similar alloy devised by William Tutin of Birmingham. Tutin, who remained in business until *c.* 1825, made spoons and other cast items such as plates bearing his touch mark. He can thus be considered to be a traditional pewterer as well as an innovator. As far as the alloys are concerned, there is in fact little to distinguish the traditional antimony-containing hard metal used from the early 18th century for quality cast items from the later alloys used for rolling and spinning.

It is the Yates family[4] who dominated the Birmingham pewter trade for much of the 19th century, and 'James Yates' is perhaps the commonest name found today on mid-19th century tavern pots and measures. Two members of the family were established as metalworkers in Birmingham by the 1780s, a James who is recorded as a brass-founder from 1781 to 1798 in Bradford Street and is variously described in trade directories as 'brass-founder and plater, coffin furniture manufacturer, looking-glass maker etc.', and Thomas who is recorded in 1780 as a die-sinker in Coach Yard off Bull Street, and from 1781 at 54, Coleshill Street, where he is referred to as 'buckle stock maker, bright engraver, spoon-moulder maker, pewterers' and glassblowers' mould maker etc.'.

Thomas died *c.* 1801 and it was his son John, born in 1788, who was the first pewterer of the family. Most of John's sons followed him in the pewter or Britannia metal trade though, as we shall see, he himself moved to other fields of metalworking in the mid-century. John established himself by 1805, at 54, Coleshill Street, as a spoon and toy maker working in pewter, Britannia metal and tutania. After moving in 1812 to Loveday Street and in 1816 to Lionel Street, he returned in 1823 to Coleshill Street, number 38, which address, together with several adjoining properties, was to be the focus of the Yates' pewtering business for the next 60 years. In 1829 he entered into partnership with Thomas Rawlins Birch and Birch's father-in-law, Lucas Spooner, to form the well-known firm of Yates, Birch and Spooner. Before 1834 the partnersip acquired Abel Grove's pewtering business and in 1838 the moulds of John Carruthers Crane of Bewdley passed to them.

John Yates' son James joined the firm in 1837 and after the death of Lucas Spooner in 1839 a new partnership of (James) Yates and Birch was formed, John having left the partnership in that year. Birch died in 1857 and until 1860 Birch's sons, Thomas Lucas and James continued as partners with James Yates. John Yates left pewtering and in the 1850s set up a business as a steel tool manufacturer, John Yates and Co., of which his son Henry and later his grandsons became proprietors in due course. After 1860 and until his death in 1881 James Yates was the sole proprietor of the business at 39–40 Coleshill Street. An indication of the range of products which he produced is given by the following extract from *Kelly's Directory* for 1872:

> 'Yates, James, pewterer and plumbers' brassfounder, manufacturer of every description of beer pulls and machines, bar fittings, measures, etc., cups, inkstands, water-closets, lift-pumps, etc., Yates Patent Protection Tap, specially adapted for use in wine and spirit vaults, stores, etc.'

The mansion where he lived in his later years, The Oaklands, Golden Hillock Lane, was demolished as recently as 1983. In his will he desired that his business be offered to his brother Thomas, Britannia metal worker, but the latter's death in 1882 resulted in it being sold to Frederick and Herbert Greenway who continued trading under the 'James Yates' name until 1899 when 'Yates and Greenway' first appears. In 1902 the firm merged with Gaskell and Chambers, successors of Peter Gaskell, who continued in business for a further seventy or more years until acquired in the 1970s by James Smellie who continued to make pewter until 1983. James Smellie could thus claim an unbroken lineage from the earliest Birmingham pewterer, Robert Wood, through Duncumb, Ingram, Crane and Yates. Many moulds from these earlier pewterers, some dating from the early 18th century, continued to be used by James Smellie, as did a number of the early touch marks. The well-nigh indestructible moulds are even now in other hands and will continue to cast pewter for many years to come. The early products of Gaskell and Chambers bear a touch mark of an open hand and the letter 'Y' in a triangle was used after 1902 to indicate that wares were made in James Yates' moulds (MPM Addenda, 1821).

Two other of John Yates' sons, George and Edwin, and later their half-brother William Joseph (son of John's second wife), were proprietors of a Britannia metal works, 'The Birmingham Spoon and Fork Works', in Pritchett Street from the 1870s. This enterprise continued under the names 'John Yates and Sons' and 'Yates Brothers' until 1900 or later, making a range of Britannia ware. Another son, George, was a spoon maker at 38, Coleshill Street in 1841 and later his brother Thomas assumed control. The firm of 'Thomas Yates' existed until the turn of the century.

Whether the Birmingham Yates' were related to Richard Yates of London (Cott. 5344) is a question still to be resolved. It is perhaps significant that James Yates is recorded in several directories as being of Birmingham and London and that there is a clear similarity between the hall marks of Richard Yates and those of Ingram and Hunt and John Carruthers Crane. All feature the Ingram arms.

Little more is heard of Thomas Lucas Birch and his brother James after their break with James Yates in 1860. For two years a brief partnership with Samuel Mason, 'Birch and Mason', existed. Thereafter for another two years they traded as 'T. and J. Birch' from 113, Coleshill Street. Samuel Mason set up his own business in 1863 and this was acquired from the Official Receiver in 1910 by Gaskell and Chambers.

The relationship between John Birch of the 18th century Birch and Villers partnership and the Birch family members involved with John and James Yates is not known. However, the Villers side of the Birch and Villers partnership continued in business under various names well into the 19th century. After the demise of the partnership in 1785, William Villers apparently continued on his own from a Moor Street address until 1805. He then formed a partnership with Edward Villers Wilkes which traded as Villers and Wilkes until 1827. Wilkes then continued on his own and in partnership with other members of the Wilkes family until his death in 1835. Edward Tertius Wilkes 'manufacturer of copper goods', died in 1862 and was followed by Alfred Salt Wilkes until 1881. The firm retained the name of E. V. Wilkes, but whether, or for how long after Edward Villers Wilkes' death it made pewter is unknown. It does, however, seem likely that the Villers and Wilkes touch marks and hall marks were used after 1827. Another member of the family, John Wilkes, of 60, Stafford Street, made beer engines in pewter, c. 1840.

Among the companies acquired by Cornelius Chambers and incorporated into Gaskell and Chambers was that of Peter Gaskell, bought in 1892. He had traded from 60, Stafford Street between 1860 and 1892, and from 1860 to 1870 was in partnership with Joseph Morgan at that address. Morgan also had a separate company, J. Morgan and Co., at 60-61 Stafford Street, from 1860 to 1872. Joseph Morgan also had a business, probably his main business, in Manchester where he is found in trades directories between 1828 and 1895, for the latter part of the period as J. Morgan and Son. It is also known that he began his life as a working pewterer in Bristol where he is recorded between 1825 and 1827.[5] It is tempting to speculate that he spent some time in Bewdley since the style of his pots is very similar to typical Bewdley ware of the earlier part of the 19th century and his hall marks (Cott. 3289) include the Ingram arms in one of the shields. Between 1854 and 1870 Joseph Morgan also operated from London where he had an address at 27, Hoxten Square. With branches in Birmingham, Manchester and London, Morgan's business was perhaps the most geographically extensive of any in the 19th century.

Another associate of Cornelius Chambers was James Meritt, who is recorded at Unity Works, 5, Lichfield Street, from 1878, and who was a partner with Chambers for some years prior to 1892 when the partnership was dissolved. It is unfortunate that the business archives of Gaskell and Chambers, which would have provided more insight into several of these Birmingham pewtering firms were destroyed in an air-raid in 1941.

Earlier in the 19th century the names of Thomas Schofield, Aaron and Thomas Meeson and Abel Grove figure prominently. Thomas Schofield has been mentioned in the previous chapter and was a partner with Edward Whitfield in 1790. In 1801 Schofield was joined by two sleeping partners, Aaron Meeson and Daniel Grove (brother of Abel I) and traded as T. Schofield & Co., Aaron Meeson died in 1807 and was succeeded as a partner by his son Thomas Cranmer Meeson, a working pewterer, who took over the firm on Schofield's death in 1811. Its name was then changed to Thomas Meeson & Co. About 1817 Daniel Grove's son, Abel II, joined the business which then became Meeson and Grove. Meeson died in 1823 and Abel Grove II eventually sold out to Yates, Birch and Spooner in 1834. The hall-marks of Abel Grove II are illustrated by Cotterell (No. 2037, first set of marks) though incorrectly attributed by him.

Clearly there were family relationships between many of the Birmingham pewtering families. It has already been remarked that Thomas Rawlins Birch was the son-in-law of Lucas Spooner, he was also a cousin of Abel Grove II. Doubtless also William Villers was related to Edward Villers Wilkes and the first wife of Daniel Grove was Sarah Meeson. Time has not, however, allowed these to be explored further, and in the industrial environment of the 19th century they are much less relevant or informative than in earlier centuries. There was no established fraternity of craftsmen with secrets to guard and anyone with an inclination in that direction could set up in business. To this category no doubt belong many of the Birmingham firms which appear and disappear from the pages of the trades directories during the middle of the century. Their names are listed at the end of this chapter, but it would add little to our understanding to attempt to pursue their activities in any detail.

As has been seen, the survivors of several of these 19th century firms, themselves the descendants of 18th century foundations, were acquired about the beginning of the 20th century by Gaskell and Chambers, a firm making a wide range of metal articles for the public house trade, including, for example, three-legged decorated cast iron bar tables. The following extract from *Gaskell and Chambers' Jubilee Booklet* of 1947 enlarges on this, and incidentally quotes a date, certainly erroneous, for the foundation of a James Yates pewter business in 1797.

'With every record of the Company destroyed on the night of April 9th, 1941, it is difficult to piece together the story of the early years.

'In 1892, Mr. Cornelius Chambers dissolved a comparatively short partnership with John Merrit and bought Peter Gaskell's well known business in Stafford Street. Thus Gaskell and Chambers came into being.

'That the young Mr. Chambers was now to be reckoned with was obvious when his august competitors, the firm of Samuel Mason, Barfitters, who had alternately threatened and withdrawn legal action for alleged patent infringement, proposed amalgamation. This Mason's continued to do at regular intervals until 1910, when the Company bought their business from the Official Receiver.

'By 1894, a sizeable firm for those days, employing 70 "hands" had been established, and three years later the Dale End Works were acquired. Meanwhile a bold step was taken in purchasing the premises and goodwill of the established firm of J. Newey & Co., of Dale End. This gave Gaskell and Chambers a commanding position in the trade and, in 1897, fifty years ago, the firm was publicly incorporated, the first Directors of the Company being Cornelius Chambers, James D. Prior and George Stephens.

'The development of Gaskell and Chambers in its early years was punctuated by the purchase of competing firms — great names now almost forgotten. One of the most important events was the amalgamation in 1902 with the century-old firm of Yates and Greenway of Coleshill Street, founded in 1797 by James Yates, the well-known pewterer, whose moulds, dating back to the 17th Century, are still in the possession of the Company and are today being used for the production of pewterware.'

By the end of the century virtually all of the others had gone, to be replaced by a few firms of general metal fabricators to whom pewter was only a side-line. For the record we may mention Lawden and Poole, whose name may be found on very late beer measures, and who do not appear to pre-date 1908, Harry Mason, and Lee and Wilkes, successors to E. V. Wilkes, both of whom date from the early years of this century. One firm only now appears to survive in Birmingham, A. & E. Williams, who claim origins in the 1780s and who retain a large collection of 18th and 19th century cast iron moulds in which their currently marketed pewterware is still made.

Of the wares made in 19th century Birmingham little need be said. They are plentiful and well marked with makers' names, and very familiar to every pewter collector. The quality of the metal is usually good — a hard antimonial alloy — and they are well-made and finished. Most frequently one finds half-pint, pint and quart beer mugs and measures, or bellied measures in sizes from a fraction of a gill up to a gallon. But flatware is also to be found, particularly plates of 9 to 10 inches diameter, though these are by no means common. Tulip-shaped drinking mugs and one and two-handled cups in a variety of styles survive. Collectors should be aware that the touchmarks of the Duncumbs, of Ingram and Hunt, James Yates, and several other long defunct pewterers have continued in use to the present day and these marks are to be found on much modern reproduction pewter.

Note

The authors are indebted to Dr. A. S. Law for his help and collaboration in compiling this chapter and for providing detailed information on the Yates family, on Joseph Morgan, and for clarification of the complexities of the Grove/Meeson/Schofield relationships.

Nineteenth Century Birmingham Pewterers

Grove, Daniel	At Prospect Place in 1802; partner with Thomas Schofield to 1811
Yates, John	At 54, Coleshill St. in 1805, 55, Loveday St in 1812; 8, Lionel St. in 1816; 38, Coleshill St. from 1823; b 1788, d 1876. (Cott. 5340a)
Claybrook, Catherine	At Moor St. in 1809
Tasker, William	At Dudley St. in 1809
Meeson, Thomas Cranmer	At Prospect Place from 1807–23; partner in Thomas Schofield & Co. Son of Aaron Meeson
Wilkes, Edward Villers	At Moor St. from 1805–35; partner in Villers and Wilkes to 1827
Grove, Abel II	At Prospect Row from 1823–34; sold out to Yates, Birch and Spooner. Son of Daniel Grove. (Cott. 2037)
Rowley, Mary	Spoonmaker in Stanley St. in 1825; successor to Sarah Rowley
Villers and Wilkes	At Moor St. from 1808–27 (*see* E. V. Wilkes). (Cott. 4876)
Yates, Birch and Spooner	Partnership of John Yates, Thomas Rawlins Birch and Lucas Spooner from 1829–39; at 38, Coleshill St. (Cott. 5349)
Yates and Birch	Partnership of James Yates with Thomas Rawlins Birch to 1857 and with Thomas Lucas Birch and James Birch to 1860; at 39–40 Coleshill St. (Cott. 5347–8)
McKenzie, William	At 13 Jennens Row from 1825–41. (Cott. 3042)
Wilkes, Edward Tertius	Partner in E. V. Wilkes from 1835 to his death in 1862; at Old Priory
Wilkes, John	Beer engine etc. manufacturer; 60, Stafford St. in 1841
Yates, George	At 38, Coleshill St. in 1841. Son of John
Jones, Henry	At 77, Cardigan St. from 1839–45; 60, Stafford St. from 1845–60. Born at Wribbenhall 1806
Yates, Thomas	At 38, Coleshill St. from 1849, died 1882. Firm of 'Thomas Yates' existed to *c.* 1900. Son of John. (Cott. 5346)
Evetts, Samuel	Successor to John Wilkes at 60, Stafford St. from 1841–5. Was succeeded by Henry Jones
Beresford, J.	At 113, Lionel St. from 1839–65
Sturgess, Elizabeth	At 26, Lichfield St. from 1835–41 in partnership with her son Richard Ford Sturgess
Sturgess, Richard Ford	*See* above. Was later at 46, Broad St. to 1860
Fridlander, David	At 134, Digbeth in 1846
Bratt, James	At 99, Mott St. from 1845–66
Mills, Thomas	At 70, Bromsgrove St. from 1845–50
Lewis, Thomas	At 31, Gospell St. in 1846
Village, William	At Court 3, Bow St. in 1851 census
Nest, Thomas	At 50, Lupin St. in 1854
Hartley, E. George	At 65, Summer Lane from 1858–65
Yates, James	In business on his own at 39–40 Coleshill St. from 1860 to his death in 1881. (*See* Yates and Birch above) (Cott. 5338)
Wilkes, Alfred Salt	Succeeded Edward Tertius Wilkes as partner in E. V. Wilkes; at Old Priory to 1881
Morgan, Joseph	Also at Manchester and London. Originated in Bristol. In partnership with Peter Gaskell at 60, Stafford St. 1860–70. In Manchester as Joseph Morgan & Son to 1895. (Cott. 3289)

Gaskell, Peter	Partner with Joseph Morgan at 60, Stafford St. from 1860–70. Succeeded by Cornelius Chambers as Gaskell and Chambers in 1892
Mason, Samuel	At 98, Lichfield St. in 1860; also in partnership with T. L. and J. Birch at 113, Coleshill St. from 1860–2. Later, until 1910, at 59, Dale End
Birch and Mason	*See* entry above
T. and J. Birch	Partnership of T. L. and J. Birch at 113, Coleshill St. from 1862–64
Motteram, T.	At 194, Bromsgrove St. from 1864–72
Stanley, James	At 185½, Cheapside from 1872–92
Mackenzie, R.	At 23, Adderley St. in 1866; in 1886 at 86, Upper St., Bordesley
Douglas, Job	At 78 (back of), Coleshill St. in 1878
Crisp, William	At 205, Aston Road in 1878
Merritt, James	At Unity Works, 5, Lichfield St. in 1878; partner with Cornelius Chambers for short time prior to 1892
Yates Brothers	Closely related to John Yates & Sons. Run by John Yates' sons, George, Edwin and William Joseph from the 1870s, originally as 'The Birmingham Spoon and Fork Works'. Traded until 1900 or later. Britannia metal makers
Chambers, Cornelius	Bought Peter Gaskell's business in 1892 to found Gaskell and Chambers. Absorbed Yates and Greenway in 1902 and bought Samuel Mason in 1910. Traded as Gaskell and Chambers until the 1970s. Bought by James Smellie
Gaskell and Chambers	*See* above entry. (MPM 1821)
Yates and Greenway	Originated with Frederick W. Greenway's purchase of James Yates in 1881. Passed to Gaskell and Chambers in 1902
McKenzie, W.	At 97, Upper Trinity St. in 1892. Partner with R. McKenzie
Lawden and Pool	Hope Works, New Town Row, 1908–
Mason, Harry	At 62, Dale End from 1912 (MPM 3104a)
Lee and Wilkes Ltd.	Brewery St., New Town Row, 1907–. Amalgamation of E. V. Wilkes with Charles Lee

NOTES AND REFERENCES

Birmingham in the 19th Century

1. Wise, M. J. and Thorne, P. O'N., 'The Growth of Birmingham 1800–1950', *Birmingham and its Regional Setting* (1952), pp. 213–6.
2. Yates, Thomas, 'Pewter and Britannia Metal Trade', *Birmingham and the Midland Hardware District* (Timmins, S., ed.) (1866), pp. 617–23.
3. The Worshipful Company of Pewterers of London, *Supplementary Catalogue of Pewterware* (1979), pp. 108–12 for lists of Britannia makers.
4. Law, A. S., 'Birmingham Pewterers of the Nineteenth Century, The Yates Family', *Journal of the Pewter Society*, Autumn 1984, pp. 105–9.
5. Law, A. S., 'The Morgan Family', *Journal of the Pewter Society*, Autumn 1982, pp. 126–8.

General

Nancy Goyne Evans, 'A Directory Survey of Pewter and Britannia Craftsmen Working in Birmingham England until 1860'. *Journal of the Pewter Collectors' Club of America*, December 1969, pp. 29–32.
Trades Directories, Pye 1785 etc., Chapman 1800 etc., Wrightson 1815 etc., Pigot 1829 etc., Dix 1858, Post Office 1845 etc., Kelly 1860 etc.
Rate Books, Birmingham Reference Library.
Census Returns, 1841–71.

WALSALL

THE TOWN OF WALSALL is an ancient one. It was a royal manor in the time of Edward the Confessor and received a charter from Henry II as early as 1159; it had a merchant guild in 1390 and two fairs from 1399. Its weekly market dates from a charter of 1417, and in 1538 it was given by Henry VIII to Robert Dudley, later Duke of Northumberland. Walsall lies centrally to a number of old market towns: Wolverhampton, Stafford, Lichfield, Sutton Coldfield, Birmingham, Halesowen and Dudley, and as early as the 14th century had coal and iron ore workings. It was then the source of the best local iron ore and remained so through the 17th century. Communications in the area were good with wagon services to neighbouring towns and beyond. Leyland, writing about 1540, described Walsall as a 'little market town' and went on to add, 'Ther be many smithes and bytte makers yn the town . . . pittes of se coles, pittes of lyme that serve South Town [Sutton Coldfield] four miles of. There is also yren ore . . .'.

Metal working was therefore established in the town in medieval times and the fact that a John Brasier was admitted as a burgess in 1377 indicates that this was not limited to iron and steel manufacture. Another brazier, Richard Marche, is described as late of Walsall in documents of the mid-15th century. Pewtering was certainly established by 1438 when there is reference to Richard Woodward of Walsall, pewterer. Indeed it is possible that the trade was carried on there in the previous century as the father of Thomas Fylkes, a London pewterer, is known to have lived in Walsall in 1399.[1] Thus Walsall may provide our earliest evidence of provincial pewtering in the area covered by this book, predating the first well documented Shrewsbury pewterer. It also supplies a series of remarkably detailed inventories of pewterers and braziers including that of Richard Parker, died 1534, which is the earliest we have examined. That Walsall supported several pewterers during the 16th century was known to Cotterell who lists four from that century and five from the seventeenth. In fact there were many more over a period of some two hundred and fifty years during which the craft of the pewterer flourished in the town. Although the Pewterers' Company searchers did not actually visit Walsall in 1640, they recorded the names of 13 Walsall pewterers whose wares were seized in neighbouring towns. Although some of the names may be duplicated in variant spellings this represents a remarkable level of activity. For a short while Walsall may have been the most important centre of the craft outside London. However this must be kept in proportion as there may have been as many as 390 working pewterers at that time in the London Company. By the time of the 1676 search there had been a dramatic change and only three names are found in the Company's records of an actual visit to the town in that year.

At the time when pewtering was in its heyday in Walsall several pewterers rose to the office of mayor, Christopher Adamson in 1576 and 1582 and Richard Adamson in 1604 and 1616 are certainly identified. A John Clarkeson was mayor in 1521, 1528 and 1536 and is probably the pewterer of that name; and William Seney, descendant of at least four generations of pewterers and himself a brazier and ironmonger, held the office in 1692, 1703 and 1705. Among braziers we find William Ebb in 1656 and Martin Pashley in 1701, William Webb, mayor in 1626, 1627 and 1649, is probably not one of the two pewterers of that name, but was presumably of the same family. The change from pewterer mayors in the 16th and early 17th century to braziers in the mid-17th and early 18th is probably indicative of the changed relative importance of the trades over that period.

The inventory of Richard Parker, pewterer of Walsall, who died in 1534, includes large quantities of both brassware and pewter and a selected extract reads:

In brasse batreware vi C and halfe at xxvi s the C	vii li x s
In pewtur and (illeg) lay mettal v C weyth	vii li
In molds and tolls to the [trade?]	iiii markes
In old brasse the weyth iiii score li and x	x s
In fine potts iiii score li and x	x s
These be the praysers of the goodes Thomas Wyrley, Henry Sporryer, Thomas Penser and John Rogers wt others.	

In his will he bequeathed to his daughter Alice his moulds and tools, and to Elizabeth his wife five hundredweights of pewter. On Elizabeth's death in 1541 the five hundred-weights of pewter was apparently intact and she bequeathed 'one hundredweight of fine hiring vessles' to Alice; another bequest was 'a platter, a dish and a saucer' to Margery Heath. Although Elizabeth describes herself as a pewterer in her will we have seen that Richard's moulds and tools passed to his daughter and it may be that his widow's business was the hiring out of the pewterware he left to her, and part of which she subsequently left to Alice. The hiring of pewter is frequently mentioned in records of the 15th to 17th centuries, either for special occasions such as banquets, or on a long term basis to the households of the rich for their servants' use.

Another 16th century inventory is that of William Nicholls who died in 1578. It is the most detailed surviving inventory from the period and lists item by item the equipment of a pewterers' shop of that time. He was a wealthy man, worth £108 18s. 0d., and possessed a dozen silver spoons among his belongings. It can be seen from his moulds that he made sadware, spoons, salts and bottles (a term of uncertain meaning) and the relevant part of this inventory (with modernised spelling) is reproduced below:

xii sadware moulds of brass iii C and xv pounds		ix li
i sadware wheel	)	
ix sadware hooks	)	
i flat	)	
i pair of great shears	)	
ii ladles of iron	)	
i pair of lifting tongs	)	
iiii pairs of bars	)	l s viii d
ii anvils	)	
i swage	)	
ii soldering irons	)	
i rapping hammer	)	
i great iron beam and scales	)	
ii cwt of leaden weights		xx s

xxix pounds of brass weights	ix s viii d
i small beam	xii d
i framing saw)	
i hand saw)	ii s
i plane)	
iiii spoon hammers)	
ii stumps)	
i little wheel)	
iv spoon moulds of brass)	xl s
ii pairs of small shears)	
(illegible) implements)	
i round salt mould)	
a pair of bars)	x s
iiii bottle moulds	ii s
lead weighing five score pounds and four	vi s viiii d
iii gross and ii dozen of spoons	xxv s iv d
xix round salts	viii s
xxiii pounds of lay metal	vi s
half dozen bottles, v half pints and i quart	ii s iiii d
old pewter i cwt	liii s iiii d
old brass i cwt and xxxii pounds	xliiii s iiii d
i houselock	iiii d
old iron lx pounds	ii s vi d
old pan brass lxxviii pounds	xxxii s ii d
old pots five score and xxi pounds	xl s
pewter going about the house lxxxv pounds	xlii s vi d
pewter pots xviii pounds	
v candlesticks)	iii s iiii d
i dozen of spoons)	

(later)

i dozen of silver spoons	iii li
vii ounces of old silver	xxx s

For a period of over a century the Nicholls family appear to have been the most prolific of Walsall pewterers. In all 10 members of the family plied the trade between

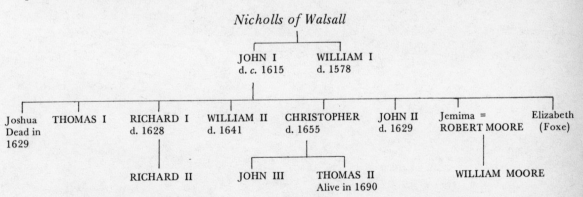

Nicholls of Walsall

Notes: 1. Pewterers shown in capital letters
2. John I had two other daughters, Joan and Alice (Lewys)
3. Christopher had another son, Christopher and two daughters, Sarah and Elizabeth (Kirkman)
4. John II's godson John Foxe was preseumably related to his brother-in-law, Elizabeth's husband.

the middle of the 16th century and the latter part of the seventeenth. William had a brother, John I, who fathered six sons and four daughters. Of the sons no fewer than five were pewterers and one of his daughters married a pewterer. The sons who followed the craft were Thomas, Richard (d. 1628), William II (d. 1641), Christopher (d. 1655) and John II (d. 1629). Christopher in turn was father to John III and Thomas II, both of whom were pewterers, and Richard's son, Richard II also followed the trade. The daughter, Jemima, married a Robert Moore whose son William Moore was left certain moulds in the will of his uncle, John II, the moulds then being in the keeping of Jemima's husband, who was therefore by inference also a pewterer.

The will of John Nicholls II also left to the use of his brothers, Christopher and Thomas, his moulds and tools until such time as his apprentice and godson John Foxe, who was to be bound to them for the rest of his term, had completed his apprenticeship. Thereafter they were to be shared between John Foxe and the testator's nephew

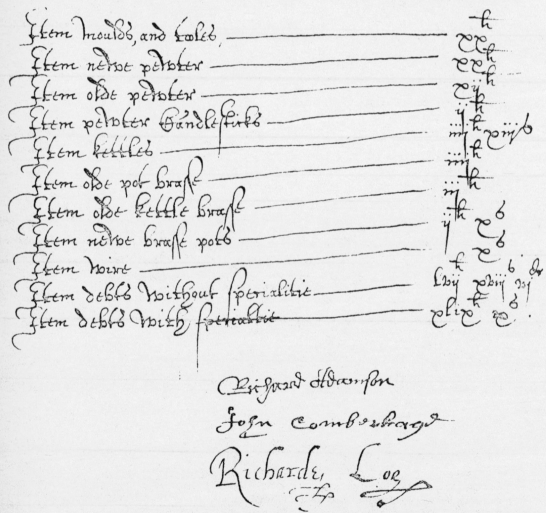

11. Extract from the inventory of Thomas Jennings of Walsall, 1615, with the signatures of his fellow pewterers Richard Adamson and John Comberlage. (Lichfield Joint Record Office).

Richard Nicholls II. The bequest however excluded a chamberpot mould and a 'garnett' mould which formed the bequest mentioned earlier to William Moore. The meaning of the term 'garnett' is unknown.

Christopher Nicholls (d. 1655) left to his son Thomas II all his moulds, tools and stock of metal, saving only that 'such moulds as my sons John and Thomas have altered unto the new fashion . . . shall be parted between my two said sons, John allowing and paying to my son Thomas half the charges of the alteration and brass'. This reference to the alteration of moulds emphasises the value of them and the cost of having entirely new ones made.

Even more prosperous than William Nicholls was Thomas Jennings who died in 1615 worth some £200. He had tools and moulds valued at £20, new pewter valued at the same amount (equivalent to about six hundred pounds in weight) and a further £20 worth of old pewter. In addition there was old pot brass worth £4 and kettle brass valued at £3, indicating brass working as well as pewtering. (*See* Fig. 11, p. 100).

Another dominant Walsall family was that of Seney who span most of the 17th and early 18th centuries. The first of several generations of the Seney family of pewterers and braziers, Joseph Seney, was far from wealthy when he died in 1630. His total inventory, which is transcribed below, reveals his assets as a mere £5 14s. 4d. It is interesting to note that two of the four appraisers were fellow pewterers.

'A true inventory of all the goods and chattels of Joseph Seney late of Walsall deceased, viewed, valued and appraised by Christopher Nicholls, Henry Rue, Thomas Chesheare and John Lucas the Twentyeth day of August 1630.'

One great saucer mould	vi s
One small mould	iv s
Two spoon moulds	vi s
One wheel, a spindle, one wheel)	
string, one tower board, 4)	x s
burnishers, six hooks, six rasps)	
2 shavers)	
2 beams and scales	iii s vi d
2 spoon hammers and one to beat the spoons in	iiii s
An anvil and three screws	vi d
A little iron kettle	xviii d
3 ladles, 2 soldering irons	xviii d
One old bed, one bolster, one blanket	viii s
2 landes of oats	xiii s iv d
One yearling calf	xvi s
Old pewter	xxii s vi d
One little kimmell [?]	vi d
2 bottle moulds, one half pint)	
mould, and one half quarter)	vi s
mould with the appurtenances)	
A little muck	vi d
His apparell	viii s
Six files and other implements	xviii d

This Joseph was followed by at least seven other members of the family who share only two Christian names, Robert and William, between them leading to some uncertainty as to relationships and identities. It appears certain that the William Sinay mentioned in the Pewterers' Company search of 1640 and the William Synaky listed in the same document are garbled versions of the name. Further members of the family may perhaps be discerned in even more garbled form in Richard Synerdy, Thomas Seneres and Robert Senores found in the same search.

Robert Seney I and Robert Seney II, described as 'senior' and 'junior' are recorded in the 1646 search and it seems reasonable to assume that they were father and son. A contemporary, William Seney I, was mentioned as a pewterer in 1640 and he died in 1673 leaving two sons, Robert III and William II and a widow Margaret who inherited his Park Street house. Both the sons became pewterers and it was William II who became mayor of Walsall in 1692 and again in 1703 and 1705. In 1671 he had married Sarah Pashley, presumably a relative of Martin Pashley, brazier, who was mayor in 1701 and Martin Pashley himself later married William II's daughter Sarah. William II had a son William III born in 1672-3 and his brother Robert had a son, Robert IV, born in 1677. Both were customers of John Duncumb in the 1720s, as was a Joseph Seney whose relationship is unknown. From this information, and with the help of the parish registers, a family tree may be constructed.

Seney of Walsall

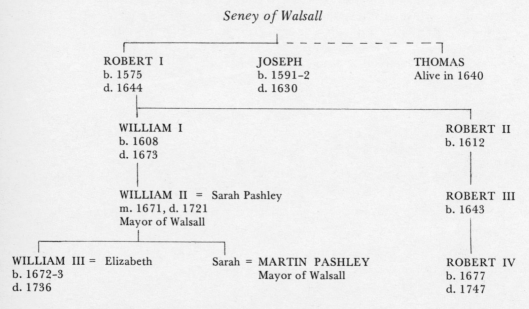

Note: Pewterers/braziers only shown.   Dotted line = conjectural.
   (We are indebted to Dr. A. S. Law for a number of dates appearing here which were too late to incorporate in the text).

William Seney II or his son William III has left for posterity an account book[2] of the period 1716-18 which was discovered in the shop he once owned. From this it is apparent that he was then primarily a brazier and ironmonger dealing in pig and pot brass and bar and rod iron, together with miscellaneous merchandise including spelter, candles, soap, butter, brushes, paper, tobacco, snuff, candlesticks, wire, sugar, whiting and rottenstone! He was nevertheless a retailer at least of pewter, being a significant customer of John Duncumb, and it is interesting that the Seney book records a payment by John Duncumb of 15 guineas on 19 June 1718, though for what is not stated. On 24 July 1717 William Seney either sold to or purchased from Hopwood Harper, the Worcester pewterer, leady tin to the value of 1s. 4½d. and in the same month purchased from one Bagnal '½G of Chargers' for 2s. 6d. Presumably half a garnish, and at a scrap price. However the book contains very little reference to pewter.

Of other early Walsall pewterers a number of inventories are to be found in the list in the *Introduction*. They reveal nothing new, but it is perhaps worth quoting from that of Christopher Nicholls, who died in 1655:

In the Shoppe

Seventeen score pounds weight of brass moulds at 8d./lb	£11 6d. 0d.
112 lbs of find metal at 9d./lb	£4 4s. 0d.
Wheels, hooks and other implements	£1 0s. 0d.

In the nearby town of Lichfield, the Pewterers' Company searchers visited the shop of the Lichfield pewterer Michael Nicken in 1640. There they found 60 pounds weight of defective pewter by six Walsall pewterers as follows:

George Gesonn	lay, stool-pans and flagons
Thomas Cheshire	porringers, spoons and saucers
Thomas Seneres [?Seney]	spoons
Thomas Gesonn	flagons
Christopher Nicholls	flagons
Robert Seneres [?Seney]	bottles

The luckless Michael was fined £2 2s. 6d.

In the earlier search of Lichfield in 1636 one John Nicken was also fined for possession of Walsall pewter by Gesonn. A Walsall pewterer, Humphrey Tudman, was fined £1 at Hatherston Fair (Warwickshire) in September 1646 for having substandard beakers and candlesticks of his own making, and also wares by Robert Seney, Snr. and Robert Seney, Jnr. A survey of the distribution of Walsall pewter of his period has been published by Hatcher and Barker.[3] From this, which is based on the 1640 Search Books, it is apparent that the Walsall pewterers sold their wares over a wide area of central England. It was found in virtually every shop in the area bounded by Abingdon, Hereford, Ashbourne and Northampton. The following table summarises their survey:

Maker	Where Found
William Nicholls	Abingdon, Hereford, Oxford, Wallingford Fair, Chipping Norton, Banbury Fair, Northampton, Coventry
Richard Nicholls	Warwick
Thomas Wilkes	Chipping Norton, Banbury Fair, Warwick, Atherstone Fair, Lichfield, Ashbourne, Coventry
William Seney (Sinay, Synaky, Senere, Senores)	Worcester, Lichfield
Thomas Cheshire	Coventry, Worcester, Lichfield, Burton-on-Trent, Atherstone
. . . Blansome	Chipping Norton, Burton-on-Trent
George Gesonn	Lichfield, Market Harborough, Leicester, Ashbourne, Burton-on-Trent, Atherstone
Thomas Gesonn	Lichfield, Derby, Atherstone Fair
Christopher Nicholls	Lichfield

Thomas Seney (Senores)   Lichfield
Richard Seney   Warwick
Robert Seney, Jnr.   Atherstone Fair, Lichfield
Robert Seney, Snr.   Atherstone Fair

The Ship Money Assessment of 29 November 1636[4] includes a number of pewterers and some measure of their relative prosperity can be deduced from the sums which they were expected to pay

Tho. Cheshire   ii s
Geo. Jesseson [?Gesonn]   v s
William Webb 'pewterer'   xii d
Mr. Richard Addamson and his son   viii s
Humphrey Tudman and his son   iii s
Robert Ebbe and his sons   3s 4d
Christopher Nicholls   iii s vi d
Wm. Ball 'pewterer'   xii d
Robert Seney   ii s

Several of them resisted payment and in January 1637 Thomas Cheshire, George Jesseson, William Ball, Robert Seney and Christopher Nicholls were threatened by the constable who was required to 'levie by distresse and sale of goods . . . the severall sumes of money whereat they are severally assessed'. The eventual outcome does not appear.

Little of this extensive trade appears to have survived the next few decades and the pre-eminence of Walsall seems to have given way to Wigan and to Bewdley as provincial focal points. In July 1676 the searchers belatedly visited Walsall itself and, as an all-too-brief note indicates, were far from welcome. Their brief record reads:

Richard Adamson   Basons; Turnspoons
William Seney   Trencher plates by Bourne of Worcester; Chamber pots by Nichols;
                         Chamber pots by ?Casterton; Chamber pots by Gorton of Birmingham

Note: Nichols and Adamson had concealed their ware.

The London Company's searchers visited the town again in *c.* 1690 and a recently discovered rough notebook of that search records a Mr. Seney and Thomas Nicholls, presumably William Seney II and Thomas Nicholls II. The entries read as follows:

At Walsall, Mr. Senyes [*sic*]: His rough spoons; Th. Nicholls porr[engers]; His saucers; His tankards; His flaggons; His upright Ch. potts; Flat handle spoons without touch, only a crown small; 'TN' candlestick; His upright Ch. potts; Salts untouched; Rnd brim Ch. potts; [two lines defective]

At Tho. Nicholls: His flaggons; His porrengers without a handle; His porrengers with handles; his tankards; His spoons; Chamber potts.

Fines totalling £1 were extracted from them for the listed substandard wares.

Clearly some pewter was being made in Walsall even at the end of the 17th century, but by then the emphasis had shifted to brass and iron ware and the town became largely a supplier of raw materials and articles to the growing Birmingham hardware industry over the following two centuries.

Walsall Pewterers and Braziers

Brazier, John	Burgess 1377, br
Fylkes, John	m 1399, ?p
Woodward, Richard	m 1438, p
Marche, Richard	m 1440, br
Clarkson, John	m 1518-28, p, mayor in 1528
Parker, Alice	m 1534, p, d. of Richard
Parker, Richard	d 1534, p and br
Parker, Elizabeth	d 1541, p, w. of Richard
Hancocks, John	m 1541, br
Worthynton, Robert	m 1550, p
Blackeburne, Robert	m 1556-78, p
Parker, Robert	d 1577, p, Cott. 3517
Adamson, Christopher	m 1576, d 1587, p, mayor in 1576, Cott. 22
Nicholls, William	d 1577, p
Peutrer, Robert	d 1578, ?p
Shaw, Jacob	m 1580, p, Cott. 4218
Woodward, *alias* Brazier, 'old mother'	d 1589, ? br
Manson, Richard	m 1592-95, p, Cott. 3090
Wright, Thomas	d 1604, p
Adamson, Richard I	m 1604-16, p, mayor in 1604 and 1616
Cheshire, Thomas	m 1609-43, p
Woodward, *alias* Brazier Margery	d 1611, ? br
Hanson, William	d 1614, p
Nicholls, Christopher	m 1615, d 1655, p, s. of John I
Nicholls, William II	m 1615-40, p, s. of John I
Jennin(g)s, Thomas	d 1616, p
Nicholls, Richard I	d 1628, p, Cott. 3393, s. of John I
Nicholls, Richard II	m 1628-40, p, s. of Richard I
Foxe, John	app 1629 to John Nicholls
Moore, Robert	m 1629, p
Moore, William	m 1629, p, s. of Robert
Nicholls, John II	d 1629, p, s. of John I
Nicholls, Thomas I	m 1629, p, s. of John I
Seney, Joseph	d 1630, p
Comberladge, John	m 1632, br
Ball, William	m 1636, p
Gesson, George	m 1636-46, p
Ebb, Robert	d 1637, br and p
Singleton, Thomas	m 1639, p
Smith, Thomas	m 1639, p
Blansome, . . .	m 1640, p
Gesson, Thomas	m 1650, p
Seney, Robert I	m 1640, d 1644, p
Seney, Robert II	m 1640, p, s. of Robert I
Seney (Seneres), Thomas	m 1640, p
Seney (Sinay), William	m 1640, p
Sinaky (= Seney?), William	m 1640, p
Sinerdy (= Seney?), Richard	m 1640, p
Wilkes, Thomas	m 1640, p
Webb, William I	d 1640, p, Cott. 5001/5014
Tudman, Humphrey	d 1647, p, Cott. 4825

Webb, William II	d 1647, p, Cott. 5011
Nicholls, John III	m 1644-1701, p, s. of Christopher
Ebbe, William	m 1656-83, br
Hancocks, Richard	m 1657, br
Seney, Robert III	b 1643, p
Comberledge, Thomas	m 1669, br
Sherwin, John	m 1670, p, Shrewsbury burgess roll
Seney, William I	d 1673, p
Collins, Edward	m 1673-1720, p
Seney, William II	m 1676, p, s. of William I, mayor in 1692, 1703, 1705, d 1721, p and br
Adamson, Richard II	m 1676, p
Deakin, Abraham	m 1689, d 1697, p
Nicholls, Thomas II	m c. 1690, p, s. of Christopher
Wright, Thomas	m c. 1690, p, Cott. 5308
Seney, William III	b 1672, p and br, alive in 1718, s. of William II
Seney, Robert IV	b 1677, p and br, alive in 1720, s. of Robert III
Pashley, Martin	m 1701, br, mayor in 1701-2
Ebb, John	d 1709, br
Barker, Samuel	m 1770, br
Heeley, John	m 1798, br
Sanders, Henry	m 1798, br

NOTES AND REFERENCES

Walsall

1. *Victoria County History of Staffordshire*, vol. 17, p. 196 for John Filkes and other early Walsall metalworkers.
2. *William Seney's daybook*, Walsall Central Library Parry Collection 33/2.
3. Hatcher, J. and Barker, T. C., *A History of British Pewter* (1974), pp. 255-6.
4. (Anon.), *Historical Collections of Staffordshire* (William Salt Archive Society, 1931), pp. 103-20.

General

Parish Registers of St Matthew's Church 1570-1649, transcribed by F. W. Williams (Walsall, 1890).
Parish Registers of St Matthew's Church 1646-1754 (Staffs. Parish Register Society, 1974-5).
Deeds at Walsall Central Library.
Trades Directories, Sketchley, 1770; Universal British, 1798.

OTHER ENGLISH TOWNS

THE EXTENT OF pewtering throughout the country towns of England is shown by the discovery of craftsmen plying the trade in many more of the market towns in the area covered by this study. Some, such as Bridgnorth and Lichfield, had guilds of metalworkers whose records survive; in other cases names have been found by chance in lists, documents and the London Company search books which were being scanned for other reasons. This chapter, though it does not pretend to be comprehensive, gathers this information together as indicative of the widespread incidence of the craft and in the hope that it may provide a starting point for future investigations of others.

BRIDGNORTH

Bridgnorth lies on the River Severn between Bewdley and Shrewsbury and is of Saxon origin. It was incorporated in 1157 and received a market charter in 1226. Historically it was a rival to Shrewsbury in the cloth and hide trades and was an early centre of ironworking. This latter trade led, during the 16th century, to the founding of a Bridgnorth Smiths' Company, the Record Book of which[1] (from 1595 to 1752), survives in the British Library. The Company described itself in the late 16th century as 'The Smiths' Company, naylors, cutters, shinglers, coopers, etc.' and first explicitly included pewterers in its title in 1610. Later it admitted as freemen members of many diverse trades including braziers, carpenters, joiners, gunsmiths, fish-hook makers, horncomb makers, locksmiths and tobacco pipe makers. It was organised with two wardens and two assistants, who were elected annually, and from 1643 also had a clerk. Its 'composition', which is mentioned in its record book, and which was renewed in 1691, appears to have been lost.

Apprentices were enrolled and normally bound for a period of seven years. Admission to the freedom cost, in the case of sons of freemen, 6s. 8d. and for those who were not freemen's sons, 13s. 4d. However, those who were admitted without having served an apprenticeship were required to pay the much larger sum of £3 6s. 8d. At least one woman was a freeman.

It is apparent from an entry in the Bridgnorth Court Leet Book[2] for a year or two later than 1500, in which the Steward of the Town ordered that 'for the time being' craftsmen might establish themselves in the town without let or hindrance, that no monopolistic guild existed at that time, though there is an implication that one was perhaps being mooted. In 1784 the wardens of the Company failed, at Shrewsbury Assizes, to prevent a grocer and haberdasher who was not free of the Company from establishing himself in the town. Its powers were therefore by then at an end. The Company was a small one, the members present at its annual meeting in 1615, whose names are entered in the record book, numbered only 36. Regrettably, though freedoms are entered regularly, trades are given only infrequently.

Though the Company included 'pewterers' in its title in 1610 the first recorded pewterer is Richard Bennett who, on 16 January 1616 'was made free of the Company of Smiths, naylors, cutlers, pewterers and shinglers to use the trade of pewterer and hath paid for his upset in lawful money of England iii li vi s viii d'. Clearly he had not served an apprenticeship and must presumably have come to Bridgnorth from elsewhere. However, in 1642, John Farr, pewterer, was fined 6s. 8d. for 'departing without a licence' and he may have been the John Farr(e) who was made free in 1604. Five members of the Farr family were freemen in 1615, including two Johns. It seems likely that the trades are only given, at least at this period, for those who did not qualify by apprenticeship. Those who were bound apprentice would be well known and it could have appeared superfluous to record their occupation.

There is a long gap, perhaps for this reason, before the next recorded pewterer, also from outside the town, in 1662. The entry reads:

'A meeting on the 20th day of November (1662) where the fraternity of Smiths and coopers, braziers and the rest of the company did meet and admit Joseph Wilkes to be a freeman of the said company of smiths. He is taken on as a pewterer and brazier and hath paid for his admittance into the company five marks [£3 6s. 8d.] and for his brotherhood he hath paid one shilling. He is taken by the consent of the company though he were a foreigner.'

This late reckoning of money in marks, which is usual in the record book even at this time, suggests a traditional sum of money dating from the time when marks were customary reckoning, and perhaps indicates the origin of the Company in the early part of the 16th century.

The next freeman described as a pewterer was also from outside. Thomas Smyth, pewterer, was admitted on 10 March 1672 and it is known from the appearance of his name on a burgess roll that he came from Bewdley. Next follows George Farr, brazier, in 1677 and then Phillip Newcomb, pewterer and brazier, in 1680. Then follow a group of entries relating to the Acton family.

The first of these records the admission, for £3 6s. 8d., of Ephraim Acton, pewterer, on 23 October 1678. We know that he was apprenticed, in London, to William Hall (probably the Birmingham pewterer of that name) in 1667–8 and would therefore have been free of the London Company by 1675. He was a warden of the Bridgnorth Company for many years. Pewter by one Edward Acton, said to be of Bridgnorth origin, was found on the premises of another member of the family, James Acton of Birmingham, at the time of the Pewterers' Company search in c. 1690.

In 1707 there is an entry which is difficult to interpret reading: 'Ephraim Acton the son of Ephrain Acton, brazier and pewterer, hath received his eldest son as an apprentice inrolled the above date [12th June]'. A further Ephraim Acton, no trade given, was admitted in 1719 and one Harvey Acton, son of Ephraim, was bound apprentice in the same year. It appears from this that there were three generations of Actons with the name Ephraim, and one of the younger ones is mentioned as a customer of John Duncumb, in the latter's day book, from 1720–4. Another son of an Ephraim, Charles, was apprenticed to Christopher Banks of Bewdley in 1712.

The Bridgnorth burgess roll[3] records Thomas Smith, Jnr., pewterer, son of the Thomas of Bewdley as a freeman admitted in 1698 but his name has not been found in the Smiths' Company records, unless he be the Thomas Smith senior, pewterer

and brazier, who was admitted on 6 February 1724, 'to follow the trade of pewterer
and brazier in the town of Bridgnorth'. Three more names can be recovered from the
Company's records:

> George Orme, pewterer and brazier, 1726
> George Pilking, pewterer and brazier, 1729
> William Pitt, brazier, 1741

From the burgess roll additional names can be obtained. Two of them from London:
Jonathan Perkins, brazier, in 1708 and Richard Pool, pewterer, in 1744. Later, in
1768, the name of John Ingram of Bewdley appears as a brassfounder and his brother,
Francis Ingram, Esq., appears in 1764 with no trade. Later burgesses include:

> Samuel Edwards, brazier, 1735
> Samuel Wall, brazier, 1766 [1746?]
> William Wall (his son), brazier, 1771
> Adrian Carver, brazier, of Broseley, 1784
> William Broadfield, brazier, 1826

It is worth recording that in 1734 one of the wardens of the Smiths' Company was
a Richard Felton, no doubt related to the Shrewsbury–Oswestry metal-working family
of that name.

It is clear that a small pewtering fraternity existed in Bridgnorth for some two
hundred and fifty years and it is unfortunate that trades appear only to be given for
'foreigners', at least for a period. With this in mind there follows here the list of names
of freemen as given in the record book in 1615 in the expectation that it may contain
some who were pewterers.

John Bradfield) Wardens	Thomas Wilde
Thomas Hill)	Richard Jukes
Francis Wesbury) Assistants	Edward Nightingale
John Millichape)	Roland Howell
John Farr	William Mather
Edward Leighton	Thomas Harper
George Farr	William Layhton
Edward Bradfield	Thomas ? Shipwaye
John Bradfield	Richard Johnson
William Powell	Richard Clagge
John Jukes	John Jukes the younger
Robert Kinseye	Richard ? Howe
William Farr	Richard Bateman
Richard Farr	Thomas Arne
Joseph Burne	William Bryante
Richard Bridge . . . ?	John Farr
John ? Burdley	Edward . . . ?
John . . . ?	(illegible)

LICHFIELD

Lichfield, an ancient cathedral city lying about sixteen miles north of Birmingham,
supported two goldsmiths in the 1570s, both of whom were country members of the
London Goldsmiths' Company. The first record of a pewterer is some sixty-five years
later when the city was visited by the Pewterers' Company searchers in 1636; then

the shop of John Nicken was found to contain pewter by Gesson of Walsall. In 1640 the searchers returned and visited the premises of Nicholas Kirkon and Michael Nickens, again seizing quantities of substandard Walsall wares. Michael Nickens is mentioned again as a pewterer in 1658 as a party to a deed. His widow is recorded as a pewterer in the 1673 search.

In common with Bridgnorth, Lichfield had a craft guild, 'The Company of Smiths, Goldsmiths, Cardmakers, Ironmongers, Pewterers, Braziers, Plumbers, Cutlers, Naylors and Spurriers.' Two record books of the Company survive[4] covering the period from 1644 to c. 1850 and from these the names of 29 pewterers and braziers can be recovered which are tabulated at the end of this chapter. Of these Jonathan Kilby (free in 1701) and John Room (free in 1718), who seems to have worked in Burton-on-Trent, are mentioned as customers of John Duncumb. Robert Ebb, to whom Thomas Cary was apprenticed, also appears in his day book and may have been of Stafford. The last pewterer appears to have been Richard Bates who is mentioned as the master of Daniel Morgan in 1719. Thereafter the entries relate to braziers. Nathanial Green, who died in 1715, mentions in his will a son Nathanial, however he was not the Nathanial Green who became a member of the London Company in 1722 (Cott. 1986). It is apparent from the Company's records that this Nathanial Green was a Londoner, son of Anthony Green of St Andrew's, Holborn. The inventory of Nathanial Green of Lichfield shows him to have been worth £63 and the value of pewter in his shop amounted to only about £5. To his wife he bequeathed only a bed 'which was hers before I was married to her', and the rest of his goods he left to be divided between his three children. Braziers were twice masters of the Company, Nathanial Green in 1710 and Thomas Meer in 1766.

LEOMINSTER

Westward, in Herefordshire, there is evidence of considerable pewtering in Leominster, a prominent wool town from the 13th century, which lies on the River Wye some fifteen miles north of Hereford. James Hales, a pewterer of Leominster, died in 1620 leaving his tools and moulds to his wife Elizabeth for her lifetime and then to his son Henry. (See Fig. 12, will of James Hales, on p. 111). We then find three generations of the Tom(p)kins family engaged in the trade. The first, Roger Tomkins, died in 1640 and he may well be the same individual as Roger Tomkyns who was recorded by Cotterell (No. 4765) as a Ludlow pewterer in 1603. He left his tools and moulds to Elizabeth his wife for her lifetime, and thereafter to be shared between his two sons, Thomas and John. Elizabeth carried on the trade for four years and died in 1644 leaving pewter and brass valued at £62 7s. 4d. 'in the shoppe'.

Both his sons continued in the craft, Thomas dying in 1667 and John in May 1677. Both their inventories survive and Thomas was worth the considerable sum of £365. His brother was a little less prosperous having goods valued at £150. The inventory of Thomas includes:

Wares in the shopp	£91	19	1
One iron beam and scales with the tools in the shopp and implements belonging to the trade	£2	10	0

In the name of God Amen the xxxth day of December 1620: in the year
of the raigne of our soveraigne Lord James by the grace of god of
England, ffraunce & Ireland, kinge defender of the faith &c the eightene: and
of Scotland the liiij. I James Hales of Leomster in the county and
Dioces of Hereff penntexter, being of perfect memory thanks be to god
mynding herefore to put that state whereof, it hath pleased god to endue
me with, in order, doe make and ordaine this my present testament
contayninge herein my last will, in manner & forme followinge
first I comend my soule to Allmyghtie god my maker Redemer
by whose death & passion I trust to be saved, and my bodie to be
buried in xpen buriall at the discretion of my executor hereafter
named./ Imprimis I give & bequeath unto my sonne Henry all my
mouldes belonge to my trade ymediatly, after the decease of Elizabeth my
wife./ Item I give and bequeath unto my sonne John ffortie shillinge
to be paid when he shall come to the age of one and twenty yeares./
Item I give & bequeath unto my daughter Margaret, ffortie shillings
to be paid to her when she shall come to the age likewise of xxxtie yeares./
and yf it shall hapen that either of them shall dye before they come to the age
of xxxtie yeares as afforesaid that then the portion bequeathed to him, or
her, so deceasinge, to be equally devided betwene the rest of my children aforesaid
then livinge./ All the rest of my goods, workinge tooles, houshouldstuffe,
and implements of what nature socever I unbequeathed I give and
bequeath unto Elizabeth my welbeloved wife whom I make & ordaine
my sole & whole executrix of this my last will & testament./

Witnesses:
Thomas ffreeman
Thomas raven
Tho: Tompkins

Signum Jacobi Hales

12. The will of James Hales of Leominster, 1620. Note the bequest of his moulds in lines 12–13 and of his tools in line 21. (Hereford and Worcester Record Office).

He also had three weeteinge (?worting) vessels, one brewing vessel, several barrels and 20 pounds of hops, suggesting brewing as a sideline. His will makes no specific mention of the tools of his trade.

John's inventory includes:

New Wares of all sorts in his house and shop	£45	0	0
Old Brass and pewter of all sorts	£18	3	8
Moulds and tools of all sorts belonging to the trade	£10	0	0

He also clearly carried on some farming and had seven pounds' worth of wheat and other grains 'in the ground', and three pounds' worth of wheat and corn in the house. He owned a mare, two pigs and a 'birdinge gun'. He was literate and had books worth 4s. 0d. He left all his tools and moulds to his son John.

13. Extract from the inventory of John Tomkins of Leominster, 1677.
(Hereford and Worcester Record Office).

The town also had a brazier in the early 17th century, John Whitcombe, who died in 1630 leaving everything to 'my newe wife Anne'. His inventory does not survive. The Pewterers' Company search of July 1677 mentions pewter made by a widow Tomkins of Leominster. It appears that this could either have been John's widow, Mary, or Thomas' widow, Elizabeth.

WELLINGTON AND NEWPORT

We have seen that the 1677 search of Shrewsbury discovered porringers by Bradshaw of Wellington on the premises of Howell Brown. Further information on the Bradshaw family comes from an article by Robert Sherlock, 'Chandeliers in Shropshire Churches'.[5] In this are given details of a brass chandelier in the church at High Ercall which is dated 1730 and inscribed 'William Bradshaw Wellington Fecit'. William Bradshaw's will was proved at Lichfield in 1763 and in it he describes himself as a pewterer. His father was John Bradshaw, pewterer of Wellington, who executed a document in 1738 in which he assigned all his possessions whatsoever to his son William, perhaps as a device to escape his creditors. He died in 1740. William Bradshaw was born in 1683 and the Bradshaw of the 1677 search was therefore his father, who was also the John Bradshaw found among the trade debtors of Sampson Bourne of Worcester.

Here is yet another self-styled pewterer who was fabricating articles in brass. William Bradshaw's competence in this metal was however obviously limited and Sherlock says of the High Ercall chandelier, 'It is difficult to imagine a greater travesty of good design . . . It copies what was typical London work of about 1705'. He goes on to describe the construction in some detail, and though it may have been an ingenious use of limited skills it was far from elegant. It is very tempting to attribute the 'William Bradshaw' touch (Cott. 549) to this Wellington pewterer despite the note in *Addenda to More Pewter Marks* that the name should read 'Birchimshaw'.

In nearby Newport there were two pewterers in the 17th century, John Poole who was buried there in 1667 and Edward Poole, perhaps his son, who is mentioned in the 1661 lay subsidy returns and in the 1672 hearth tax returns.

LEDBURY

Ten miles east of Hereford lies Ledbury, about midway to Tewkesbury. Here, in 1597, died James Walcroft, alias Pewterer. His will does not give his trade, but we can assume that his alias describes it. Unfortunately this voluminous document says nothing about his moulds or tools, but it does indicate considerable wealth. He lived in High Street and owned or leased a number of other properties which went to his son John, together with the residue of his estate.

TEWKESBURY

From the Company's searches it can be seen that Tewkesbury, standing virtually at the junction of the Avon and Severn, supported three pewterers in 1689, Samuel Spirow, William Jones and William Leight. A Mr. Jones is mentioned in 1677, and one William Tudman also appears in that year. An undated pewter token for one farthing, inscribed 'Samuel Canner in Tewkesbury, Pewterer', is recorded by Cotterell and it is apparent that the town was a not unimportant centre of the craft in the latter part of the 17th century. The search of 1702 shows that William Jones was still in business in that year and a new name, Elizabeth Spirers (probably a corruption of Spirow), appears. She was perhaps Samuel's widow.

SOUTH OF BIRMINGHAM

Southwards from Birmingham we find mention of Matthew Briggs of Bromsgrove in the searches of 1677 and c. 1690, and of John Perks of Henley-in-Arden in 1676. In Stratford-on-Avon, William Baker is recorded in the searches of 1676 and c. 1690 and John Scrivens, Richard Perks and Thomas Badger appear in 1702. Richard Perks may be the pewterer of that name recorded in Alcester *c.* 1690 and Thomas Badger was a customer of John Duncumb in the 1720s. Evesham boasted several 17th century pewterers. Cotterell records Samuel Tudman (No. 4826) and William Barber (No. 252), and the latter is found in the *c.* 1690 search. This document also names William Hamson and Richard Perks. A deed of 1704 records Phillip Brooks (Cott. 610) as then resident in Bridge Street, Evesham.[6] In the nearby Shipston-on-Stour, John Scruby (? Scroby) is mentioned in the Warwick Quarter Sessions for 1663[7] as being appointed a searcher, along with William Brookes of Warwick, 'to enter into and make search in the day-time in the house, shop, cellar, warehouse or other place of or belonging to any pewterer or brazier inhabiting in any borough, town or village within the said County of Warwick . . . and there put to view all vessels of what sort soever made or to be made to be put to sale of pewter or of brass and all such vesells as they shall find made of mixed or deceitful metals . . . to seize . . . '. Clearly he was a craftsman of some standing in the trade.

Later in Shipston we find Charles Wareing who was born in Shipston, the son of Francis Wareing, but who was apprenticed in London to Charles Halifax of the London Company in 1678. He became free in 1685 and presumably returned straight away to his native town where he is recorded as a pewterer in the *c.* 1690 search. He was a maker of some substance as his wares were found quite widely in that search and the one of 1692. In the latter year he is found also as the holder of a booth at Stow-on-the-Wold Fair. His own shop in 1690 contained flagons, porringers, tankards, saucers and chamberpots of his own making. He died in 1697 leaving no sons and his will makes no specific provision in respect of his business. This passed to a Joseph Wareing who is recorded in the 1702 search. Almost certainly the mark of Charles Wareing and the hall-marks of Joseph are to be seen in Cott. Nos. 4965a and 5999.

Alcester also provided a searcher, Richard Parshouse, appointed at the Warwick Quarter Sessions in 1664.[8] Two later Pershouse [*sic*] pewterers or braziers figure among the customers of John Duncumb *c.* 1720 and may also be of Alcester; they were Richard and Thomas. The *c.* 1690 search also mentions a Mr. Perks and a Mr. Scroby of Alcester.

THE ENVIRONS OF BIRMINGHAM

In what is now the industrial midlands, the only town which appears to have had a 19th century pewter trade is Wolverhampton. Pewterware by Palliser of Wolverhampton dates from *c.* 1860–80, and another firm, T. Bailey, is mentioned in trade directories for 1850. The extent of Wolverhampton's earlier pewter trade is conjectural. A probable pewterer's trade token of John Comberladg of Wolverhampton is extant and is dated 1664. This is noted by Cotterell and bears the device of a flagon on one side and of a bell on the other, suggesting a dual trade. The token is of pewter and members of the Comberlidge family were known to have been pewterers in Warwick and Walsall in the 17th century. A brazier, John Southwick, appears in the parish registers between 1636 and 1654, and Rowlands notes John Ebb who died in 1667–8.[9]

In Stourbridge in 1702 the Company's searchers noted a William Pitt, perhaps connected with the William Pitt of Bridgnorth and Shrewsbury, and also recorded William Seney with the note 'Goods sent to fair yesterday'. He must have been William Seney II or III of Walsall who appears from this entry to also have had interests in Stourbridge.

In nearby Wednesbury early evidence of pewtering is found in the Shrewsbury records where 'William Jenins, son of Thomas Jenins of Wedisburye in the County of Stafford, pewterer' was made free in the trade of pewterer in 1548-9.

GLOUCESTER AND BRISTOL

In view of the importance of the River Severn, a trade artery for Shrewsbury, Bridgnorth, Worcester and Tewkesbury, it is relevant to look briefly farther downstream at Gloucester and Bristol. The city of Gloucester was the subject of a search as early as 1505 and the names of two pewterers, William Henshaw and Richard ap gWillym are found. There is a very long gap before the next surviving search, that of 1636. Between 1636 and 1641 the searchers visited Gloucester no less than five times and the eight pewterers whose premises were searched are listed at the end of this chapter. In 1636 the goods of Robert Plumer were found good 'but he did not burnish his handles and joints of his flagons and for that the wardens fined him two shillings'. Six months later the same Robert Plumer denied entry to the searchers, as did a fellow pewterer, Robert Knowles. As has been seen earlier much pewter by Sampson Bourne and Thomas Nichols of Worcester was found in the city at this time. It appears that Gloucester then had a Company of Metalmen which included goldsmiths, pewterers, braziers, coppersmiths, wiredrawers, cardmakers, pinmakers and plumbers.[10] From the search in 1689 five further Gloucester pewterers can be identified, Alan Prior (whose pewter was found widely in various midland towns at this time and also in 1677), William Harwood, Robert Davis, Mr. Knowles and Mr. Marris. Harwood, Davis and Knowles, together with Alice Prior (presumably successor to Alan) are also found in the later search of 1692. In 1702 Alice Prior and William Harwood were still in business and the additional names of Richard Crump, and John Browne are found. Even from this rather superficial information it is apparent that Gloucester was a pewtering centre of some significance for two hundred years or more.

Bristol has a much better documented record of pewtering, and indeed one of the earliest recorded provincial pewterers, John Peutrer, resided in the city in 1343.[11] The Bristol guild of pewterers were granted ordinances in 1456-7 and these have been published by Cotterell in *Old Pewter its Makers and Marks*. Such was its importance in the 15th century that it was one of the places searched in the first country search carried out by the London Company in 1474. This followed immediately on the grant of rights of search and seizure to the Company through its first charter of 1473-4. This gives the names of four Bristol pewterers, William White, John Caulse, Alson Caylye and John Avys. Two centuries later, in 1674, 13 Bristol craftsmen are named by the searchers, in 1683, 18, and in 1702, 20. In York at that time we find 16 names and in Wigan, 18. Clearly Bristol was one of the three main provincial pewtering centres in the later 17th century, and no doubt a major port for the export of wares to the

American colonies and elsewhere. Indeed links existed between the Bewdley firms of John Ingram and Ingram and Hunt and the Bristol firm of Willshire. Not only does some Willshire pewter bear the hall-marks of Ingram and Hunt (as recorded in Cotterell) but an undoubtedly Bewdley plate has been discovered with the Willshire touch and the earlier hall-marks of John Ingram. Apparently wares were factored by Willshire for the Bewdley concerns and possibly were shipped from Bristol to other parts of the country by sea as being more convenient than land transport.

From the searches the names of 10 Bristol pewterers not recorded by Cotterell have been found and these are listed at the end of this chapter.

In 1697 the London Company was engaged in one of its periodic attempts to secure legislation requiring beer to be sold only in pewter pots of standard capacities, and abolish the use of earthenware and other materials for this purpose. The Bristol pewterers rose to the support of their London colleagues and wrote on 3 April 1697 as follows:[12]

> Wee the pewterers of the City of Bristoll having understood by information from London of your care and diligence in promoting the consumption of Tinn, together with the intrest of the pewterers of England in the present juncture of the Parliament's inclination for the promoting thereof; Doe gladly joyne with you in soe good a work and wold desire a few lines from you how farr you have proseeded in this worke if you thinke fitte and whatt may be proper for uss to doe in our stattion and in you pleas to send uss a copy how farr you have proceeded in it; for you are nott unsencible what grate disadvantages the woorking parte of our trade hath layne under this many years by reason of the retayling of liquear in uncertayne measures which iff it cann be remedyed will promote the consumption of Tinn and employ many poor workemen that are in grate distreess with uss for want of employment. This is what ofers at present from your obliged friends and servants Thomas Bayly, Erasmus Dole, John Jones, John Batchelor, Thomas Cave, Theo. Newton, Arthur Thomas, Jno. Peters. Subscribed in behalf of our selves and others nott presentt.

THE WELSH BORDER

Turning now to the Welsh border area, rather centrally placed is the old market town of Kineton (now Kington) in Herefordshire. Here, in 1677, Thomas Arndale had a well stocked shop with a range of ware including:

Spoons; Saucers; Porringers; Blood Porringers; Salts; Flagons; Bellied Cups; Small pots; Tankards made by Brown [? Howell Brown of Shrewsbury]; Candlesticks; Dishes made by Prire of Gloucester; Chamber pots.

He was probably related to Elizabeth Arndale of Ross-on-Wye (*see Introduction*) and to an earlier Thoms Arindale [*sic*] mentioned in the 1640 search of Ross. Also in Ross on-Wye in 1677 was another pewterer, William Bennett. His shop stocked a number of wares by Prire as well as a good range of his own making. Cotterell (No. 2409) also mentions a Samuel Hopton of Ross *c.* 1730.

There is scope for much further research in many of these towns where we have only scratched the surface by summarising readily accessible records, or where we have found the names of a few individuals by chance.

Bridgnorth Pewterers and Braziers

Note: f = Free of the Bridgnorth Smiths' Company.

Bennett, Richard	f 1616, p
Farr, John	f 1642, d 1672, p
Wilkes, Joseph	f 1662, p and br
Smyth, Thomas I	f 1672, p (of Bewdley)
Farr, George	f 1677, br
Acton, Ephraim I	f 1678, p
Newcombe, Phillip	f 1680, p and br
Acton, Edward	m 1690, p
Perkins, Jonathan	B 1708, br (from London)
Acton, Ephraim II	f 1719, d 1759, br, ? s. of Ephraim I
Acton, Harvey	app 1719, p, s. of Ephraim II
Smyth (Smith), Thomas II	B 1698, f. 1724, p and br, s. of Thomas I
Orme, George	f 1726, p and br
Pilking, George	f 1729, p and br
Edwards, Samuel	B 1735, br
Pitt, William	f 1741, br (from Shrewsbury)
Pool, Richard	B 1744, br (from London)
Wall, Samuel	B 1766 (? 1746), br
Wall, William	B 1771, br
Carver, Adrian	B 1784, br (of Broseley)
Bradfield, William	B 1826, br

Lichfield Pewterers and Braziers

Note: f = Free of the Lichfield Smiths' Company

Nicken, John	m 1636, p
Kirkon, Nicholas	m 1640, p
......, Edward	f 1644, p and br
Nickins, Michael I	m 1640-58, p
Webb, Robert	f 1657, p
Baggeley, William	f 1667, p
Nickins, Widow	m 1673, p
Nickins, Michael II	f 1677, p and br
Leane, Thomas	f 1678-9, br
Mosely (Mousely), Samuel	f 1680-1, p and br
Greene, Nathanial	f 1695, p (app to Sam Mousely)
Kilby, Jonathan	f 1701, p and br (app to Edward Linthwait of Mansfield)
Marshall, George	f 1703, p and br (app to Jon. Kilby)
Bates, Richard	f 1707, br (app to Nathn. Greene)
Motteram, Thomas	f 1708, p and br
Room, John I	f 1709, p and br (app to Jon. Kilby)
Greene, Thomas	f 1718, br, s. of Nathanial
Marshall, George	f 1718, br (app to Jon. Kilby)
Room, John II	f 1718, br (app to Jon. Kilby)
Morgan, Daniel	f 1719, p and br (app. to Rd. Bates)
Arnis, Thomas	f 1726, br (app to Nath. Greene)

Cary, Thomas	f 1731, br (app to Robert Ebb*)
Kilby, Richard	f 1733, br, s. of Jonathan
Meer, Thomas I	f 1761, br
Meer, Thomas II	f 1766, br, s. of Thomas I
Alkin, Richard	f 1799, br and tinman
Evans, William	f 1801, br (ousted in 1802)
Hawkins, William	f 1802, br
Hardy, Charles	f 1803, br

* Robert Ebb, brazier and pewterer of Stafford, was a major customer for the
   pewter of John Duncumb in the 1720s.

Leominster Pewterers and Braziers

Hales, James	d 1620, p
Whitcombe, John	d 1630, br
Tompkins, Roger	d 1640, p
Tompkins, Elizabeth	d 1644, p, w. of Roger
Tompkins, Thomas	d 1667, p
Tomkins, John	d 1677, p
Tompkins, Widow	m 1677, p

Gloucester Pewterers

Note: All the following are from the Pewterers' Company Search Books.

Henshaw, William	m 1505, p
gWillym, Richard ap	m 1505, p
Hall, Thomas	m 1636-7, p
Plummer, Robert	m 1636-7, p
Robartes, Robert	m 1636-7, p
Knowles, Robert	m 1636-41, p
Younge, Thomas	m 1636-7, p
Everes, Thomas	m 1636, p
Browne, William	m 1640-1, p
Prise, Robert	m 1640-1, p
Prire, Alan	m 1677, p
Prire, Alice	m 1692-1702, p
Harwood, William	m 1689-1702, p
Davis, Robert	m 1689-92, p
Knowles, Mr.	m 1689-92, p
Marris, Mr.	m 1689, p
Browne, John	m 1702, p (Cott. 635a)
Crump, Richard	m 1702, p

Bristol Pewterers Not Listed by Cotterell

John Peutrer	m 1343–1350s, p
White, William	m 1474, p
Caulse, John	m 1474, p
Caylye, Alson	m 1474, p
Avys, John	m 1474, p
Barnes, William	m 1676, p
Betton, Robert	m 1676, p
Mearse, Richard	m 1683, p
Bailey, Mr.	m 1683, p
Bourge, Anthony	m 1683, p
Bartholomew, John	m 1683, p
Britten, Robert	m 1683, p
Bayley, Thomas	m 1702, p
Sell(?eck), Richard	m 1702, p
Goen, Richard	m 1702, p

Of these the last, Richard Goen, may perhaps have been the father of the well-known Richard Go(e)ing (Cott. 1909) whom Cotterell records as free in 1715.

NOTES AND REFERENCES

Other English Towns

1. *Bridgnorth Smiths' Company Book*, British Library Add. MS. 38834.
2. Skeel, C. A. J., 'The Bridgnorth Company of Smiths', *English Historical Review*, vol. 35 (1920), p. 248 note.
3. *Bridgnorth Burgess Rolls*, MSS. at Shropshire Local Studies Library.
4. *Lichfield Smiths' Company Book*, Lichfield Joint Record Office, D77.
5. Sherlock, Robert, 'Chandeliers in Shropshire Churches', *Transactions of the Shropshire Archaeological Society*, vol. 57, Part 3 (1964), pp. 241-64. This article contains much about braziers who were working in the 18th century.
6. *Deeds* at Birmingham Reference Library, 280054, 280190, 281031.
7. Ratcliffe, S. C., and Johnson, H. C. (eds.), *Warwick Quarter Sessions Order Book 1657-65* (1938), p. 251.
8. *Warwick Quarter Sessions*, p. 302.
9. Rowlands, M. B., *Masters and Men in the West Midland Metalworking Trades before the Industrial Revolution* (1975), p. 38, ref. 39.
10. Fisher, F. J., *Provincial Guilds*, London M.A. thesis (1931). Although of general background value this thesis does not concern itself, except incidentally, with metalworking guilds.
11. *Calendar of Close Rolls 1343-6*, p. 124.
12. Pewterers' Company, uncatalogued archives at Pewterers' Hall.

WALES

THE LATE CHRISTOPHER PEAL in introducing the section on Wales in his popular book *British Pewter and Britannia Metal* said, 'most regrettably, I can find no evidence whatsoever of pewter manufacture in Wales'. This bold statement was, until very recently, so near the apparent truth that it could not be challenged. Although it has long been known that a number of Welshmen worked as pewterers in England, notably in Bristol, but also in other towns and cities such as Ludlow, Shrewsbury and Chester; only one reference to a pewterer definitely resident in Wales is included in Cotterell's *Old Pewter its Makers and Marks*, William Thomas of Haverfordwest.

This statement by Peal implies a number of obvious questions. Was pewter widely used in Wales as it was in the neighbouring counties of the Marches and the West Midlands? If pewter were used in any quantity, where was it made and how was it retailed to the consumer? Finally, what features of economic and social life in the Principality can account for any differences which may have existed.

There is ample evidence that pewter was used in Wales in the 17th and 18th centuries, both for domestic and ecclesiastical purposes. To cite but a few examples, in March 1665-6 an Inventory was taken of the property of Sir Edward Lloyd who lived just outside Llanidloes in mid-Wales. This indicates that he owned 348 pounds of pewter, priced at 8d. a pound and worth in total £6 12s. 0d.[*sic*][1] Moving to another century and another part of Wales, Elizabeth Morgan, the mistress of Henblas on the island of Anglesey, recorded in 1735 that the household property included four dozen plates with arms and three dozen plates without arms, a dozen soup plates, five new large dishes with crests, five soup plates, six old dishes and two very large dishes with crests.[2] Over fifty years later an inventory, taken on 1 October 1796 at Pwllywrach in Glamorgan, includes a pewter noggin measure, 14 hot water dishes, 80 pewter plates and dishes, a pewter cheese stand, a fish strainer, and (surprisingly) a pewter baking pan.[3] Another example of the use of pewter is found in the records of the Montgomeryshire Quarter Sessions for 7 October 1819.[4] An order was issued by visiting magistrates for the purchase of 24 pewter chamber pots from Mr. Jones of Welshpool for use in the local jail. Many other examples can be found of the use of pewter by the gentry and their tenants. That it was also used in the taverns and public houses is amply shown by the number of surviving 19th century measures bearing Welsh verification stamps.

Moving from these examples of domestic use to the ecclesiastical usage of pewter we find much convincing evidence that pewter was widely used in the churches of Wales. If the various inventories and lists of church plate in the Welsh diocese are studied the widespread distribution of church pewter is apparent. That for Bangor, published in 1906, includes between eighty and ninety pieces of pewter,[5] while in the two counties of Pembroke and Carmarthen, in 1905 and 1907 respectively, it was recorded that the local churches still possessed well over a hundred and forty pieces, 80 per cent. of which was flatware. Although the numerical spread of pewter in churches in other parts of Wales seems to have been much the same,[6] the proportion of flatware to hollow-ware is frequently different. Compared with some neighbouring areas more pewter seems to survive in Welsh churches, and possibly more may have been used in the first place. However as in other parts of the country, investigation of the current position indicates the steady disappearance of the pewter recorded in earlier surveys.

Having established that there is adequate evidence for the use of pewter in Wales from the 17th to the 19th centuries, the second (and more difficult) of the three questions posed at the beginning of this chapter needs to be faced: who supplied the market? One obvious source was the various sizeable border towns such as Chester, Oswestry, Gloucester, Hereford, and the prolific pewtering centres of Bewdley and Worcester. Most of these towns had an area of commercial influence which spread across the border into the Principality. Further, the gentry and the more prosperous Welshmen came to these urban centres for purposes of business, trade or leisure, or passed through them on their way to London or elsewhere.

Evidence for the part played by at least one of these towns is found in the order books of the Ingram and Hunt partnership of Bewdley. This firm, who increasingly dominated the trade in the latter part of the 18th century, supplied various retail outlets in the following Welsh towns, Abergavenny, Bridgend, Brecon, Caerphilly, Cardiff, Carmarthen, Denbigh, Haverfordwest, Holywell, Knighton, Llandeilo, Llanelly, Machynlleth, Monmouth, Montgomery, Neath, Pontypool, Swansea, Usk, Welshpool and Wrexham, and possibly in others.

This cannot, however, be the whole answer to the question at issue. Before the construction of the turnpike roads and canals large areas of Wales were effectively isolated by poor roads and a mountainous terrain from these border towns. Road travel was at most times difficult and the carriage of heavy goods over any distance very costly. The only available contemporary solution to this problem was transport by water, either the sea or one of the limited number of navigable rivers. The survey of pewter mentioned above in Pembroke and Carmarthen lists between forty and fifty pieces which were made in Bristol. There can be little doubt that these were imported by sea and that such trade had been going on over a long period.

The Welsh Port Books for the period 1550 and 1603 have been in part published.[7] They record the imports and exports of the main Welsh ports, including details of the cargoes carried, the ships used and sometimes the merchants owning the goods. Remembering that these records are only partially available and that the efficiency with which they were kept may be in some doubt, the picture they give is most illuminating. Pewter and brass were being imported into Carmarthen and Milford Haven from Bristol and Barnstaple and from Chester into the Anglesey port of Beaumaris. Between 1592 and 1603, 15 ships' cargoes carried from Chester to Beaumaris included pewter. Interestingly, no pewter is recorded in this period as being landed in Caernarvon. In the South Wales area, eight part cargoes are listed as being carried from Bristol to Carmarthen and six to Haverfordwest, while two were imported into Carmarthen from Barnstaple. Also, scrap metal was being conveyed back to the English ports.

HAVERFORDWEST

Two of the most interesting entries in the Elizabethan Port Books refer to Thomas Thomas of Haverfordwest, who is described as a pewterer. These entries reveal that on 19 October 1586 Thomas Thomas despatched seven hundredweight of brass and pewter on board the ship *Michael of Pill* to Ireland. On 18 December of the same year, he imported on the ship *Peter of Milford* six hundredweight of old brass and pewter from Ireland. Here, then, is evidence for a Welsh pewterer and one who was sufficiently enterprising and who had sufficient capital to undertake a trading mission to Ireland. Unfortunately there is no data at present available to suggest whether this was an isolated incident or part of a regular pattern of trade.

Haverfordwest, which is on the Cleddau River at the head of the Milford Haven, is an ancient borough. This part of Wales was subject to early settlement during the Anglo-Norman penetration of Wales and Haverfordwest received privileges as a corporate community which were extensive for a town which was never large. The information which is available for the study of the town and its history is as a result extensive, well-catalogued, and of great value to the researcher.

A study of the borough's archives[8] has produced a list of names of pewterers and braziers active over a period of more than a hundred years:

> David Thomas, pewterer, *c*. 1540
> Thomas Thomas, pewterer, *c*. 1565–90
> William Thomas, pewterer, *c*. 1595–1602
> William Cattell (Kattell, Cattle, Cetell), pewterer, *c*. 1585–1600
> Thomas Colton, pewterer, *c*. 1650
> William Lewis, pewterer, *c*. 1650
> Richard Bevans, brazier, *c*. 1647
> John Bevans, brazier, *c*. late 1650s
> Edward Morrell, brazier, *c*. 1657

The William Thomas mentioned here is the William Thomas already referred to as being the sole Welsh pewterer listed by Cotterell. However, there is an entry (Cott. 343) recording that an Arnold Beavins of Haverfordwest was apprenticed as a pewterer to John Knowles of Bristol on 30 December 1657. Making due allowance for the variations in spelling which occur and the difficulties experienced by English clerks in rendering Welsh names, Arnold Beavins was almost certainly a member of the same family as the John and Richard Bevans listed above.

Unfortunately, after the Restoration in 1660 the borough records change character and the recovering of information about the occupations of residents becomes more difficult. This lack of further detail cannot obscure the fact that this small and distant Welsh town was able to sustain two master craftsmen of the pewterer/brazier type continuously for a large part of the 16th and 17th centuries.

CARMARTHEN AND BRECON

This discovery prompted a study of a number of other Welsh towns. The choice of the towns to be investigated was partly determined by what has been published about urban growth and development in Wales before the Industrial Revolution, and partly by the accessibility of the necessary records. Starting initially in South Wales, two urban centres, Brecon (pop. in 1801 — 2,576) and Carmarthen (pop. in 1801 — 5,548), were selected for more detailed study. Of these, Carmarthen was for most of the time under consideration probably the largest town in the Principality.

Carmarthen had a Company or Fraternity of Hammermen which existed as early as 1575 and its Rules were approved by the Borough Corporation in 1633 and were entered in the Council Order Book. The Rules show that membership of the Company included Goldsmiths, Ironsmiths, Cutlers, Pewterers, Plummers, Mettallers and Tinkers. This document states that the Company may elect a Master, carry out searches, make rules, decide on the admission of craftsmen from outside the town, and determine questions of apprenticeship. For these privileges, they had to make an annual payment of 13s. 4d. to the Corporation as well as a share of various other fines and payments. A transcription of the Rules of the Company of Hammermen is to be found in the Appendix to this chapter.[9]

A list of the original members of the Fraternity is included in the Rules, although their occupations are not given. It is a reasonable assumption that all the crafts were represented in this list. The Port Books already discussed record a number of Carmarthen men trading in pewter and brass at this time. Among those mentioned is David ap Ievan, whose name is entered twice in 1566. David ap Ievane and Ievane ap Ievane are found among the first members of the Carmarthen Company of Hammermen and it seems likely that they were pewterers. The other Carmarthen men mentioned in the Port Books as trading in pewter and brass are Richard Lewis Hopkins and Thomas Davies.

In 1651-2 the Town Order Book contains another and even more significant reference to the Company of Hammermen in the following terms:

> 'One composition, grant, order and decree made by the said Mayor [David Edwards] unto Thomas Hobson, pewterer, and others to an association or fraternity of pewterers or mettle-men paying therefore to the Chamberlain for the time being the rent of 15/- at every St Michaels, yearly.'.

Thomas Hobson or Hopson was Sheriff of the borough in 1663 though he did not afterwards become Mayor. He was also mentioned in 1657 in another context. This Thomas Hobson must be the same pewterer who was made free of Bristol in 1647 (Cott. 2346).

The names of other pewterers who were active in the 16th and 17th centuries have not been found, but several 18th century braziers have been identified: David Davies — Sheriff in 1723; John Blome — Sheriff in 1738; William Philips — Sheriff in 1759 (died in office); David Williams — Sheriff in 1772; plus others in the later part of the century and in the early 19th century.[10] An interesting reference survives in the 1907 survey, *Church Plate in Carmarthenshire*, to a nine and three-eighth inch pewter plate in the church of Llanfihangel Aberconwin with a worn mark 'DAV . . . VIES'. This would seem to be the mark of the above brazier. The quantity of pewter in this survey and that of the adjoining old county of Pembrokeshire which in the period 1675 to 1800 was made in Bristol, suggests that these braziers were retailing pewter made in that city and brought by sea to West Wales. Implicitly some came unmarked and the importer added his own touchmark.

The other South Wales town initially chosen for study was Brecon. Some municipal records survive for the 17th and 18th centuries and the registers of St Mary's Church give the occupations of the great majority of the 17th and 18th century residents. From these and other sources, the names of several pewterers and braziers have been extracted. The earliest of these is Mathias Berrow or Berrowe, a pewterer who appears in the rent roll of burghal tenants compiled in 1664 and amended in 1676.[11] Mathias, however, does not seem to have been a member of one of the ancient burghal families. He was, nevertheless, a man of some economic standing, occupying several burghal tenements or part tenements in the commercial area of the town and was one of those responsible for the preparation of the rent roll.

Mathias' son John, and his grandson of the same name, both followed the same trade. The elder John died in 1706 and his executor applied for probate at the Brecon Archdeaconal Court in whose records the inventory of his property, made on 18 July 1706 by a Mathias Berrow and Llewellin Jones, still survives. In total, his movable property was valued at £56 10s. 0d. which included brass pans and kettles in the shop worth £10, pewter in the shop worth £10, and moulds and working tools valued at £1 10s. 0d. John Berrow, if this inventory is to be taken at face value, also dealt in grocery, tallow and general merchandise. This is the only probate document of this type which has so far been traced for a Welsh pewterer or brazier, and is consequently at this moment unique. Although it is not certain, the Mathias Berrow who acted as one of the appraisers could well be John's father.

The third generation of the Berrows is represented by John junior, who was apprenticed to John Bacheler, pewterer, of Bristol in 1703 and was made a freeman in April 1711 (Cott. 411). The evidence suggests that he did not return to his native town but set up in business in Bristol, being mentioned in a Bristol Poll Book as late as 1739. However, in 1721, he was made a burgess of Brecon implying a continued link with the town.

The Berrows were not the only pewterers who traded and worked in Brecon, since the parish registers include a Thomas Vaughan, pewterer and brazier, between 1705 and 1717.[12] Thomas was trained in his craft in Bristol where he was apprenticed to Thomas Bailey and his wife Alice in June 1695 (Cott. 4864). The same registers also list a John Vaughan, brazier, in 1716; a Thomas Vaughan, ironmonger, in 1739 and 1741; and William Vaughan and Walter Vaughan, both braziers in the 1760s. The family clearly kept its link with this particular occupation for many years. Other braziers entered in the registers include John Bloom in 1732 (who could be the same person as John Blome of Carmarthen), John Williams in 1752 and 1762, and a family surnamed Powell in the late 18th and early 19th centuries.

CARDIFF, SWANSEA AND MONMOUTH

The positive results obtained in Brecon and Carmarthen led to the investigation of a number of other South Wales towns. In two of these, Cardiff and Swansea, evidence has been obtained of working pewterers producing their own wares. These now major cities were, at the time in which we are interested, both comparatively small and insignificant. The first traceable pewterer in Swansea was a certain Marmaduke Devereux who was permitted to settle in the town in 1649.[13] He is mentioned several times in the following 10 years, as are his sons, and he was employed periodically to repair the Market House. How he fared in Swansea after that is unclear, but one must have a certain sympathy for a man with his name who had to make his living in a small and isolated town when the predominant language was Welsh!

After Marmaduke Devereux, at least two pewterers and two braziers are recorded, including one pewterer who worked on well into the third quarter of the 18th century. This was Richard Matthews, whose active career seems to have spanned the years 1739 to 1770. He was apprenticed on 1 February 1724 to Thomas Cave of Bristol and was made free on 14 May 1734. He is noted by Cotterell (No. 3136), and was apparently still alive in 1774. Spanning some of the gap between these two was Owen Williams, pewterer, who was sworn a burgess of Swansea on 2 September 1657. He had earlier been apprenticed to John Knowles of Bristol and again is noted by Cotterell (No. 5179). A brazier, Walter Williams, whose relationship to Owen, if any, is unknown, is mentioned in 1775 and his death is reported in the *Gloucester Journal* in 1779 in terms which indicate that he was also involved with pewter.

Cardiff also produces evidence of a pewterer who was trained in Bristol, George Mower (Cott. 3314), whose apprenticeship to Robert Belton of Bristol Cotterell records. The register of St John's Church, Cardiff, records the baptism of his daughter and entered in a contemporary hand above his name is 'pewterer'; George Mower is found in other records between 1697 and 1708 and of all the pewterers in South Wales so far identified, he is the only one for whom pieces of pewter are known to survive.[14]

A century earlier Thomas Jones is mentioned as a pewterer in the court records of Monmouth for the mid-1580s. In addition a number of braziers are recorded in the town in the early 18th century. Unfortunately few town records survive for the intervening years.

DENBIGH

In North Wales the initial approach was also concentrated on those towns known to have been of local importance, and for this reason Denbigh was chosen. As in Carmarthen, Denbigh had a Company or Guild of Hammermen, although their rules have not survived. The borough records in February 1678-9 indicate that the Company embraced blacksmiths, whitesmiths, nailers, tinmen and braziers.[15] The same records show that pewterers as well as braziers were members of this company. In December 1612, John Cotterell, pewterer, was admitted as a Burgess of Denbigh, being a foreigner (i.e. not a native of the town). For this privilege, he paid the very considerable sum of £5. Later in the same century another pewterer is mentioned, Edward Roberts. He appears in the borough records in 1685 and in 1686 when the enigmatic note is made against his name 'At London'. The London Pewterers' Company gave leave to an Edward Roberts to strike his Touch in 1686 (London Touchplate number 425), and reference to their records reveals that Edward Roberts, son of Thomas Roberts of Denbigh, gentleman, was apprenticed to Robert Harding of London on 2 August 1672. He was made free on 14 August 1679.

A brazier, Richard Thomas, who was a contemporary of Edward Roberts, is listed in the Borough Book on 13 September 1679 when he became a burgess and in February 1694-5 when he fathered an illegitimate child. No further pewterers or braziers have been found in these borough records until 1784 when Robert Green, brazier, became a burgess. Robert Green was a customer of Ingram and Hunt of Bewdley.

WREXHAM AND CONWAY

Wrexham, another North Wales town near to Denbigh, has produced evidence of pewtering. The London Company's Searchers in 1677 noted a Francis Nicholls, pewterer, in that town. This is their only known visit to a pewterer resident in Wales, although they included also Welshpool and Montgomery in the itinerary of their search, without apparently finding any pewter in either of these towns. Nicholls was making spoons, porringers, flagons and saucers and possibly other items, and buying pewter from Wigan, Shrewsbury and Worcester. Unfortunately Wrexham was at this time an unincorporated town and remained so until 1857. This makes research into the tradesmen of the town somewhat difficult. Fortunately, a 19th century local historian carried out an extensive study of the town on the basis of property and property owners or occupiers, and this provides details of an 18th century family of braziers and pewterers named Hughes.[16]

Ellis Hughes	Resided at Yspythy, Wrexham, dead by 1733
John Hughes	Resided at High Street, Wrexham, married 10 February 1719-20, buried 29 July 1730
John Hughes	Probably his son. Resided at Chester and at Stantsy near Wrexham. Married 1734 and buried at Wrexham February 1749-50.

These Hughes' appear also in the lists of freemen of the city of Chester. Ellis Hughes, pewterer and brazier, became a freeman in the year 1697-8, and John Hughes in 1719-20 when he was described as the son of John Hughes, Wrexham, County Denbigh, brazier and pewterer. These details suggest that there may have been four generations of Hughes rather than the three recorded in Wrexham, or alternatively John Hughes may have married twice. Certainly, the available information indicates the Hughes to have been a family of some standing with connections with the Cheshire gentry. With the death of the last John Hughes in 1749-50, involvement with the trade of pewterer and brazier ceased, though the family continued to reside in Wrexham and to have links with the town until the 1780s. By the 1750s, another brazier was resident in the town, Peter Hurst, who was living in Hope Street in 1757.

Indications of pewter production have been found in Conway, where a pewterer, Hugh ap Meredith, is recorded in the 1580s,[17] and there are possible indications of the trade (implicit in the London Company's visit in 1677) in Welshpool and Montgomery. Interestingly the Conway parish registers record the burial on 28 August 1610 of 'Richard Mackeroche, pyauterer of Chester'. Presumably he was the Richard Meycock who was free as a pewterer in Chester in 1572-3.

In the late 18th century, and particularly in the early 19th many braziers were active in Wales, where, in the latter period, some two-thirds of the world's copper was smelted. Thus Pigot's trade directories of 1828-9 list between sixty and seventy braziers, though most of them are also described as 'tinmen', that is tinplate workers, none is described as a pewterer. However it is known that many of them sold pewter and other items bought in from the larger manufacturers. The substantially improved transport in the 19th century facilitated this change in the organisation of the trade. One other feature of the marketing of pewter in Wales has been identified, that is through the local fair, already familiar in England. William Bulkely of Brynddu in Anglesey noted in his diary in 1735, 'A very great fair today at Llanfechall, plenty of young horses for harrowing to be sold in this fair, Pewter, Brass, Shoes, Hats, Woollen and Linen cloth in abundance, money very scarce, no great buying'. Doubtless pewter and brass were available for purchase at many such fairs throughout the Principality.[18]

Two of the three questions posed at the start of the chapter have now been answered so far as existing information permits. As has been demonstrated, there is ample evidence that pewter was used in Wales and that the demand so created was met by imports by sea, river and land from England, as well as by resident and native craftsmen. Sufficient evidence now exists to be able to identify certain characteristics of the local pewter trade. It was numerically weak and relied heavily on outside resources for training and for the provision of craftsmen. A very significant proportion of those whose names have been discovered either went to Bristol or one of the other border towns to be apprenticed (and one indeed to London), or were English immigrants who chose to seek their fortunes in Wales. As the market for pewter declined in the 18th century with the introduction of new materials, and the available means of transport improved, the local industry, such as it was, declined even further and the market was increasingly dominated by a few major pewtering concerns in centres such as Bewdley, Birmingham, and Bristol.

The manufacture of pewter was, with one or two exceptions, an urban activity, and the explanation for the weakness of the Welsh industry can be found in the state of urban development in Wales in the 16th and 17th centuries. Before the Anglo-Norman invasion the country was virtually without towns. Most historic Welsh towns were founded in the 12th and 13th centuries, largely by the Anglo–Normans, or by native Welsh lords, although some were founded on sites where incipient urban development had already been initiated. The motivations for this period of intense urban development were political, military and administrative, financial and to some extent religious. Some of the new towns did not survive the long period of conquest and conflict, but a good proportion, with the active support of the Crown and the Marcher Lords, prospered and grew. Following the final victory of Edward I over the Princes of Gwynedd, conditions began to change. The level of political support for the new towns began slowly to decline; many were subject to periodic epidemics and some to destruction in the 15th century military campaigns during the wars of Owain Glyndwr. In this context it is interesting to note that one Geofrey Pewterer provided solder for work on Newcastle Emlyn castle in the early 15th century.[19]

From the early decades of the 15th century, without the stimulus of military necessity, outside investment declined and the development of urban life in Wales became progressively dependent on the strength of the local economy alone. This trend continued and was probably further strengthened by the more stable conditions brought about by the political union with England in the 1530s. Lacking external stimulus the economy of Wales appears to have been unable to support the further development of the urban hierarchy which had been created. Some towns stagnated, some contracted and some declined over the centuries to a point at which it can be seen that they were no longer performing an urban function.[20] To quote perhaps one of the more extreme examples, Trelech, in Eastern Gwent, contained 378 burghal plots and tenements in 1288 and 265 tenements in 1314, yet by 1861 only 29 houses remained. Although an extreme example, it highlights the general trend.

Thus, during the two or three centuries preceding the Industrial Revolution, which was the heyday of the British pewter industry, Wales was a backward area with a largely pastoral rural economy. Lacking the urban infrastructure and prosperity of England the essentially urban craft of pewtering failed to become self-sustaining and indigenous pewter manufacture remained a marginal activity.

Welsh Pewterers and Braziers

Geofrey Pewterer	Newcastle Emlyn	early 1400s, p
Thomas, David	Haverfordwest	m 1540, p
Thomas, Thomas	Haverfordwest	m 1565–90, p
ap Ievane, David	Carmarthen	m 1566–75, ?p
ap Ievane, Ievane	Carmarthen	m 1575, ?p
ap Meredeth, Hugh	Conway	m 1581, p
Jones, Thomas	Monmouth	m 1580s, p
Cattel, William	Haverfordwest	m 1585–1600, p
Thomas, William	Haverfordwest	m 1595–1602, p
Cotterel, John	Denbigh	m 1612, p
Bevans, Richard	Haverfordwest	m 1647, br
Devereux, Marmaduke	Swansea	m 1649–59, p
Lewis, William	Haverfordwest	m 1650, p
Colton, Thomas	Haverfordwest	m 1650, p
Bevans, John	Haverfordwest	m late 1650s, br
Hobson, Thomas	Carmarthen	m 1651–63, p
Williams, Owen	Swansea	m 1657, p
Morrel, Edward	Haverfordwest	m 1657, br
Berrow(e), Mathias	Brecon	m 1667–76, p
Nicholls, Francis	Wrexham	m 1677, p
Jones, John	Swansea	m 1677–1707, br
Thomas, Richard	Denbigh	m 1679–95, br
Roberts, Edward	Denbigh	m 1685–6, p
Price, Benjamin	Welshpool	m 1690, br
Berrow(e), John I	Brecon	m 1694, d 1706, p
Mower, George	Cardiff	m 1697–1708, p
Vaughan, Thomas	Brecon	m 1707–17, p and br
Jones, Edward	Monmouth	m 1709, br
Berrow(e), John, II	Bristol/Brecon	m 1711–39, p
Vaughan, John	Brecon	m 1716, br
Agedon, Henry	Monmouth	m 1722, br
Davies, David	Carmarthen	m 1723, p and br
Hughes, John I	Wrexham	m 1719–20, d 1730, br
Hughes, Ellis	Wrexham	d by 1733, p and br
Bloom, John	Brecon	m 1732, br

Phillips, Edward	Monmouth	m 1733, d 1746, br
Evans, David	Conway	m 1733–56, br
Blome, John	Carmarthen	m 1738, br
Hughes, John II	Wrexham	d 1749–50, p and br
Mathews, Richard	Swansea	m 1739–70, p and br
Philips, William	Carmarthen	d 1750, p
Hurst, Peter	Wrexham	m 1757, br
Green, Alexander	? Anglesey	m 1758, br
Williams, John	Brecon	m 1760s, br
Vaughan, William	Brecon	m 1760s, br
Williams, David	Carmarthen	m 1772, br
Roberts, Daniel	Carmarthen	m 1772, br
Williams, Walter	Swansea	d 1779, p and br
Green, Robert	Denbigh	m 1784, br
Bastud, Thomas	Cardiff	m 1788, br
Edwards, John	Abergavenny	m 1793, br
Morgan, William	Brecon	m 1793, br
Tollman, Richard	Cardiff	m 1793, br
Evans, Thomas	Cardigan	m 1793, br
Williams, John	Carmarthen	m 1794, br
Beavans, James	Haverfordwest	m 1798, br
Hopkin, John	Welshpool	m 1798, br
Bowen, William	Haverfordwest	m 1798, br
Baldwin, William	Carmarthen	m 1822, br
James, Abraham	Carmarthen	m 1828, br
Jones, William	Carmarthen	m 1828, br
Lloyd, John	Carmarthen	m 1828, br
Morgan, Isaac	Carmarthen	m 1828, br
Morris, John	Carmarthen	m 1828, br

APPENDIX

The Ordinances of the Hammermen of Carmarthen

At which Daie (8th February 1569) fforasmuch as it appeared unto the said Maior, the Recorder, Towne clarke and Councell, burgesses and cominaltie of the said towne, That sundrie the handie crafts men of this Towne, as Goldsmithes, Iron Smithes, Cuttlers, Pewterers, Plummers, Metellers and Tynkers are greatlie diminished and empaired by the resorte of others, light and vagrante persons (devoide of skill and cunning, bearinge the name onelie of men of the same occupacions or misteries), wanderinge and goinge from one Towne to another, and from place to place, as such as have no certaine abode, who withoute controllement of anie heretofore, have sett open their shoppes at their pleasure, in anie place within the said Towne, and there have ussed hade and practised moche decepte in utteringe of light and deceivable stuffe, to the greate deceapt lose and hinderance of the Queen's Mats. Subjects within the said Towne. Therefore and for other consideracions . . . it is at this present daie ordered statuted and enacted . . . That from henceforthe Lewes ap Owen, Thomas Walter Emonde,* Elias Shaller, John ap Hoell, Lewes Walter, Thomas David, Ievane Morgan, Thomas Cuttler, John Salsbury, John Cotton, David ap Ievan, Rice ap Ithell, and Ievane ap Ievane, shalbe one Associacion or ffraternitie of themselves and called and knowne by the name of the fraternie hambermen within the said Towne of Carmerddin And that they and their successors may yearlie amonge them upon the five and twentith daie of June choose one able person to be maister of the said occupacions within the said Towne, and twoo others meete persons to be wardens of the said occupacions, and that Lewis ap Owen be maister of the said misteries or occupacions for this present yeare.

Which maister and every one of them, shall have full power to see, search and peruse that everie one of the severall misteries or occupacions foresaid be bothe experte and skillfull in his said particular crafte or misterie and that all such stuffe as shalbe brought or carried unto them be well and sufficientlie wrought and made, takinge for the workmanship thereof that shall be reasonable, meete and agreeable to good conscience. And that they do sell no kind of wares but such as is good, sufficiant and lawfull, without puttinge in anie thinge that they shall happen to make or worke, anie kinde of slight or deceitful stuffe. And do sell the same at convenient prices. And if they shall finde anie person offend to the contrarie of any the premisses Then he (so offendinge) to pay for everie such default or offence such fyne . . . as by the said maister . . . shalbe levied.

And further it is . . . ordered that the maior for the tyme beinge shall not suffer any foreyener or burges to sett up any of the severall occupacions or misteries aforesaid eyther privilie or openlie within the said Towne or liberties of the same, unless he agree with the maister for the time being, and the more parte of the fellowship of the said Associacion, and be by them therunto admitted and received, and also be a burgess of the said Towne and payenge for his admittance such somme of money as the said maister and fellowship shall assesse. Provided nevertheless that he that hath byn an

---

* The reading here is uncertain. It should probably be, Thomas Walter, Edmonde (surname wanting), Elias etc. . . .

apprentice in the said Towne to anie of the said occupacions, by the space of seven yeares, and well and truelie served out his yeares, shall paie for his admittance but three shillings four pence.

(Here follow fines for offending, provisions for the fraternity to make its own rules, an undertaking by the mayor and other officers to uphold the ordinances).

And in respect of this graunte the said associacion or fraternitie (of) hambermen do binde themselves and their successors to paie at every feast of St. Michaell tharchangell yearlie to the maior, bailiffs and cominaltie of the same towne, to the use of the Corporacion of the said Towne, the summe of thirteen shillings four pence of lawfull English money. In witness etc. . . . .

NOTES AND REFERENCES

Wales

Note: NLW = National Library of Wales.

1. *The Montgomeryshire Collections*, vol. 61, p. 147.
2. Evans, G. Nestor, *Social Life in mid-18th Century Anglesey* (1935), p. 38.
3. Twiston-Davis, L. and Lloyd-Johnes, H. J., *Welsh Furniture* (1950), p. 49.
4. *Montgomeryshire Quarter Sessions Records*, NLW Q/AG1.
5. Jones, E. A., *The Church Plate of the Diocese of Bangor* (1906).
6. Evans, J. T., *The Church Plate of Pembrokeshire* (1905) and *idem, The Church Plate of Carmarthenshire* (1907).
7. Lewis, E. A. (ed.), *The Welsh Port Books 1550–1603* (1927).
8. Charles, B. G., *Calendar of the Records of the Borough of Haverfordwest 1539–1660.*
9. Evans, C., *Transcript of the Records of the Corporate Borough of Carmarthen . . .*, NLW 12858D.
10. *Journal of the Carmarthenshire Society and Field Club*, Part 16, p. 43 and Part 26, pp. 83–4.
11. Jones-Davis, J., *An Essay towards the History of Breconshire* (1967).
12. *Registers of St Mary's, Brecon*, NLW.
13. Thomas, W. S. K., *History of Swansea 1485–1662*, thesis at NLW.
14. Mathews, J. H., *Cardiff Records, Materials for a History of the Borough* (1898–1911) and *Registers of St John's Church, Cardiff*, Cardiff Record Office.
15. Williams, J., *Ancient and Modern Denbigh* (1856).
16. Palmer, A. N., *The History of the Town of Wrexham . . .* (1893).
17. Clark, Charles, J. (ed.), *Parish Registers of Conway 1541–1793* (1900).
18. Evans, G. Nestor, *ibid.*, p. 110.
19. Lloyd, J. E., *A History of Carmarthenshire* (1935), vol. 1, p. 302.
20. Soulsby, Ian, *The Towns of Medieval Wales* (1983) and Griffiths, R. A., *Boroughs of Medieval Wales* (1978).

General

Source records for Wales are scattered in many locations. Although much material is available at the National Library of Wales the following list gives the locations of the original records of the most important towns discussed in the text.

Brecon. Brecknock Borough (District) Council Offices, Brecon, Powys.
Cardiff. The Record Office, County Hall, Cathays Park, Cardiff.
Carmarthen. The Carmarthenshire Record Office, County Hall, Carmarthen, Dyfed.
Denbigh. The Record Office, 46, Clwyd Street, Ruthin, Clwyd.
Haverfordwest. The Pembrokeshire Record Office, The Castle, Haverfordwest, Dyfed.
Monmouth. The Monmouth Museum, Priory Street, Monmouth, Gwent.
Swansea. The Record Office, County Hall, Swansea, West Glamorgan.

A FINAL NOTE

THERE IS CONSIDERABLE documentary evidence, though few surviving artefacts, which attest to the use of pewter in England as early as the 12th century. However, pewtering cannot be discerned as an identifiable craft in London before the early 14th century and in the area covered by this book before the last years of that century and the early years of the next. From the previous chapters, the reader will have been able to see how the craft developed, changed, prospered and finally withered. In simple terms the history of pewter making in the West Midlands could be described as follows: the 15th century saw its introduction, the 16th its consolidation and expansion, the 17th its greatest prosperity, the 18th its initial decline and the 19th a final flourish. Today, although pewter is still being made and sold, it no longer has many practical uses. Such production as continues is mainly directed to the quality souvenir and gift market, which market justifiably benefits from the historical associations attaching to the alloy.

In the *Introduction* attention was drawn to the main discoveries and conclusions stemming from our study and there is little point in reiterating these. There would however seem to be some value in concluding with a brief summary of the economic and social development of the craft in the provinces so far as they are now apparent.

It is clear that pewter making was for a considerable time a well established craft industry in most of England and at least to some extent in Wales. The industry was never however a large one. Although most market towns were able to support one or two master craftsmen the total number employed can never have been substantial in terms of contribution to the town's economy.

The craft was essentially an urban one, which is particularly relevant to its partial failure in Wales, and it did not, at least in its heyday, succeed in establishing itself outside the bounds of the corporate town. This meant that the industry remained subject to the restrictions and regulations which operated through the guild system, reinforced by the provincial activities of the London Company. Technical innovation would be difficult to introduce in such an environment and slow to spread. Eight of the towns we have covered are known to have had guilds or companies which included pewterers and braziers but all the evidence points to the fact that these trades were never the dominant ones. All the organisations were either general fraternities of hammermen and metalworkers, or even broader groups of urban craftsmen linked by traditions the origins of which may even then have been obscure. The strong bonds through family ties and apprenticeship, the shared social and religious obligations and the closely interwoven trade links, all provided factors which limited competition and innovation.

At least as early as the 1530s there is evidence that provincial pewterers made and traded in wares fabricated from copper-zinc alloys. As the supply of these alloys and the techniques for their working developed in Britain, so the part played by brass in the provincial pewterers' businesses grew. At the beginning of the 18th century, when the market for pewterware began to contract, some of those who survived the economic challenge did so by placing more emphasis on that part of their activities described by the term 'brazier'. The techniques used for the making of pewterware remained unchanged, as they do to the present day. The challenge presented in the 18th century by the growing competition from pottery, brassware and tin-plate could not be met by improved technology and the competitive pressures proved too much for the traditional craftsman.

A few, like the wealthy John Duncumb and his successors at Bewdley, and those who established themselves in Birmingham outside the confines of a corporate town, pioneered new business methods and organised their production so as to compete successfully in the changed environment. Unfortunately the means by which they achieved this are not fully apparent, but cheap non-guild labour, an outwork system and factory methods all no doubt played a part. The records of Ingram and Hunt reveal the use of a travelling salesman and of catalogues and samples described by number, an approach to marketing which is very familiar today. The probate inventory of Sampson Bourne II of Worcester shows that these trends had had their origins even before the close of the 17th century. He, in common with John Duncumb, had considerable wealth which would have enabled capital intensive business methods beyond the means of most contemporary provincial craftsmen.

Not even the economic expansion of the 19th century brought significant improvement to the industry or major technical changes, though increasingly iron and steel moulds were used in place of the expensive traditional bronze ones. The one important discovery made, that the antimony-containing alloy which had formed the pewterer's 'hard metal' from the late 17th century could be rolled and spun, was made in Sheffield by innovators not associated with the traditional craft. Their new products, designed to mimic the elegance of silver, appealed to the growing numbers of fashion-conscious customers and were marketed in a manner designed to avoid any connection with the traditional hand-cast pewter. Britannia metal, though indeed pewter in metallurgical terms, has only in recent years come to be seriously appreciated by collectors.

By the mid-19th century traditional manufacture was almost entirely restricted to London and Birmingham and was largely confined to drinking pots and measures for the public house trade. Though Birmingham had many Britannia metal makers the two industries were viewed as distinct and the industrial production of Britannia metal on power presses and lathes sets it apart entirely from the craft which has been our concern.

Little now remains except for the historian and collector to seek to understand the documents and artefacts which survive and to interpret and preserve them for posterity.

LIST OF WILLS AND LETTERS OF ADMINISTRATION (LA) CONSULTED

The date given is that of the will and not that of probate.

Abbreviations:

HWRO	Hereford and Worcester Record Office
LJRO	Lichfield Joint Record Office
LRO	Lancashire Record Office
NLW	National Library of Wales
PRO	Public Record Office

Acton, Ephraim	Bridgnorth	1759	LJRO
Baker, Edward	Oswestry	1608	PRO
Banks, Robert	Wigan	1692	LRO
Banks, William	Bewdley	1795	HWRO
Baysie, John	Worcester	1585	HWRO
Birch, George	Birmingham	1770	PRO
Birch, Thomas Rawlins	Birmingham	1857	PRO
Bourne, Sampson I	Worcester	1674	PRO
Bourne, Sampson II	Worcester	1689	PRO (LA)
Bradnock, Joseph	Birmingham	1684	LJRO
Bradshaw, John	Wellington	1740	LJRO (Deed of assignment)
Bradshaw, William	Wellington	1763	LJRO
Burges, Thomas	Shrewsbury	1758	LJRO
Charlemont, Agnes	Worcester	1536	HWRO
Collins, Richard	Shrewsbury	1611	LJRO (LA)
Collins, Rowland	Shrewsbury	1654	PRO
Cooke, White	Shrewsbury	1782	PRO
Deakin, Abraham	Walsall	1697	LJRO (LA)
Duncombe, Joseph	Birmingham	1792	PRO
Duncumb, John	Bewdley	1739	PRO
Duncumb, Stynt	Bewdley	1762	HWRO
Farr, John	Bridgnorth	1672	LJRO
Felton, Gwen	Oswestry	1678	NLW
Felton, James	Oswestry	1716	PRO
Felton, John	Shrewsbury	1708	PRO
Felton, Philip	Oswestry	1732	NLW
Felton, Thomas	Oswestry	1675	NLW
Forster, Thomas	Shrewsbury	1718	LJRO
Goode, Henry	Bewdley	1726	HWRO (LA)
Gorton, Michael	Birmingham	1722	LJRO
Gorton, Thomas	Birmingham	1683	LJRO
Green, Harry	Worcester	1586	LJRO
Green, Margery	Worcester	1571	HWRO (LA)
Green, Nathanial	Lichfield	1715	LJRO
Greenbank, Dickenson	Worcester	1713	HWRO (LA)
Greenbank, Francis	Worcester	1689	HWRO
Greenbank, James	Worcester	1603	HWRO
Greenbank, John	Worcester	1680	HWRO (LA)

Greenbank, John	Worcester	1698	PRO
Greenbank, Margaret	Worcester	1604	HWRO
Greenbank, William	Worcester	1637	HWRO
Hales, James	Leominster	1620	HWRO
Hall, William	Birmingham	1723	LJRO
Hanson, William	Walsall	1614	LJRO
Harper, Hopwood	Worcester	1732	HWRO
Harrop, Samuel	Shrewsbury	1777	PRO
Hill, Stephen	Bewdley	1699	PRO
Hopkins, William	Worcester	1602	HWRO (LA)
Hughes, Ellis	Wrexham	1730	NLW (LA)
Hughes, John	Wrexham	1730	NLW (LA)
Ingram, John	Bewdley	1799	HWRO
Jennings, Thomas	Walsall	1615	LJRO
King, Francis	Worcester	1719	HWRO
Laugher, Russell	Worcester	1749	HWRO
Leeth, Edward	Worcester	1746	HWRO (LA)
Letsome, Sampson	Worcester	1737	HWRO
Meeson, Aaron	Birmingham	1806	LJRO
Meeson, Thomas	Birmingham	1822	LJRO
Mountford, William	Kidderminster	1680	PRO
Nicholls, Christopher	Walsall	1653	PRO
Nicholls, Edward	Walsall	1668	LJRO
Nicholls, John	Walsall	1629	LJRO
Nicholls, Joshua	Walsall	1615	LJRO (Deed of assignment)
Nicholls, William	Walsall	1577	LJRO
Parker, Elizabeth	Walsall	1541	LJRO
Parker, Richard	Walsall	1534	LJRO
Parkhouse, William	Hereford	1722	HWRO (LA)
Philips, Edward	Monmouth	1746	HWRO
Plummer, Richard	Ludlow	1697	HWRO
Reynolds, Michael	Shrewsbury	1739	PRO
Roberts, Thomas	Shrewsbury	1730	PRO
Rosengrove, John	Shrewsbury	1601	LJRO
Schofield, Thomas	Birmingham	1806	LJRO
Seney, William	Walsall	1673	LJRO
Spooner, Lucas	Birmingham	1839	LJRO
Sherwin, Humphrey	Shrewsbury	1684	LJRO
Smith, Thomas	Bewdley	1709	HWRO
Tomkins, Elizabeth	Leominster	1644	HWRO
Tomkins, John	Leominster	1677	HWRO
Tomkins, Roger	Leominster	1640	HWRO
Tomkins, Thomas	Leominster	1677	HWRO
Trapp, Francis	Worcester	1633	HWRO
Trapp, Francis	Hereford	1689	HWRO (LA)
Trapp, Francis	Hereford	1699	HWRO (LA)
Trapp, John	Worcester	1675	HWRO (LA)
Trapp, John	Worcester	1713	HWRO (LA)
Walcrofte, James	Ledbury	1597	HWRO
Wareing, Charles	Shipston-on-Stour	1696	PRO
Whitcombe, John	Leominster	1630	HWRO
Wood, Robert	Birmingham	1637	LJRO
Wood, Thomas	Birmingham	1734	PRO
Wood, William	Birmingham	1644	LJRO
Wood, William	Birmingham	1726	PRO

ILLUSTRATIONS OF MARKS

Many of these marks which appear in Cotterell are either not attributed or not located by him and are here fully identified for the first time.

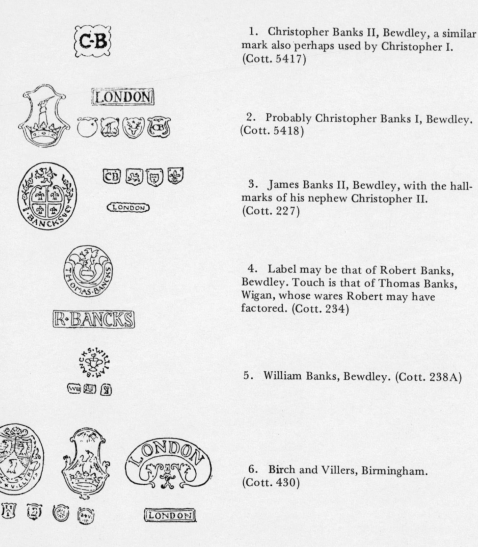

1.   Christopher Banks II, Bewdley, a similar mark also perhaps used by Christopher I. (Cott. 5417)

2.   Probably Christopher Banks I, Bewdley. (Cott. 5418)

3.   James Banks II, Bewdley, with the hall-marks of his nephew Christopher II. (Cott. 227)

4.   Label may be that of Robert Banks, Bewdley. Touch is that of Thomas Banks, Wigan, whose wares Robert may have factored. (Cott. 234)

5.   William Banks, Bewdley. (Cott. 238A)

6.   Birch and Villers, Birmingham. (Cott. 430)

7.   Sampson Bourne I, Worcester. (Cott. 5463)

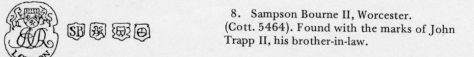

8.   Sampson Bourne II, Worcester. (Cott. 5464). Found with the marks of John Trapp II, his brother-in-law.

9.   Perhaps Edward Bowen, Worcester. Appears on pewter at *The Fleece*, Bretforton.

10.   Edward Box, Banbury. (Cott. 538)

11.   Probably William Bradshaw, Wellington. (Cott. 549)

12.   John Brain(e) I or II, Worcester. (Cott. 555)

13.   Thomas Burgess of London and perhaps also the Thomas Burgess of Shrewsbury. (Cott. 704)

14.   Josiah Clark of London and perhaps also the Josiah Clark of Shrewsbury. (Cott. 938)

15.   Perhaps White Cook of Shrewsbury rather than his Bristol namesake. (Cott. 1095)

16.   James Carruthers Crane, Bewdley. (Cott. 1197)

139

 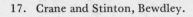

17. Crane and Stinton, Bewdley.

18. John Duncumb, Birmingham and Bewdley.
The upper left-hand mark is probably that of
his Birmingham period, his adoption of the
Duncumb crest following his inheritance of
the family estates in 1719. (Cott. 1465)

19. Stynt Duncumb, Bewdley. (Cott. 1466)

These appear to be marks of the Felton family, Shrewsbury and Oswestry. Five of them had the initials 'IF' making attribution difficult. Nos. 21 and 22 appear on pewter in churches in mid-Wales (21 on a plate dated 1684). Tentative attributions are,

20. James I or II (Cott. 1649A)

21. John I (Cott. 5591)

22. John I (Cott. 5585)

23. James II, Jeremiah or John II (Cott. 607 (Cott. 6072)

24. Gaskell and Chambers, Birmingham. A late 19th century mark, the 'Y' signifies pewterware cast in ex-James Yates moulds.

25. Richard Green, Worcester.

26. John Greenbank II, Worcester. Found with the hall-marks of his son William II q.v. (Cott. 5619)

27. William Greenbank II, Worcester. (Cott. 1992)

28. Abel Grove II, Birmingham. (Cott. 2037)

29. Probably Samuel Harrop, Shrewsbury. (Cott. 5681)

30. John Ingram, Bewdley. (Cott. 5725)

31. Ingram and Hunt, Bewdley. (Cott. 5708)

32. Russell Laugher, Worcester. (Cott. 4077)

33. Perhaps Sampson Letsome I or II, Worcester. (Cott. 6037)

S. MASON

34. Samuel Mason, Birmingham.

MORGAN

35. Joseph Morgan, ?Bewdley, Birmingham and Manchester. The hall-marks are found earlier than the touch, which is perhaps Manchester. (Cott. 3289)

36. George Mower, Cardiff. (Cott. 3314)

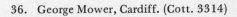

37. Perhaps Christopher Nichols, Walsall. (Cott. 5809)

38. Edward Roberts, Denbigh and London. (Cott. 3953)

39. John Trapp II, Worcester. (Cott. 5977). His marks appear with those of Sampson Bourne II, his brother-in-law.

40. William Tutin, Birmingham.

41. John Underhill, Worcester.
(MPM. 4856a)

42. Villers and Wilkes, Birmingham.
(Cott. 4876)

43. Charles Wareing, Shipston-on-Stour. The set of hall-marks with the initials 'IW' are of Joseph Wareing, his successor. (Cott. 4965A and 5999)

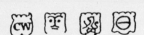

44. William Wood II, Birmingham.

45. James Yates, Birmingham. (Cott. 5338)

46. John Yates, Birmingham. (Cott. 5340A)

47. Thomas Yates, Birmingham. (Cott. 53
(Cott. 5346)

48.   Yates and Birch, Birmingham.
(Cott. 5347)

49.   Yates, Birch and Spooner, Birmingham.
(Cott. 5349)

50.   Yates, Birch and Co., Birmingham.
(Cott. 5348)

51.   Unattributed. The three leopards' heads
appear in the arms of Shrewsbury and of
Stratford-on-Avon. Commonly found on
pewter in the midlands area. (Cott. 6046)

GLOSSARY

A number of the expressions found in the inventories in this book are obscure or uncertain in their meaning. The following list gives definitions of some of the commonest terms used.

Ashes	The scum of oxide which forms on the surface of molten pewter. It was collected and smelted to yield new metal.
Brass	The word 'brass' was used, until the 18th century, to mean both brass and bronze.
Fine Metal	A superior quality of pewter comprising tin hardened with copper or antimony. Sometimes denoted by the letter 'X'. The same as hard metal.
Flatware	Plates, dishes and the like.
Garnish	A set of plates or dishes; frequently a dozen.
Hard Metal	*See* 'Fine Metal'.
Hollow-ware	Flagons, measures, tankards and vessels in general.
Kettles	Open cooking pots, cf. the modern 'fish kettle'. Wired kettles presumably had rims rolled over iron wire reinforcement.
Lay Metal	A cheaper and softer pewter alloy consisting of tin and up to about 25 per cent. of lead.
Porringers	Small bowls, with one or sometimes two decorative 'ears', from which semi-solid food was eaten. Silversmiths used the word in a different sense.
Sadware	The same as flatware.
Saucers	Small plates, 4–6 inches in diameter, used for sauces.
Shruff	Scrap metal, often in the form of shavings.
Tin Glass	The metal bismuth, added in traces to improve the working characteristics of pewter.
Trifle	A pewter alloy intermediate in quality between fine and lay metals. Hence 'trifles' for wares made from it.

BIBLIOGRAPHY OF RECENT GENERAL WORKS ON PEWTER

Brett, V., *Phaidon Guide to Pewter* (1981)

Hatcher, J. and Barker, T. C., *A History of British Pewter* (1974)

Homer, R. F., *Five Centuries of Base Metal Spoons* (1975)

Homer, R. F. and Shemmel, S., *Pewter, A Handbook of Selected Tudor and Stuart Pieces in the Museum of London* (1983)

Hornsby, P., *Pewter of the Western World* (1983)

Hornsby, P., *The Arthur Negus Guide to Pewter, Copper and Brass* (1981)

Michaelis, R. F., *Antique Pewter of the British Isles* (1955)

Michaelis, R. F., *British Pewter* (1969)

Peal, C. A., *British Pewter and Britannia Metal* (1971)

Peal, C. A., *Pewter of Great Britain* (1983)

INDEX OF PLACES

NAME INDEX OF PEWTERERS AND BRAZIERS

The spelling used in this index for a number of names is chosen arbitrarily from among several contemporary variants; it may therefore differ at times from that found in the text.